Development Centre Studies

Is Informal Normal?

TOWARDS MORE AND BETTER JOBS IN DEVELOPING COUNTRIES

Edited by
Johannes P. Jütting and Juan R. de Laiglesia

OECD

DEVELOPMENT CENTRE OF THE ORGANISATION
FOR ECONOMIC CO-OPERATION AND DEVELOPMENT

ORGANISATION FOR ECONOMIC CO-OPERATION AND DEVELOPMENT

The OECD is a unique forum where the governments of 30 democracies work together to address the economic, social and environmental challenges of globalisation. The OECD is also at the forefront of efforts to understand and to help governments respond to new developments and concerns, such as corporate governance, the information economy and the challenges of an ageing population. The Organisation provides a setting where governments can compare policy experiences, seek answers to common problems, identify good practice and work to co-ordinate domestic and international policies.

The OECD member countries are: Australia, Austria, Belgium, Canada, the Czech Republic, Denmark, Finland, France, Germany, Greece, Hungary, Iceland, Ireland, Italy, Japan, Korea, Luxembourg, Mexico, the Netherlands, New Zealand, Norway, Poland, Portugal, the Slovak Republic, Spain, Sweden, Switzerland, Turkey, the United Kingdom and the United States. The Commission of the European Communities takes part in the work of the OECD.

OECD Publishing disseminates widely the results of the Organisation's statistics gathering and research on economic, social and environmental issues, as well as the conventions, guidelines and standards agreed by its members.

The opinions expressed and arguments employed herein do not necessarily reflect the official views of the Organisation, the OECD Development Centre or of the governments of their member countries.

Also available in French under the title:

Études du Centre de Développement
L'emploi informel dans les pays en développement
UNE NORMALITÉ INDÉPASSABLE ?

Cover illustration:
© Fotolia /Yali Shi/J-F Perigois/Ploum1/Charles Taylor/Mirek Hejnicki

Corrigenda to OECD publications may be found on line at: *www.oecd.org/publishing/corrigenda*.
© OECD 2009

Development Centre

The Development Centre of the Organisation for Economic Co-operation and Development was established by decision of the OECD Council on 23 October 1962 and comprises 23 member countries of the OECD: Austria, Belgium, the Czech Republic, Finland, France, Germany, Greece, Iceland, Ireland, Italy, Korea, Luxembourg, Mexico, the Netherlands, Norway, Poland, Portugal, Slovak Republic, Spain, Sweden, Switzerland, Turkey and the United Kingdom as well as Brazil since March 1994, Chile since November 1998, India since February 2001, Romania since October 2004, Thailand since March 2005, South Africa since May 2006 and Egypt, Israel and Viet Nam since March 2008 and Colombia since July 2008. The Commission of the European Communities also takes part in the Centre's Governing Board.

The Development Centre, whose membership is open to both OECD and non-OECD countries, occupies a unique place within the OECD and in the international community. Members finance the Centre and serve on its Governing Board, which sets the biennial work programme and oversees its implementation.

The Centre links OECD members with developing and emerging economies and fosters debate and discussion to seek creative policy solutions to emerging global issues and development challenges. Participants in Centre events are invited in their personal capacity.

A small core of staff works with experts and institutions from the OECD and partner countries to fulfil the Centre's work programme. The results are discussed in informal expert and policy dialogue meetings, and are published in a range of high-quality products for the research and policy communities. The Centre's *Study Series* presents in-depth analyses of major development issues. *Policy Briefs* and *Policy Insights* summarise major conclusions for policy makers; *Working Papers* deal with the more technical aspects of the Centre's work.

For an overview of the Centre's activities, please see www.oecd.org/dev

ISBN: 978-92-64-05923-8 - © OECD 2009

4

Foreword

Employment has a key role to play in reducing poverty and improving well-being. In the context of the OECD Development Centre's Programme of Work 2007-2008, this study sheds new light on an old topic: how can we deal better with the reality of labour markets in developing countries with a view to achieving the Millennium Development Goals? The study synthesises and builds on three country reports – Informal Employment in Romania; Internal Migration and Labour Markets in China; and Integrating the Employment and Social Development Agendas in Mexico. It also draws on insights from an international policy dialogue event on "Creating more and better jobs: What do we know, what can we do?", jointly organised in Rabat, Morocco, by the OECD Development Centre and the World Bank in May 2008. The result is a report that makes concrete recommendations on how to provide incentives for formalisation while improving productivity and social protection for those who will remain informal for a long time to come.

ISBN: 978-92-64-05923-8 - © OECD 2009

Acknowledgements

This document has benefited from inputs and comments from colleagues both inside and outside the OECD. To all of them we express our warm thanks. We would like in particular to extend our gratitude to Danielle Venn from the Employment, Labour and Social Affairs Directorate of the OECD, who provided useful insights on informal employment within OECD countries. Special thanks also go to Jante Parlevliet who participated in the writing of background material for this volume.

This volume benefited from the generous support of the Mexican Ministry of Social Development (SEDESOL) for the completion of the background studies, which is gratefully acknowledged.

We also thank participants in presentations of parts of this work for their suggestions and comments. Previous versions of this work have been presented at IZA-World Bank meetings in Bonn, Rabat and Washington D.C., at the ILO in Geneva, Bath University and at IDS at the University of Sussex. Special thanks go to the review committee: Arjun Bedi (ISS), Martha Chen (Kennedy School of Governance and WIEGO), Gary Fields (Cornell University), Henrik Huitfeldt (SIDA), Ralf Hussmanns (ILO), Naila Kabeer (IDS), Bill Maloney (World Bank), Pierella Paci (World Bank), Uma Rani Amari (Institute of Labour Studies) and Victor Tokman.

We extend our thanks to our colleagues at the Development Centre: Denis Drechsler, Estelle Loiseau and Espen Pryzd for their comments on earlier versions, for providing and editing statistics, and for ensuring the smooth running of the logistics related to this project.

The volume has been edited by Johannes Jütting and Juan R. de Laiglesia (OECD Development Centre). We thank Stephen Jessel for giving the manuscript its final form and Magali Geney and Vanda Legrandgérard for preparing the volume for publication.

Table of Contents

PREFACE 9

EXECUTIVE SUMMARY 11

CHAPTER ONE 17
Employment, Poverty Reduction and Development: What's New?
Johannes Jütting and Juan R. de Laiglesia

CHAPTER TWO 27
Concepts, Measurement and Trends
Jacques Charmes

CHAPTER THREE 63
Persisting Informal Employment: What Explains It?
David Kucera and Theodora Xenogiani

CHAPTER FOUR 89
Women in Informal Employment: What Do We Know and What Can We Do?
David Kucera and Theodora Xenogiani

CHAPTER FIVE 115
Moving Out of Bad Jobs – More Mobility, More Opportunity
Jason Gagnon

CHAPTER SIX 143
Dealing With Informal Employment: Towards a Three-Pronged Strategy
Johannes Jütting and Juan R. de Laiglesia

ISBN: 978-92-64-05923-8 - © OECD 2009

Preface

The financial and economic crisis that started in 2008 has deep implications for employment across the planet. It is virtually certain that both jobs and wage levels will suffer in many developing countries. Most workers in the developing world are employed informally: without access to developed social security mechanisms, they are particularly vulnerable and face increasingly severe risks. Their numbers are likely to grow in times of economic crisis, as informal employment plays the role of a buffer, providing families with an alternative source of income. Some of them are very visible: the vast array of petty traders, shoe-shiners and casual labourers that fill the streets of the cities of the world. Many are less obvious: skilled professionals evading regulation, industrial outworkers, piece-rate factory workers and a myriad of different occupations.

As part of its 2007-2008 Programme of Work, the OECD Development Centre set out to encourage peer learning on the impact of social policies on development and well-being. The work undertaken through case studies in China, Mexico and Romania and through extensive data collection presented here provides a rich new data set on informal employment across the developing world. This work complements the OECD Development Centre's Gender, Institutions and Development Data Base, which features social institutions as key determinants for employment outcomes along gender lines. It also puts the wealth of knowledge generated by recent research into the context of its implications for policy. As such, the conclusions found in this book are a major contribution to facilitating evidence-based policy dialogue in an area hitherto characterised by preconceived notions and sketchy evidence.

The authors find that informal employment is the norm, rather than the exception, in most developing countries. Moreover, growth has not reduced the proportion of people working informally. However, there is great mobility in labour markets, even in low-income countries, and that mobility can be an avenue to improved livelihoods if better jobs are created. The authors propose a policy framework built around three objectives: creating more and better jobs, providing better incentives for formality, and protecting and promoting informal workers.

Where people have chosen to leave the formal sector, they need incentives to rejoin it. Benefits should be linked to social contribution levels, while administrative procedures should be simplified. While reducing informal employment also implies strengthening enforcement mechanisms, policies also need to address those who have no choice but to work informally.

Employment is a permanent feature on the development agenda. As policy makers get to grips with the evolution of labour relations and the transformations that globalisation brings to them, they will face new challenges. The OECD Development Centre will contribute to meeting these challenges in its overarching Global Economic Outlook programme by analysing the impact on employment in the developing world of shifts in the centre of global economic gravity. Understanding how employment policies can lead to wider distribution of wealth and the creation of stable, sustainable development is critical to achieving fairer globalisation and more coherent societies. This is in the interests of both OECD and non-OECD countries; that is, of all citizens of the planet.

Javier Santiso,
OECD Chief Development Economist and
Director, OECD Development Centre
Paris
January 2009

ISBN: 978-92-64-05923-8 - © OECD 2009

Executive Summary

The financial and economic crisis that started in 2008 is bound to have profound implications for employment across the planet. As economic growth slows down, capital flows dry up and export markets weaken in many developing countries, it appears certain that both jobs and wage levels will suffer. This volume shows that most workers in the developing world are employed informally: without access to developed social security mechanisms, they are particularly vulnerable and face increasingly severe risks. Their numbers are likely to grow in times of economic crisis, as informal employment plays the role of a buffer, providing families with an alternative source of income.

In the context of the unfolding crisis it is important that the commitment to poverty reduction – as stated in the Millennium Development Goals (MDGs) – is maintained. To make employment work to reduce poverty, the challenge is not only to create jobs, but also to create better jobs: those that offer adequate pay and a sufficient level of social protection. Jobs in the informal sector frequently fail to offer just that. In many parts of the world, being employed informally constitutes the norm, not the exception. Informal employment refers to jobs or activities in the production and sales of legal goods and services which are not regulated or protected by the state. On a worldwide average, more than half of all jobs in the non-agricultural sector can be considered informal. In some regions, including sub-Saharan Africa and South Asia, this rate reaches at least 80 per cent. As shown in this study, informal employment constitutes a large and growing segment of the world's labour markets. Its persistence limits the effectiveness of employment as a tool for poverty reduction and has serious repercussions on social and economic development.

For developing countries, high rates of informal employment mean narrow tax bases and insufficient capacity to address pressing social objectives such as the provision of health and unemployment protection. They also imply an inadequate use of available human resources as informal jobs are believed to be associated with lower efficiency and productivity. For individuals, being informally employed often means being locked in low-paid, high-risk and precarious activities – a situation particularly challenging in the developing world considering that labour is by far the most important productive asset of the world's poor.

IS INFORMAL NORMAL?

When informal employment was first recognised in the 1970s, the discussion focused on a small set of low-income countries. Inefficient public institutions, cumbersome registration processes and a general distrust of the government – all factors that spur the creation of a market outside a country's formal structures – were seen as the epitome of under-development. Furthermore, it was assumed that these factors – and hence informal employment – would disappear in the course of economic development.

The reality today looks different. Informality is increasingly becoming normal, not least in middle and even high-income countries. In some cases, the share of jobs performed outside a country's formal structures may be more than half of all non-agricultural jobs, and up to

ISBN: 978-92-64-05923-8 - © OECD 2009

90 per cent if agricultural jobs are included – in spite of economic growth. The development in selected countries in Southeast Asia and Latin America is telling in this respect: over the last 30 years, growth in these countries was accompanied by increasing, not falling, informal employment (see Figure 0.1).

Figure 0.1. Informal Employment and GDP in Latin America and Southeast Asia

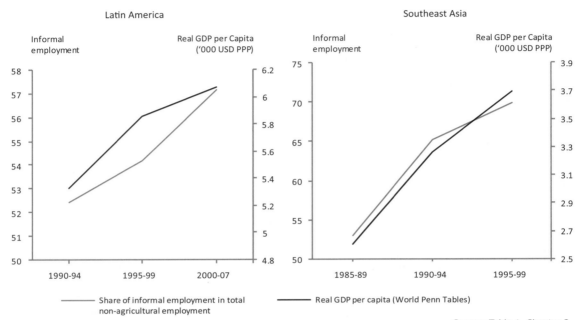

Source: Table 1, Chapter 2

StatLink http://dx.doi.org/10.1787/533114034365

Even in OECD countries a growing tendency to an "informalisation" of working conditions creates informal employment, partly because of increasing international competition in the course of globalisation. An example in this respect is the recent phenomenon of "false self-employment", whereby individuals sub-contract every day to the same employer – voluntarily or not – and thus operate as self-employed contractors to bypass the legal requirements of a normal working relationship.

INFORMAL EMPLOYMENT: PROBLEMATIC AT BOTH THE INDIVIDUAL AND SOCIETY LEVELS

Many people depend on informal employment for a living, but informal employment has serious consequences at the levels of both the individual and society. Beyond earning levels, informal employment makes basic rights vulnerable and difficult to defend. As such, it can be a major cause of poverty in dimensions other than income. Most of those who work informally are insufficiently protected from the various risks to which they are exposed: illness or health problems, unsafe working conditions and possible loss of earnings.

At the level of society, pervasive informal employment undermines the ability of the state to ensure that workers have fair working conditions, including appropriate working hours and safety regulations, and receive adequate pay – in the sense of equal pay for equal jobs or skills. Persistently high levels of informality, furthermore, reduce fiscal revenues and the ability to develop social security systems based on taxes and contributions.

ISBN: 978-92-64-05923-8 - © OECD 2009

In addition, the size and composition of informal employment have an influence of the growth pattern of an economy. Whether or not informal employment represents a "drag on productivity" or could at least temporarily be an "engine of growth" is debatable. For example, many observers argue that a high degree of informal employment may reduce the competitiveness of an economy as informal firms: *i)* prefer to stay small; *ii)* have less access to inputs; and *iii)* cannot engage in formal business relationships, factors which consequently reduce their productivity. Others emphasise that in emerging economies, such as China, informal employment allows the necessary flexibility to produce innovative entrepreneurs who boost growth. Disregarding the validity of these two opposing views – i.e. small firms characterised by low-productivity vs. innovative entrepreneurs with high levels of flexibility – it is widely accepted that informal employment is an important issue to which policy makers need to respond.

INFORMAL EMPLOYMENT IS CLOSELY LINKED TO POVERTY

In spite of its growing importance even in OECD countries, informal employment remains particularly problematic in developing countries. The majority of the 1.7 billion poor in the world depend exclusively on their labour for survival, emphasising the key importance of employment for poverty reduction and economic development.

A general lack of formal employment and the limited coverage and effectiveness of social security systems imply that the poor often have to undertake any type of job in order simply to sustain themselves and their families. Dismissed workers frequently have to move to the first available job even if it is of a lower quality than the one they have just lost.

Moreover, certain groups, such as young people and women, require specific attention as they are over-represented among the informally employed. Women seem to be especially susceptible to informal employment. Until recently researchers and policy makers concentrated chiefly on gender differences in labour market participation and the barriers women face in employment. Although this remains an important concern, a second dimension of labour market outcomes should be added: gender differences in the quality of jobs and inequality in terms of access to good, secure and well-paid jobs. Understanding why women are over-represented in informal work is of primary importance in the design of more effective policies that allow a country's workforce – including women – to engage in productive activities.

Even though it is becoming increasingly the norm in low and middle-income countries, informal employment cannot therefore be accepted from a development perspective. However, simply abolishing micro-enterprises or informal wage work is also not a sustainable policy response. On the contrary, such measures would cause significant social costs and represent a huge challenge for public expenditure.

REASONS FOR INFORMAL EMPLOYMENT

Informal employment occurs in various types and shapes, making it difficult to grasp this complex phenomenon. Similarly, levels of informal employment vary widely across countries, reaching the highest shares in sub-Saharan Africa, followed by Southeast Asia and Latin America.

What are the reasons for this situation? Informal employment can be a result of both people being excluded from formal jobs and people voluntarily opting out of formal structures. In many middle-income countries, for example, incentive structures are conducive to driving individuals and businesses out of the formal sector. In Latin America, formal workers are often required to pay for a mandatory bundle of programmes, some of which they do not even want. Likewise, many businesses opt out of formal structure as a result of inefficiencies in business registration and social security administration.

ISBN: 978-92-64-05923-8 - © OECD 2009

Economic development also plays an important role in determining the prevalence of informal employment. Episodes of rapid economic expansion often coincide with sharp increases in informality. However, sustainable economic development can also contribute to the reduction of informal employment. Long-term increasing per capita income, for example, is clearly associated with lower levels of informality. Is economic development therefore driving informality, or is the use of informal channels, conversely, fostering growth? The answers to these questions are complex.

In some countries, the use of informal channels may indeed have positively affected economic development. If cumbersome registration procedures and other administrative red tape undermine the creation of formal businesses, for example, informality may be a tool to unleash entrepreneurial behaviour. Informal minibuses in South Africa are a prominent example of how the evasion of formal structure (e.g. route concessions, licence requirements, safety regulations) has contributed to the establishment of a multi-million-dollar industry.

In other instances, the use of informal structures may be driven less by a voluntary decision than necessity. For many people informal employment is an important livelihood strategy and thus plays a critical role in order to alleviate poverty and social hardship. Besides the fact that being informally employed usually also means being without adequate social protection, informality also traps people in unproductive and precarious jobs. In these instances, the lack of formal structures is rather a reason for, not the solution to, lagging economic development.

WHAT CAN WE DO?

As suggested in the book's title, informality can be expected to influence labour markets for many years to come. Governments should face this reality and incorporate informal employment into their policy making. The overall focus of policy interventions should rest on providing jobs that are more productive and offer adequate social protection. To better link employment, growth and poverty reduction, the following factors play a crucial role: a macroeconomic framework that guarantees stability, while not toning down public investment, to improve social protection; structural policies aiming at promoting sectors with a high potential for creating formal employment as well as easing mobility; and poverty alleviation policies that provide improved risk management and social protection, in particular for the poor.

TOWARDS A THREE-PRONGED STRATEGY

Effectively addressing informal employment needs to start by reinforcing the advantages of the formal sector. Where people have chosen to leave the formal sector, they need to be given incentives to rejoin it. Benefits should be linked to social contribution levels, while administrative procedures such as business and workers' registrations should be simplified. Apart from positive incentives, reducing informal employment also implies strengthening enforcement mechanisms. However, policies also need adequately to address those who have no choice but to work informally. Such people need a different approach from those who voluntarily opt out of the formal sector. Poverty-alleviation programmes can tide over people whose options for entering the labour market are limited.

A better understanding of the complexity of informal employment and a more nuanced approach to address the specific needs of informal workers are urgently needed. Informal employment comprises different phenomena that require distinct policy approaches. *Is Informal Normal?* therefore calls for a three-pronged strategy that should be adapted depending on the specific situation in a country. The following components can be identified:

ISBN: 978-92-64-05923-8 - © OECD 2009

1) For the world's poor, working informally is often the only way to participate in the labour market. Policies should consequently try to unlock these people from their low-productivity activities, enable them to be more productive and provide them with opportunities to climb the social ladder. Specific recommendations include active labour market policies, such as training and skill-development programmes, that reopen the doors to formality.

2) If informal employment is a deliberate choice to avoid taxes or administrative burdens, governments should aim to establish efficient formal structures that have the potential to encourage people to join or rejoin the formal market. Countries should aim to introduce formal structures that can offer the same (or higher) levels of the flexibility and efficiency that informal channels occasionally may provide. In this way, informal workers, who frequently have strong innovation and growth potential, can more effectively contribute to the overall competitiveness of a country. Needless to say, targeting those who voluntarily opt out of the formal sector also involves the establishment of credible enforcement mechanisms. *Is Informal Normal?* therefore advises countries to spend more resources on labour inspections, for example, which will help identify law-breakers and increase compliance with a country's rules and regulations.

3) In many low-income countries, finally, informal employment is mainly a consequence of insufficient job creation in the formal economy. *Is Informal Normal?* thus also recognises the need for a general push for more employment opportunities within the formal sector. Governments should support small businesses to comply with formal requirements and encourage large companies to create formal employment opportunities.

THE BIGGER PICTURE – BUILDING TRUST IN THE STATE

Informal employment is back on the policy agenda after many reforms in the past have failed to deliver successful results. In particular, policies were insufficiently targeted at the different types of informal employment that we can observe today. Clearly, finding the right balance between guaranteeing social security for those who are excluded from formal structures and encouraging those who voluntarily left the formal sector is of primary importance.

Policies can go a long way, but they are no substitute for trust. Informality is above all an expression of the lack of trust in public institutions, the negative perception of the role of the state and the limited understanding of the benefits derived from social security. It is basically a sign of a broken social contract. Long-term sustainable change requires a transformation of people's attitudes and beliefs. More innovative policies, such as information campaigns on the benefits of formal work and the risks of informality, can gradually change people's opinions. While these things will not happen overnight, governments need to pave the road with the right policies and regulations now.

ISBN: 978-92-64-05923-8 - © OECD 2009

CHAPTER ONE

Employment, Poverty Reduction and Development: What's New?

Johannes Jütting and Juan R. de Laiglesia

ABSTRACT

The main aim of this volume is to initiate a policy dialogue on how to deal with this phenomenon. It makes three main contributions to the policy debate. First, it presents comparable data on the evolution of informal employment and its most significant components for a wide array of countries and over time. Second, it discusses what determines informal employment, its persistence over time, and its gender dimension. It also considers the strategies of individual workers in seeking to increase their earnings within informal employment and across the divide between informal and formal employment. Third, it argues for a three-pronged strategy better to deal with informal employment and its consequences.

ISBN: 978-92-64-05923-8 - © OECD 2009

THE RATIONALE FOR THIS VOLUME

The economic crisis of 2008 has deep implications for employment across the planet. It is impossible now to put an accurate figure on its effect, but it appears certain that both jobs and wage levels are going to suffer in many countries. The crisis brings to an end a period of relatively strong and sustained growth accompanied by the creation of many more jobs. World employment in 2007 was almost one third higher compared with 1990 (ILO, 2008).

Despite these successes in the last decade in creating more jobs in the course of economic expansion, welfare gains vary widely between countries and individuals. An increasing concern, all the more important during an economic downturn, is whether these jobs are "good" jobs that can provide a minimum standard of living and protection against risks. Indeed, the ILO and others argue that the newly created jobs are often "bad" jobs, locking people into a vicious circle of low pay, high risks and limited mobility. As further developed in this study, a large majority of bad jobs are closely linked to informal employment.

Informal employment refers to jobs or activities in the production and sales of legal goods and services which are not regulated or protected by the state[1]. Most of the world's workers are informally employed. According to the latest data available, in the average country over 55 per cent of non-agricultural employment is informal. Moreover, in sub-Saharan African or South Asian countries, proportions are higher and closer to 80 per cent – 83 per cent of Indian non-agricultural workers are informally employed – or even 90 per cent, as is the case of Chad, with 95 per cent informal employment in non-agricultural activities.

The quality of the jobs created is a key concern for developing countries but a growing issue in developed countries as well. Indeed, it is not only an issue of the quality of new jobs created. In developed countries, where formal employment predominates, the recent trend towards a shift from formal jobs into informal ones presents an additional challenge. The transformation of labour relations arising from the globalisation of value chains and the prevalence of outsourcing, especially in the case of industrial activities, has far-reaching effects on the employment conditions of workers across the world.

Why Should We Care About Informal Employment?

Distinct arguments can be put forward: poverty reduction, efficiency and public finance concerns.

First, equity and poverty reduction considerations. Informal jobs are often precarious, have low productivity and are of a low general quality. Most of the informally employed are exposed to various risks – health, safety at work, loss of earnings – without adequate protection. This is true in particular for most of those working on their own account and of wage employees within the informal sector. Unable to afford spells of unemployment, many people in developing countries use informal employment as a survival strategy. Moreover, certain groups, such as the young and women, seem to be over-represented within this category of jobs. Quite apart from earnings levels, informal employment is also associated with vulnerability in the field of basic rights and a limited capacity to defend those rights. As such, it can be a major cause of poverty in areas other than that of simple income.

With the adoption in 2000 of the Millennium Development Goals (MDGs) by more than 190 heads of state and government leaders, the reduction of poverty has become a key issue for policy makers in developing and developed countries alike. The debate about how best to achieve the MDGs has also prompted interest in looking again at the role of employment in poverty reduction (Islam, 2006; Cook *et al.*, 2008; Lundström and Ronnas, 2006) and examining ways to create not only more jobs but also better ones (Paci and Serneels, 2007)[2].

Second, productivity considerations. There is no consensus in the literature on whether or not informal employment represents a "drag on productivity" or could, at least temporarily, present an engine of growth. One side of the argument is that a high degree of informal employment

ISBN: 978-92-64-05923-8 - © OECD 2009

reduces the competitiveness of the economy as informal firms prefer to stay small or are compelled by the threat of inspections to do so, have less access to inputs (credit, training), cannot engage in formal relationships and accordingly also exhibit a lower productivity (OECD, 2004; Levy, 2008; La Porta and Shleifer, 2008). In emerging economies such as China, on the other hand, informal employment is sometimes seen as a positive phenomenon (admittedly a temporary one) and an engine of growth. Hu (2004) argues that informal employment growth since the early 1990s has been the main driving force of job creation in China and is seen as extremely flexible, dynamic and innovative. While this debate is not settled yet, the link between productivity and informal employment is an important one that deserves close attention.

Third, public finance considerations. Persistent and high levels of informality reduce tax revenues and the ability to develop contribution-based social security systems. Furthermore, those workers who are rationed out or excluded from formal jobs and who depend on informal employment, either as micro-entrepreneurs or informal wage workers, for income generation represent a huge challenge for public expenditure (OECD, 2004). Ultimately, the prevalence of informal employment is not only a fiscal issue: it can be interpreted as a sign of a dysfunctional social contract between the state and its citizens. The state is not delivering the public goods in the quantity and quality desired by its citizens, while in parallel citizens are evading taxes, social security contributions and the like in actions which undermine the capacity of the state to deliver those goods.

19

INFORMAL EMPLOYMENT: WHAT'S NEW?

Rediscovering the Importance of Employment for the Growth-Poverty Nexus

Many studies analysing "pro-poor growth" find that functioning labour markets are essential in transforming growth into effective poverty reduction (Osmani, 2005; Islam, 2006; Lundström and Ronnas, 2006). Most of the nearly 1.7 billion extremely poor people in the world[3] depend on their labour for survival as it is often their only asset. The opportunities they have to use their labour productively are a crucial element in determining how they will benefit from growth or suffer from a downturn. That said, it is increasingly recognised that it is not good enough simply to provide more jobs. Many workers are locked into low pay, high risk and precarious activities often related to informal employment. The issue lies not so much in having a job but in having a bad job. Unemployment rates in a country such as India are lower than those of most OECD countries and most of the non-employed are relatively better off as they can afford not to work. Most people, though, have to work to earn their living and with an estimated 83 per cent of non-agricultural jobs qualifying as informal, and many of them being of poor quality, there is a need to make these jobs better, especially for women and young people[4]. The International Labour Organization (ILO) (2008) estimates that there are 190 million people out of work in the world, but as many as 487 million workers living under the international one-dollar-a-day poverty line. The great majority of these are informally employed and work in the informal sector.

Informal Employment Concerns Very Heterogeneous Groups

The economic literature, both theoretical and empirical, has evolved substantially from the view of informal employment as an undistinguished mass of underemployed "reserve" workers in the spirit of the Lewis (1954) model. It is now accepted, and indeed embedded in the successive attempts to establish a consensus definition, that informal employment refers to a very widely varying set of employment relations. As data on the earnings of informal workers from developing countries have become available and been studied, the heterogeneity of informally employed workers has become evident (Chapter 2). The recognition that not all informal workers are poor, unproductive workers, without access to more productive forms of employment, matters

ISBN: 978-92-64-05923-8 - © OECD 2009

not only for accurately describing informal employment, but also for determining what policies to adopt to improve welfare and reduce poverty.

There are many possible classifications of workers within informal employment. Subdivisions of it have been proposed that account for differences in work conditions or employment status. The Women in Informal Employment: Globalizing and Organizing (WIEGO) network and its members have proposed several classifications based either on the place of work or the status of employment (www.wiego.org/). In particular, distinguished by status of employment, the informally employed can be further classified into several groups. Among those self-employed it is possible to distinguish: *i)* an entrepreneurial class among the self-employed; *ii)* a majority of micro-entrepreneurs and own-account workers with no intention of, or scope for, potential growth; and *iii)* unpaid family workers. Among informal wage employees, there is also a wide range of workers; including *iv)* regular wage employees in the informal sector; *v)* casual and day labourers in the informal sector (particularly in agriculture and construction); *vi)* other wage employees, including in formal sector enterprises, without employment-based protection. Finally, a category of workers who are neither fully dependent wage workers nor fully independent self-employed workers can be singled out, including *vii)* industrial outworkers and other dependent contractors.

Why Does Informal Employment Persist? Old and New Controversies

Based on available information, informal employment today accounts for up to 47 per cent of total non-agricultural employment in West Asia and in North Africa, 70 to 90 per cent in sub-Saharan Africa, more than 50 per cent in Latin America, nearly 70 per cent in South and Southeast Asia and 24 per cent in transition economies. So "informal is normal" describes very accurately a key feature of today's labour markets in the world.

It is interesting to note that in the early 1970s a debate had already begun about informal employment, often focusing on the informal sector and informality and its impact on the economy (Hart, 1973). Over the years, a number of different schools of thought have emerged, giving rise to discussion about the nature and the *raison d'être* of the informal sector and informal employment. More than three decades later some progress had been made in defining and measuring the "Informal Sector Elephant" (Mead and Morrisson, 1996). Much less has been achieved when it comes to understanding the persistence of informality and what this means for policy making (Maloney, 2004). Recent evidence, however, points to the need to revisit the representation of the realities that such a concept encompasses, in terms of theories, modelling and policy prescriptions. Many of the early debates on informality focused on the relationship between the formal and informal sectors. Four stylised polar views can be identified:

1) The dualist school sees the informal sector as a set of marginal subsistence activities that have no link to the formal sector (Hart, 1973). In that view, informal work is the only option for surplus labour in the sense of the Lewis (1954) model. Informal activities are seen as operating in separate spheres and in segmented labour (and product) markets.

2) The structuralist school (Moser, 1978; Castells and Portes, 1989) sees informal activities as subordinated to the formal sector and therefore as a means for formal enterprises to reduce their costs.

3) The legalist school, associated in particular with the work of de Soto (1989, 2000), highlights the role of excess regulation or the cost of formal sector activity in driving potential entrepreneurs to operate informally.

4) Finally, a parasitic school (associated with Lewis, 2004) puts the emphasis on the illegality of informal activities and presents them as a means to gain an unfair advantage in their competition with formal counterparts. While in essence closely related, the legalistic and parasitic strands of literature differ markedly, depending on whether the emphasis is placed on excessive regulation on the part of the state (de Soto, 1989) or parasitic behaviour on the part of informal entrepreneurs (Lewis, 2004).

ISBN: 978-92-64-05923-8 - © OECD 2009

The type of interaction between the formal and the informal sectors is critical to understanding the effects of policy on the economy as a whole. Using the stylised views above, it is possible to see how the assessment of a particular policy would vary. As an example, it is possible to imagine policies that would make subcontracting easier: for example, through value added tax (VAT) exemptions. Dualists would take a benign view of formal sector enterprises subcontracting to the informal sector, as this would provide new opportunities for informal sector firms, possibly leading to increases in wages for the workers. On the other hand the parasitic school would oppose such a move as it results, in its view, in informal firms benefiting from their illegal status. Structuralists would also oppose it, but for quite different reasons: such a policy would enshrine the unequal links between sectors, and would therefore be unlikely to have a positive effect on informal workers.

While in the past the focus of the debate has been very much on an assessment of the implications for society as a whole of informal employment, the debate since the 1990s has moved on to discuss the causes of informal employment, taking a micro-perspective and looking at the motivation of individuals. The key question is whether people or firms voluntarily exit from formality or are excluded from the formal edifice of rights and obligations. Two dominant schools of thought can be identified according to the alternatives proposed in the 2007 World Bank publication: *Informality: Exit and Exclusion* (Perry *et al.*, 2007).

The *exit* or *voluntary* view argues that the majority of entrepreneurs and, to a lesser degree, of employees, choose to work informally as the result of weighing the costs and benefits brought by formality. Empirical analysis along these lines has been carried out mostly in studies on Latin America (Perry *et al.*, 2007; Maloney, 2004). This view can focus on the evasion of taxes (Lewis, 2004) but in its more complete version the recent literature also highlights the reality that individuals or firms that are voluntarily informal may choose to be so not only to evade tax but for many other reasons. These factors may be financial, such as compliance costs or the value-for-money of social security services, or non-financial, such as greater freedom in self-employment or entrepreneurship.

In sharp contrast, the *exclusion* view claims that informal workers are denied access to formal jobs. This view is consistent with the dualist school, which focuses on labour market segmentation but also with the legalistic school (de Soto, 2000) for which the origin of the segmentation is the prohibitive cost of formality imposed on a subset of the population. Ultimately, the crux of the debate rests on the relative importance of incentives and segmentation in the *raison d'être* of informal employment.

Recently, a *third view* has emerged combining aspects of both exclusion and exit. Fields (2005) and others argue that in urban informal labour markets in developing countries there exist an "upper tier" and "lower tier" (or free/easy entry sector, following Fields [1990]). The upper tier has access requirements that make it unavailable to workers in the lower tier. This upper tier comprises the competitive part, i.e. those who voluntarily choose to be informal, and the lower tier consists of individuals who cannot afford to be unemployed but do not have access to more productive employment in either the formal or the informal sector. Such a two-tiered view of the informal sector highlights the existence of segmentation *within* informal employment.

THE POLICY AGENDA: TOWARDS A THREE-PRONGED STRATEGY

This volume argues for a three-pronged strategy towards informal employment: *i)* creation of more formal jobs; *ii)* providing incentives to become formal to those who are located in the upper tier of informal employment; *iii)* giving the necessary means (legal, financial, social) to those who are excluded from the formal labour market, to enable them to become more productive, while at the same time helping them in improving their risk management through providing basic social services and fostering institutions for social security.

ISBN: 978-92-64-05923-8 - © OECD 2009

This strategy deviates substantially from a conventional approach to growth and poverty reduction, which focuses exclusively on growth as an objective of structural policies and sites poverty solely in the social policy realm, to be addressed through handouts and other social assistance interventions. It also differs markedly from views of informal activities that aim to "formalise" the sector, narrowly focusing on the effect of business and labour regulations and their enforcement.

This study argues for an integrated framework in which specific policy responses should differ more according to the type of informal employment prevalent than to the specific country context. The key point is the need for policy makers to have two different policy packages when dealing with each of the different tiers. For the lower tier – and this tier will comprise in most developing countries more than half of the working population – a productivity/social protection agenda is required. Increasing productivity, improving skills, enhancing upward mobility and, most importantly, creating good jobs – jobs that protect workers from falling into poverty – take precedence. The agenda for the upper tier looks different. Here there is a need to provide appropriate incentives through lower transaction costs related to business creation and operation and increased benefits of formalisation, and lending credibility to established regulation.

The study says that it is important to note that the transition to formal employment will take a very long time and that in many countries of the world "informal is normal" will remain the reality for decades to come. The key challenge is to increase productivity and social protection in informal employment while at the same time making easier the transition towards formal employment. To put this strategy into practice means to differentiate clearly between the upper tier part of informal employment and the lower tier. Within the upper tier, formality has to become more attractive through a reduction of costs and an improvement of the benefits; for the lower tier the creation of more and better jobs is the main concern.

Finally, the report argues that informal employment needs to be seen in the larger context of a need to build or repair a social contract between the state and its citizens. A redefinition – indeed often *the* definition – of the social contract between the state and its citizens is at stake. To achieve this, the report argues for more policy coherence and a whole-of-government approach that addresses informal employment. In particular, it calls for a stronger reflection of employment issues and outcomes in the Poverty Reduction Strategy Papers (PRSP) process and, more generally, for better co-ordination between employment, social and economic policies.

OUTLINE

This volume covers five topics: *i)* the size and evolution of informal employment; *ii)* determinants and causes of its persistence; *iii)* the gender dimension of informal employment; *iv)* the role of mobility; and *v)* policy implications.

In Chapter 2, Jacques Charmes presents an overview of the size of informal employment as well as trends in the last three decades, relying on both already collected and new data. This chapter presents a thorough picture of informal employment in the developing world. The findings are sobering: informal employment constitutes a remarkably high proportion of employment in many countries for which data are available. Moreover, although there is no consistent trend for all countries, overall informal employment in non-agricultural activities is increasing in a great many cases. Chapter 2 also collects data on the characteristics of informal employment in terms of job status and earnings separately for men and women. The findings show that earnings differentials between formal and informal work depend dramatically on the status of workers. In particular, they differ markedly between informal entrepreneurs and employees. The former seem to benefit from their informal status, while the latter, in the best of cases, have earnings comparable to the prevailing minimum wage, and in certain cases much lower.

Having shown that informal employment is persistent, and even increasing, the study turns to the light recent evidence has shed on the phenomenon of informal employment. In Chapter 3,

David Kucera and Theodora Xenogiani discuss the relationship between growth and the prevalence of informal employment. They review theories and evidence that underpin the view that there is dualism within informal employment. The authors suggest that once the diversity that exists within informal employment is recognised, the way that certain forms of informal employment are complementary to economic growth provides one answer to the puzzling persistence of informal employment.

Chapter 3 also examines what accounts for the persistence of informal employment by exploring three different hypotheses. The first emphasises the amount and pattern of growth, the second identifies labour market institutions and regulations as a main factor explaining persisting informal employment, while the third concentrates on broad institutions and culture. In respect of labour institutions and regulations in particular, the authors advocate going beyond the debate about regulation versus deregulation, and thinking rather about the optimal design and implementation of labour regulations in country and time-specific contexts.

Chapters 4 and 5 study two topical themes in informal employment that are of particular interest in painting a picture of who is informally employed in the developing world and why. Women are often over-represented in low quality, often informal jobs. In particular important gender differences exist in terms of sector of employment and pay, as well as non-monetary payoffs. In Chapter 4, David Kucera and Theodora Xenogiani seek to explain why this is so and what can be done about it. Women are found to be over-represented in the worst forms of informal employment, if not necessarily in informal employment taken as a whole. The factors that underlie the blatantly unequal outcomes between men and women in informal employment appear to be the same as those that are responsible for the low labour force participation rates found among women in the developing world. They include discrimination – shaped by informal institutions and social norms – in particular in forms that limit women's access to the labour market, and unequal access to resources (education, land, capital, networks). Finally, structural changes, driven in particular by globalisation, determine how many participate in labour markets and how. Policy implications include recommendations that are valid also for men, in terms of improving education outcomes, mobility and access to labour markets. However, specific-gendered policies that reach out to women, and take into account the specific barriers they face, and how these change over a woman's life, can further enhance the options open to women.

In a second topical chapter, attention is drawn towards the role of mobility. As panel data have become available in a limited number of developing countries, studies have found that mobility in developing country labour markets is quite high, including between formal and informal work, dispelling views of labour markets in low and middle-income countries as stagnant and inefficient. In Chapter 5, Jason Gagnon looks at forms of mobility and their implications for workers. The apparent paradox that average earnings in informal employment are penalised while moves from formal to informal employment are usually privately beneficial can be reconciled by acknowledging the diversity of informal employment. This interpretation also suggests that mobility can be welfare-enhancing even *within* informal employment. Focusing on improving the quality of jobs, and in particular those to which poor people have access, has important implications for how both the poor and informal workers are regarded by labour and social policy. The chapter pays particular attention to geographical mobility, including both internal and international migration, as a response to poor working conditions.

Finally, Chapter 6 presents a policy strategy for development that integrates policy lessons drawn from the literature and from experiences in both developing and OECD countries. It proposes a three-pronged strategy to deal with informal employment. This strategy has three basic aims: *i)* creating more good formal jobs; *ii)* protecting and promoting those without access to formal work; and *iii)* establishing incentives – through better service and enforcement – for more jobs to become formal.

Accordingly, three policy approaches are presented: a fundamental approach to enhance job creation, a second directed towards the lower tier of informal employment based around measures to increase the productivity of those workers and provide them with means better to deal with risk, including social protection, and finally a third approach using carrots and sticks to enhance the incentives to become formal for those in the upper tier of informal employment, including employers in the informal sector. The key underlying hypothesis is that while a one-size-fits-all approach will not work, the ingredients for each country's recipe are not all that different. In fact, policy approaches need to correspond to the form of informal employment and such forms are recognisable from one country to the next. However, the mix needs to be adjusted to suit conditions in each country.

NOTES

1. Chapter 2 in this volume discusses in detail the definition of informal employment and the statistical process of turning abstract concepts into observable and measurable quantities.

2. International organisations and research institutes dealing with poverty, aid and employment have set up specific programmes and initiatives. For example. the OECD Poverty Network set up a dedicated Task Team in 2006 on employment, poverty reduction and growth and the World Bank initiated in 2008 a Trust Fund on informality.

3. According to the one-dollar-a-day poverty line (adjusted to USD 1.45 in 2005 prices; see Chen and Ravallion, 2008).

4. The ILO launched in June 2008 within its "decent work" agenda a focus on gender equality.

ISBN: 978-92-64-05923-8 - © OECD 2009

REFERENCES

CASTELLS, M. and A. PORTES (1989), "World Underneath: The Origins, Dynamics and Effects of the Informal Economy", *in* A. PORTES, M. CASTELLS and L.A. BENTON (eds.) *The Informal Economy: Studies in Advanced and Less Developed Countries,* Johns Hopkins University Press, Baltimore, MD, pp. 11-40.

CHEN, M. and M. RAVALLION (2008), "The Developing World is Poorer than We Thought, but no Less Successful in the Fight against Poverty*", Policy Research Working Paper* No. 4703, World Bank, Washington, D.C.

COOK, S., J. HEINTZ and N. KABEER (2008), "Economic Growth, Social Protection and 'Real' Labour Markets: Linking Theory and Policy", *IDS Bulletin* No. 39, pp. 1-10.

FIELDS, G.S. (1990), "Labour Market Modelling and the Urban Informal Sector: Theory and Evidence", *in* D. TURNHAM, B. SALOMÉ and A. SCHWARZ (eds.), *The Informal Sector Revisited*, Development Centre Seminars, OECD, Paris.

FIELDS, G.S. (2005), "A Guide to Multisector Labour Market Models", *Social Protection Discussion Paper Series* No. 0505, World Bank, Washington, D.C.

HART, K. (1973), "Informal Income Opportunities and Urban Employment in Ghana", *The Journal of Modern African Studies,* Vol. 11(1), pp. 61-89.

HU, A. (2004), "Economic Growth and Employment Growth in China (1978-2001)", *Asian Economic Papers*, spring/summer 2004, Vol. 3, No. 2, pp. 166-176.

ILO (2008), *Global Employment Trends*, International Labour Office, Geneva, January.

ISLAM, R. (2006), "Fighting Poverty: The Development-Employment", p. 521, Lynne Rienner Publishers, Boulder, CO.

LA PORTA, R. and A. SHLEIFER (2008), "The Unofficial Economy and Economic Development", *Brookings Papers on Economic Activity*, August.

LEVY, S. (2008), "Good Intentions, Bad Outcomes", The Brookings Institution, Washington, D.C.

LEWIS, A. (1954), "Economic Development with Unlimited Supplies of Labour", *The Manchester School of Economic and Social Studies*, May.

LEWIS, W.W. (2004), *The Power of Productivity: Wealth, Poverty and the Threat to Global Stability*, Chicago, Ill., University of Chicago Press, Chicago.

LUNDSTROM, S. and P. RONNAS (2006), "Integrated Economic Analysis for Pro-Poor Growth", *SIDA Methods Document,* SIDA, Stockholm.

MALONEY, W.F. (2004), "Informality Revisited", *World Development,* Vol. 32(7), pp. 1159-1178.

MEAD, C. and C. MORRISSON (1996), "The Informal Sector Elephant", *World Development,* Vol. 24(10), pp. 1611-1619.

MOSER, C. (1978), "Informal Sector or Petty Commodity Production: Dualism or Dependence in Urban Development?", *World Development*, Vol. 6, Issues 9-10, September-October, pp. 1041-1064.

OECD (2004), *World Employment Outlook,* OECD, Paris.

OSMANI, S.R. (2005), "The Role of Employment in Promoting the Millennium Development Goals", *Issues in Employment and Poverty Discussion Paper* No. 18. ILO/UNDP, Geneva/New York, October.

PACI, P. and P. SERNEELS (eds.) (2007), *Employment and Shared Growth: Rethinking the Role of Labor Mobility for Development*, World Bank, Washington, D.C.

PERRY, G., W. MALONEY, O. ARIAS, P. FAJNZYLBER, A. MASON and J. SAAVEDRA-CHANDUVI (2007), *Informality: Exit and Exclusion*, World Bank, Washington, D.C.

SOTO, H. DE (1989), *The Other Path: The Invisible Revolution in the Third World*, Harper & Row, New York, NY.

SOTO, H. DE. (2000), *The Mystery of Capital: Why Capitalism Triumphs in the West and Fails Everywhere Else*, Basic Books, New York, NY.

26

ISBN: 978-92-64-05923-8 - © OECD 2009

CHAPTER TWO

Concepts, Measurement and Trends
Jacques Charmes

ABSTRACT

Measuring informal employment has remained a challenge and requires the use of a variety of sources and methods, including the use of data for self-employment as a proxy indicator. Although patterns are not uniform, informal employment persists at a high level in all parts of the developing world, with the highest level seen in sub-Saharan Africa where more than two-thirds of people in the non-agricultural sector are working in informal jobs. Important gender differences can be seen in informal employment, with patterns in job status and earnings differing distinctly between men and women. Moreover, the differences in earnings between formal and informal work depend on the job status with informal entrepreneurs being better off relative to informal employees.

ISBN: 978-92-64-05923-8 - © OECD 2009

INTRODUCTION

The concept of informal employment has become widely accepted in the analysis of labour markets in developing countries. The controversies and debates around its importance, determinants and policy implications referred to in Chapter 1 result to some degree from different concepts, definitions and measurement approaches. To resolve these ambiguities, this chapter identifies recent progress in harmonising the measurement of informal employment at the international level. If the trends in informal employment and in its main components are to be assessed the concepts used for defining informality, as well as for measuring its characteristics, need to be clarified.

The particular contribution that this chapter brings to the discussion is the publication of new data related to informal employment and self-employment, their trend over time and gender component, as well as new data about earnings and wages. By so doing, the chapter is laying the groundwork for the chapters that follow. While important progress in respect of data quality and availability has been made, one major conclusion from this chapter is to underline the need for further improvements. Existing data-sets are often still scattered, quality issues remain and some data published are already out of date. For some new phenomena such as informal employment in formal sectors and false self-employment, or for the different categories of workers within informal employment, no international comparable data yet exist.

CONCEPTS

The informal sector as a concept continued to be controversial in academic circles long after it was discovered in the early 1970s (Hart, 1973; ILO, 1972) and internationally defined by the International Conference of Labour Statisticians in 1993 (15th ICLS, ILO, 1993a and 1993b). The controversy centred on the failure of the "informal sector", as defined, to capture the dramatic increase of unprotected jobs within the formal sector itself. Eventually, the 17th ICLS (2003) provided guidelines for the definition and measurement of *informal employment*, a concept capturing unprotected jobs in both the formal and informal sectors[1].

The definition of informal employment is concerned with the characteristics of jobs, rather than the economic units to which they belong. *The operational criteria for defining informal employment are mainly that the job has no written contract and lacks social protection*. The guidelines approved by the 17th ICLS provide more substantive characteristics of this type of work. Besides informal self-employment, the guidelines define informal wage jobs as those in which:

> "the employment relationship (...) is not subject to national labour legislation, income taxation, social protection or entitlement to certain employment benefits (advance notice of dismissal, severance pay, paid annual or sick leave, etc.). The reasons may be the following: non-declaration of the jobs of the employees; casual jobs or jobs of a limited short duration; jobs with hours of work or wages below a specified threshold (e.g. for social security contributions); employment by unincorporated enterprises or by persons in households; jobs where the employee's place of work is outside the premises of the employer's enterprise (e.g. outworkers without an employment contract); or jobs for which labour regulations are not applied, not enforced, or not complied with for any other reason."

The criteria are to be determined "in accordance with national circumstances and data availability".

The 1993 ICLS resolution provides a *substantive definition* of the informal sector as:

> "consisting of units engaged in the production of goods or services with the primary objective of generating employment and incomes to the persons concerned. These units typically operate at a low level of organisation, with little or no division between labour and capital

as factors of production and on a small scale. Labour relations – where they exist – are based mostly on casual employment, kinship or personal and social relations rather than contractual arrangements with formal guarantees."

The *operational definition* refers to the characteristics of economic units. Criteria for defining the informal sector are: the legal status of the economic unit (unincorporated enterprises, not corporations); non-registration of the unit; non registration of its employees; size (fewer than five or ten permanent employees): and at least some production for the market. Given this last characteristic, household production exclusively for own final use and the unpaid care economy are excluded from the scope of the present study.

To summarise the definitions, an assessment of the size and trends of informal employment and of its main components can use the following definitions:

— Informal employment in the informal sector as comprised of:

  - Self-employed: own-account workers, employers, contributing family workers.

  - Employers and paid employees in micro-enterprises with fewer than five workers or employees.

— Informal employment in the formal sector as comprised of:

  - Paid employees without social protection in enterprises with five workers (or employees) or more.

  - Paid domestic workers without social protection.

Hussmanns (2001) has proposed a useful and detailed framework to understand the coverage and meaning of the two concepts which is reproduced in Diagram 2.1 and explained on the next page.

Diagram 2.1. Components of the Informal Sector and of Informal Employment

Production units by type	Jobs by status in employment									
	Own-account workers		Employers		Contributing family workers	Employees			Members of producers' co-operatives	
	Informal	Formal	Informal	Formal	Informal	Informal	Formal		Informal	Formal
Formal sector enterprises					1	2				
Informal sector enterprises[a]	3		4		5	6	7		8	
Households[b]	9					10				

Notes:

a) As defined by the 15th International Conference of Labour Statisticians (excluding households employing paid domestic workers).

b) Households producing goods exclusively for their own final use and households employing paid domestic workers.

In Diagram 2.1, cells shaded in light grey refer to formal jobs. Unshaded cells represent the various types of informal jobs. Cells shaded in dark grey refer to jobs which, by definition, do not exist in the type of production unit in question.

In summary, informal employment is captured by jobs in cells 1 to 6 and 8 to 10. Employment in the informal sector is captured by cells 3 to 8, which include formal jobs in informal sector enterprises (cell 7). Informal employment outside the informal sector is captured in cells 1, 2, 9 and 10.

ISBN: 978-92-64-05923-8 - © OECD 2009

MEASUREMENT, SOURCES AND PROXIES

Because *informal employment* is measured through individual or job characteristics, labour force surveys are the best data sources for measuring it. Recent labour force surveys, especially those that have benefited from technical support from the ILO, have included an adequate set of questions to measure both informal employment and informal sector employment.

Employment in the informal sector has been measured through direct surveys since the 1980s. Before this period, it was measured (and is still measured in those countries where labour force surveys are lacking) by indirect methods called "residual methods", which consist of subtracting registered employment from total employment, industry by industry.

These methods are also used for measuring informal employment where labour force surveys have not yet included the questions necessary to identify this category. Many *ad hoc* surveys have been conducted at various periods in developing and transition countries for the measurement of informal sector and informal employment (see Charmes, 2004). It is also in these *ad hoc* surveys that data on income and salaries in the informal sector can be found, to be compared with the legal minimum wage, the average wage in the public and/or the private sector or with the GDP per worker (for comparison purposes between countries and over time) as well. Furthermore, the ILO bureau of statistics has been collecting data on informal employment and informal sector employment from a questionnaire survey sent to member countries (in 2004).

While data on employment in the informal sector are now available for a large number of countries, data on informal employment are only available for selected countries in more recent periods. For this reason, the use of proxies is still necessary for understanding trends in informal employment, especially trends over the past four decades.

Self-employment is such a proxy, or indicator, for informal employment. Self-employment is the complement to wage employment (employees) in total employment and comprises own-account workers, employers, contributing family workers and members of producers' co-operatives. The growth of wage employment has traditionally been taken as an indicator of modernisation, as it corresponds to the integration of labour into firms. The growth of self-employment similarly can be interpreted as an indicator for the growing importance of less codified labour relations and therefore of informalisation. Self-employment is only a proxy because it comprises workers who are formal, such as (self-employed) professionals, whose number, however, is small in developing countries. Figure 2.1 observes the strong correlation between self-employment and informal employment and supports the use of self-employment as a useful indicator for informal employment.

ISBN: 978-92-64-05923-8 - © OECD 2009

Figure 2.1. **Self-Employment and Informal Employment**

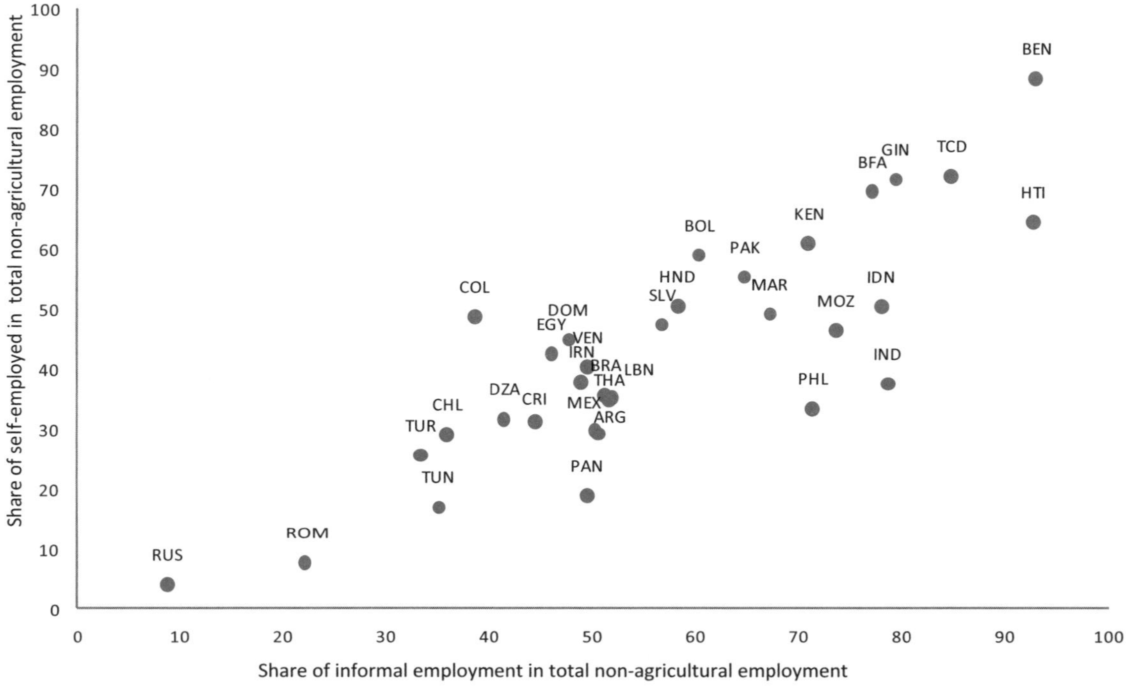

Source: See Tables 2.1 and 2.3.
StatLink http://dx.doi.org/10.1787/533140181104

Self-employment has been measured in population censuses since the early 1960s and in labour force surveys since the 1980s. As a proxy for the main component of the informal sector, the concept of self-employment is the most suitable for measuring the trends over the past four decades. Data are available for more than 110 countries, compiled from the database of the United Nations Population Division for population censuses (United Nations, 1994) and from the database LABORSTA from the ILO bureau of statistics, completed by national sources.

Useful tables are those cross-classifying the employed population by industries (International Standard Industrial Classification, ISIC) or by occupations (International Standard Classification of Occupations, ISCO) and by employment status (International Classification by Status in Employment, ICSE) and by gender.

The main challenge is to classify paid employees and, if possible, employers by formal/informal sector or formal/informal employment. The characteristics of the economic unit in which paid employees work are, therefore, needed. Very few countries collect both sets of variables necessary to measure both informal employment and the informal sector.

Disaggregating figures for informal employment and self-employment between agriculture and non-agriculture (rather than rural/urban) is of primary importance because it makes it possible to take into account major structural changes in developing countries (see Box 2.1).

ISBN: 978-92-64-05923-8 - © OECD 2009

Box 2.1. Informal Employment Excluding or Including Agriculture?

There are several reasons why informal employment – although including agricultural activities by definition – is measured excluding agriculture, animal husbandry, fishery and forestry. The first reason is that the criteria for defining the informal sector (though it is less true for informal employment) are not adapted in the case of agriculture and usual data collection systems do not often distinguish formal and informal (or modern and traditional) agriculture. The second reason is that the shift from agricultural to non-agricultural activities is a sign of modernisation. Therefore, we must distinguish between agriculture and non-agriculture (rather than rural/urban) to take account for major structural changes in developing countries: to be acknowledged and understandable, the trends in informal employment as well as in self-employment must distinguish between agriculture and non-agricultural activities. This is because the shift from the former to the latter results in a decrease of agricultural self-employment or agricultural informal employment and an increase of non-agricultural informal employment or non agricultural self-employment.

In many countries some gaps persist in the application of international definitions and it is therefore necessary to use categories that are not strictly comparable. For instance, the time series prepared for most countries in Latin America by the "Panorama Laboral" of the ILO regional office do not fit exactly with the international definition because they are based on size of the unit and not the legal status.

And there are still many countries where *indirect methods* of estimation are the only means for assessing the size of informal employment. In particular, the "residual method", traditionally implemented by national accountants in their attempt to build labour input matrices for imputing production to specific categories of employment, was widely used in the 1970s and in the 1980s.

Details for the methodologies used for the data presented in this study are available in Annex 2.A2 (informal employment) and Annex 2.A3 (self-employment).

TRENDS AND CHARACTERISTICS

Estimates of informal employment have existed since it was first tentatively defined in the mid-1970s. Most of the estimates for the 1970s and 1980s result from the application of indirect methods based on the comparison between total employment and employment in registered establishments or activities. From the end of the 1980s *ad hoc* informal sector surveys based on mixed household/establishment data collection were launched, as well as adapted labour force surveys or household surveys.

As seen in Figure 2.2, on average, informal employment accounts for more than 47 per cent of total non-agricultural employment in West Asia and in North Africa, and more than 70 per cent in sub-Saharan Africa, more than 50 per cent in Latin America, nearly 70 per cent in South and Southeast Asia and 24 per cent in transition economies.

ISBN: 978-92-64-05923-8 - © OECD 2009

Figure 2.2. **Share of Informal Employment in Non-Agricultural Employment**

Share of informal employment in total non-agricultural employment

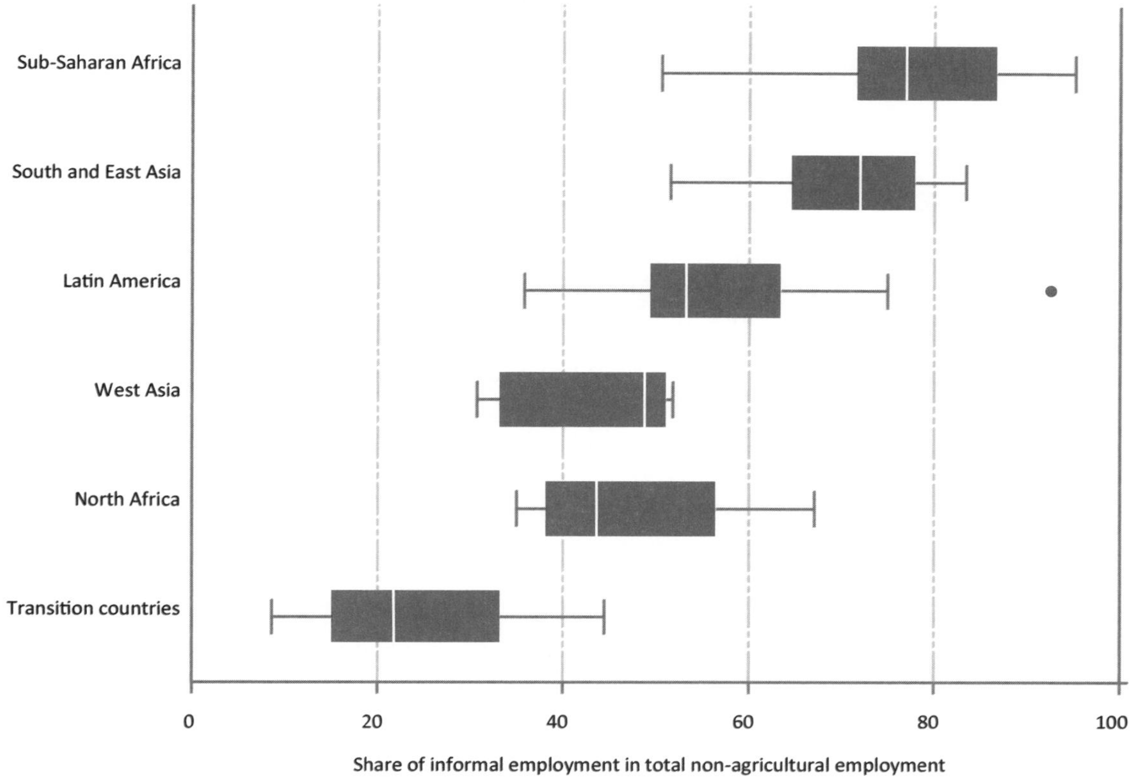

Note:
The box chart shows the range of informal employment as share of total non-agricultural employment by region, based on the latest available observation for each country. The edges of each box correspond to the upper and lower quartiles, with the vertical line inside indicating the median value for each region. The 'whiskers' outside the box show the upper and lower adjacent values of the data. The outlier value in Latin America is Haiti.

Source: See Table 2.1.
StatLink http://dx.doi.org/10.1787/533451351643

The share of informal employment in total non-agricultural employment is presented in Table 2.1. Albeit not uniform, the data show an upward-oriented trend of informal employment in all regions (for the last period, however, the number of observations is too small to be representative in some regions).

Sub-Saharan Africa is characterised by the highest levels of informal employment, increasing regularly and rapidly over time, from 70 per cent of non-agricultural employment in Burkina Faso in mid-1985 to 77 per cent in 1994. Informal employment reached a high point of 94.1 per cent of total non-agricultural employment in Mali at the end of the 1990s (from 63.1 per cent at the end of the 1970s, 78.6 per cent at the end of the 1980s and 90.4 per cent at the beginning of the 1990s) before dropping to 81.8 per cent in 2004, probably because of changes in the definition. Another example of rapid growth of informal employment is Guinea, from 64.4 per cent at the beginning of the 1980s to 71.9 per cent in the early 1990s and 86.7 per cent at the end of the 1990s. In these countries informal employment has been the main, if not the sole, source of employment creation, absorbing the labour surplus resulting from population growth.

Trends in *North Africa* are more mixed: they are in general an example of the countercyclical behaviour of informal employment and of its components. The case of Tunisia is typical in this regard: after a period of rapid growth during the early 1970s, followed by a decline at the end of the 1970s, informal employment increased again in the late 1980s as a result of

ISBN: 978-92-64-05923-8 - © OECD 2009

the structural adjustment programmes, then the take-off of industrialisation in the 1990s re-initiated a rapid growth of informal employment until the end of the decade, while the figure has declined in the 2000s.

In *Latin America*, the share of informal employment in non-agricultural employment peaked at 54.2 per cent in 1995-99 and remains high where data are available for 2000 onwards, with considerable increases seen in Ecuador, Panama and Venezuela, but also significant rates of decrease in Mexico and Brazil.

Similar trends are observed in *South and Southeast Asia*, but at a higher level. Informal employment was 69.9 per cent of total non-agricultural employment in the period 1995-99: high rates of increase can be observed in India, Indonesia and Pakistan. Thailand, as an emerging economy, experienced a decrease in informal employment over the whole period, even if a small increase was observed during the financial crisis of the end of the 1990s. In *West Asia,* the small sample in past decades does not make it possible to assess the trends: the share of informal employment was at 43.2 per cent in the mid-2000s.

Recent measures in *transition economies* show a level of informal employment at an average of 24.1 per cent in the 2000s, ranging from 8.6 per cent in Russia to 44.4 per cent in Kyrgyzstan.

34

Table 2.1. Share of Informal Employment in Total Non-Agricultural Employment by five-year period and by country and region

	1975-79	1980-84	1985-89	1990-94	1995-99	2000-07
North Africa					47.5	47.3
Algeria	21.8		25.6		42.7	41.3
Morocco		56.9			44.8	67.1
Tunisia	38.4	35	39.3		47.1	35.0
Egypt	58.7		37.3		55.2	45.9
Sub-Saharan Africa				76.0		
Benin				92.9		
Burkina Faso			70	77		
Chad				74.2	95.2	
Guinea		64.4		71.9	86.7	
Kenya			61.4	70.1	71.6	
Mali	63.1		78.6	90.4	94.1	81.8
Mauritania		69.4	80			
Mozambique				73.5		
Niger	62.9					
Senegal		76				
South Africa						50.6
Zaire (now Democratic Republic of Congo)		59.6				
Zambia				58.3		
Latin America					54.2	
Argentina				47.5	53.3	
Bolivia				56.9	63.5	
Brazil				60	60	51.1
Chile					35.8	
Colombia					38.4	
Costa Rica					44.3	

ISBN: 978-92-64-05923-8 - © OECD 2009

Dominican Republic				47.6	
Ecuador				53.5	74.9
El Salvador				56.6	
Guatemala			56.1		
Haiti				92.6	
Honduras				58.2	
Mexico			55.5	59.4	50.1
Panama				37.6	49.4
Paraguay				65.5	
Peru					67.9
Venezuela			38.8	46.9	49.4
South and Southeast Asia				**69.9**	
India		76.2	73.7	83.4	
Indonesia		39.2		77.9	
Pakistan		39		64.6	
Philippines			70.5	72	
Thailand		57.4	51.4	51.5	
West Asia					**43.2**
Iran		43.5			48.8
Lebanon					51.8
West Bank and Gaza Strip					43.4
Syria			41.7	42.9	30.7
Turkey				30.9	33.2
Yemen			57.1		51.1
Transition countries					**24.1**
Kyrgyzstan					44.4
Moldova					21.5
Romania				5.4	22.0
Russia					8.6

Sources: Charmes (2002), for the ILO *Women and Men in the Informal Economy*, 2002. For the most recent period: Heintz and Chang (2007) for the ILO, and for West Asia: Charmes (2007 and 2008). For detailed sources, see Annex 2.A4.
StatLink ᔏᔑ⬚ http://dx.doi.org/10.1787/533451351643

Table 2.2 below shows the composition of non-agricultural informal employment by status in employment (self-employment/wage employment) for the 1990s and the 2000s for selected countries. Unfortunately this type of disaggregation is not possible for most estimates from the 1970s and the 1980s and also for some recent estimates. The number of countries for which data for several years are available is small, and consequently it is possible to present representative trends for these indicators only for the past two decades. Tables 2.4 and 2.5 present these indicators in a gender perspective.

During the 1990s, sub-Saharan Africa was the region with the lowest share of wage employment in informal employment (28.3 per cent). The regional average would be even lower if Kenya and South Africa were not taken into account (15.7 per cent). South and Southeast Asia show a much higher share (42.6 per cent) of paid employment in informal employment. Latin America has a share of 38.8 per cent for paid employment. Finally, informally paid employees represent 37.7 per cent of informal employment in North Africa and with a similar regional average in West Asia (but substantially lower if Turkey is not considered).

ISBN: 978-92-64-05923-8 - © OECD 2009

After the year 2000, it appears that the share of paid employment in informal employment is on the rise in North Africa and sub-Saharan Africa. For Morocco, the figure is 32.2 per cent (against 18.7 per cent in the 1990s) and 64.5 per cent for Egypt (against 50.3 per cent); Mali shows 81.8 per cent of informal employment and only 21.9 per cent of paid employees and South Africa with 79.2 per cent of paid employees in informal employment (against 74.8 per cent in the 1990s). In Latin America, the share of paid employees in informal employment increased in Mexico and Panama, but the ratio decreased in Brazil and Venezuela. In Western Asia, informal employment has grown in Iran and Turkey, but decreased in Yemen. Finally, transition countries show very high shares of informal paid employment (56.7 per cent) for a relatively modest (but increasing) size of informal employment.

Table 2.2. Informal Employment by Status in Employment
countries and regions, 1990s and 2000s

Regions/Countries	% self-employed in informal employment		% paid employees in informal employment	
Years	1990s	2000s	1990s	2000s
North Africa	**62.3**		**37.7**	
Algeria	66.6		33.4	
Morocco	81.3	67.8	18.7	32.2
Tunisia	51.6		48.4	
Egypt	49.7	35.5	50.3	64.5
Sub-Saharan Africa	**71.7**		**28.3**	
Benin	95.4		4.6	
Burkina Faso	86.9		13.1	
Chad	92.7		7.3	
Guinea	95.0		5.0	
Kenya	42.0		58.0	
Mali		78.1		21.9
Mauritania	72.8		27.2	
Mozambique	63.3		36.7	
South Africa	25.2	20.8	74.8	79.2
Latin America	**61.2**		**38.8**	
Argentina				
Bolivia	81.3		18.7	
Brazil	41.5	52.8	58.5	47.2
Chile	52.4		47.6	
Colombia	38.2		61.8	
Costa Rica	55.2		44.8	
Dominican Republic	73.8		26.2	
Ecuador		45.4		54.6
El Salvador	65.2		34.8	
Guatemala	60.2		39.8	
Haiti	68.5		31.5	
Honduras	71.7		28.3	
Mexico	53.7	52.1	46.3	47.9
Panama	65.5	56.5	34.5	43.5
Paraguay				
Peru		60.1		41.2
Venezuela	68.7	71.7	31.3	28.5

ISBN: 978-92-64-05923-8 - © OECD 2009

South and Southeast Asia	**57.4**		**42.6**	
India	52.3		47.7	
Indonesia	63.0		37.0	
Philippines	48.3		51.7	
Thailand	66.0		34.0	
West Asia				
Iran	65.7	74.5	34.3	25.5
Lebanon		46.8		53.2
West Bank and Gaza Strip		62.0		38.0
Syria	65.5		34.5	
Turkey	10.7	37.3	89.3	62.3
Yemen	89.2	88.6	10.8	11.4
Transition countries				
Kyrgyzstan		53.4		46.4
Moldova		32.1		67.9
Russia		44.2		55.8

Sources: Charmes (2002), for the ILO *Women and Men in the Informal Economy*, 2002. For Western Asia: Charmes (2007) and (2008). For detailed sources, see Annex 2.A4.
StatLink ᝏ᠍ http://dx.doi.org/ 10.1787/533470660737

37

Non-Agricultural Self-Employment

At the global level, non-agricultural self-employment increased continuously in absolute and relative terms from the 1970s through the 1990s, with somewhat more ambiguous trends after 2000 when data availability is limited. Self-employment represented 22.5 per cent of total non-agricultural employment in the 1970s, 26.8 per cent in the 1980s, 31.3 per cent in the 1990s and it is expected to remain at this level in the 2000s, when the data for West and Central Africa become available.

In *Africa,* the most rapid increases in non-agricultural self-employment are observed in North Africa (from 28.6 per cent in the 1990s to 35.1 per cent in the 2000s), and in Southern Africa (from 12.2 per cent to 32.8 per cent during the same period). The lack of recent data for West and Central Africa, two regions where informality rose during the 1990s (to 49.6 per cent and 69 per cent respectively), do not allow for a definitive picture of recent trends in the region.

In *Latin America,* non-agricultural self-employment is generally declining in South America (from 40.8 per cent in the 1990s to 36.5 per cent in the 2000s) and also dropping back in Central America from 38.0 per cent to 28.8 per cent), so that overall at regional level, a decrease of more than 8 percentage points is observed (from 41.8 per cent to 33.7 per cent).

In *Asia,* self-employment is increasing, from 32.5 per cent to 33.1 per cent during the last decade, in East as well as in Southeast Asia (especially in Cambodia, from 49.4 per cent in the 1990s to 56.9 per cent in the 2000s). Emerging economies of Southeast Asia, which experienced a fall in self-employment in the 1990s, are experiencing an increase in the 2000s (Thailand, Singapore and Hong Kong, China), while others (Philippines, Indonesia, Korea) continue along their downward trend. Further data for individual countries can be found in the supplementary database, published alongside this volume.

ISBN: 978-92-64-05923-8 - © OECD 2009

Figure 2.3. **Share (per cent) of Self-Employed in Non-Agricultural Employment**

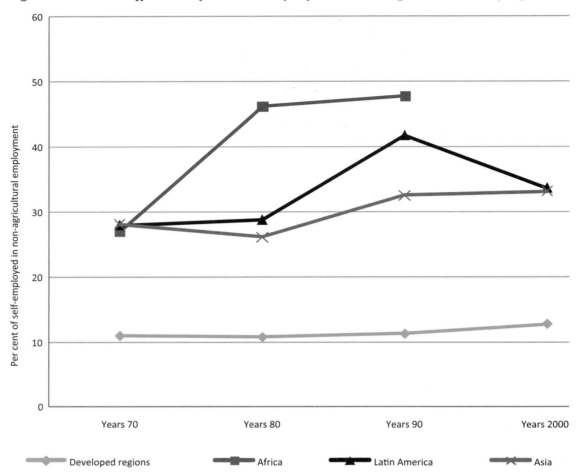

Source: See Table 2.3

StatLink ⬛ http://dx.doi.org/10.1787/533180710606

ISBN: 978-92-64-05923-8 - © OECD 2009

Table 2.3. Trends in Self-Employment and Female Self-Employment by Region

	% of self-employed in non-agricultural employment				% of self-employed in female non-agricultural employment				% of women in total non-agricultural self-employment			
	1970s	1980s	1990s	2000s	1970s	1980s	1990s	2000s	1970s	1980s	1990s	2000s
Developed regions	**11.0**	**10.8**	**11.3**	**12.8**	**9.6**	**8.7**	**9.3**	**9.7**	**29.1**	**29.1**	**34.5**	**45.6**
Eastern Europe	3.5	3.4	7.2	10.6	3.5	2.7	6.1	8.5	39.2	31.2	35.6	47.3
Western Europe	13.3	12.5	14.2	14.4	11.1	9.7	11.3	10.6	26.5	28.3	32.8	44.6
- Northern Europe	9.4	6.8	8.5	9.6	7.1	5.2	6.5	6.5	24.4	29.5	34.2	47.3
- Southern Europe	20.6	21.8	23.6	22.4	16.7	16.7	19.4	18.1	21.3	22.4	31.0	41.3
- Rest of Western Europe	11.6	10.9	10.6	11.4	10.8	8.9	8.0	7.7	31.6	31.2	33.3	45.5
Other developed countries	10.0	10.1	10.7	13.2	9.7	9.2	9.0	9.8	28.9	30.4	36.8	45.1
Africa	**27.0**	**46.2**	**47.7**	**36.7**	**36.8**	**59.9**	**50.6**	**41.6**	**20.4**	**38.2**	**35.9**	**34.8**
North Africa	19.2	23.3	28.6	35.1	16.1	23.3	29.6	41.1	13.2	18.6	20.6	22.8
Sub-Saharan Africa	28.5	51.1	52.3	39.2	41.9	68.7	56.9	42.8	22.1	42.2	40.8	42.9
- East Africa	15.9	28.1	50.4	45.7	20.0	45.6	61.1	47.9	13.8	20.7	43.7	47.4
- Central Africa	33.9	49.3	49.6		54.7	76.3	52.9		23.3	43.2	29.5	
- Southern Africa	17.6	12.3	12.2	32.8	45.8	25.5	15.9	37.8	56.4	43.6	56.4	38.4
- West Africa	40.0	72.9	69.0		48.4	87.7	74.0		19.9	50.6	38.1	
Latin America	**28.0**	**28.8**	**41.8**	**33.7**	**27.6**	**29.6**	**49.5**	**34.9**	**32.8**	**33.5**	**47.4**	**44.7**
Central America	25.1	28.7	38.0	28.8	25.3	29.8	48.5	31.0	34.9	32.4	52.0	43.0
South America	29.2	28.9	40.8	36.5	27.6	29.4	45.3	37.2	30.2	31.0	41.6	45.7
Caribbean	31.4	28.9	54.8		33.3	29.9	66.9		35.8	41.0	56.3	
Asia	**28.1**	**26.2**	**32.5**	**33.1**	**26.9**	**23.6**	**31.1**	**33.5**	**17.8**	**15.0**	**25.4**	**31.0**
East Asia	21.8	22.6	18.6	22.2	22.5	20.5	23.2	18.5	27.8	28.2	47.8	43.5
Southeast Asia	33.6	33.9	33.2	34.2	40.3	37.8	39.6	37.2	39.7	35.9	47.2	42.6
South Asia	38.4	40.1	52.5	51.5	35.6	37.7	53.7	53.8	13.6	8.8	17.7	15.7
West Asia	19.5	13.0	23.6	23.4	14.4	6.4	9.9	20.1	5.5	3.8	5.9	19.0
WORLD	**22.5**	**26.8**	**31.3**	**24.7**	**23.7**	**29.0**	**32.2**	**24.0**	**25.6**	**28.7**	**34.8**	**40.5**
World without Africa (Central and West)	**22.3**	**23.4**	**28.5**	**24.4**	**23.1**	**24.1**	**29.6**	**23.7**	**26.8**	**27.3**	**35.3**	**40.0**

StatLink ᔈᔈᔈ http://dx.doi.org/10.1787/533488150022

Note: For regional groupings used above, see Annex 2.A5.
Figures in italics are averages based on an incomplete set of countries.

Source: International compilation of population censuses and labour force surveys, by J. Charmes, prepared for the ILO programme "Improving the Quality of Women's Employment", based on ILO (1990), completed with the UN (1994), and for the recent period (years 2000s) on LABORSTA, the ILO database available on-line, ILO (2008).

ISBN: 978-92-64-05923-8 - © OECD 2009

GENDER AND EMPLOYMENT TRENDS

Women's share in total non-agricultural self-employment rose from more than 25 per cent in the 1970s to more than 40 per cent globally in the 2000s. Data presented in Figure 2.4 and Tables 2.4 and 2.A1 (Annex 2.A1) show that during the 1990s in sub-Saharan Africa, women's participation in informal employment was generally higher than men's. A regional average for sub-Saharan Africa shows that in the 1990s 84.1 per cent of women employed outside agriculture were in informal employment, against 63 per cent of men. In Latin America also, women in the 1990s were relatively more often employed in informal activities than men (56.2 per cent against 47.1 per cent).

In South and Southeast Asia, the gap between women and men was very narrow in the 1990s with only 2 percentage points separating women from men in the regional average. But in West Asia, where all countries show relatively low levels of participation in informal employment, lower levels are observed for women than for men (except in Lebanon). In Yemen, for example, the gap was nearly 20 percentage points in the 1990s and increased to 22 percentage points in 2004. The gap between women and men is also very considerable in the West Bank and Gaza with more than 26 percentage points in 2006. Over the period, Turkey was the only country that improved the indicator: from 19.1 per cent for women against 29.1 per cent for men in the 1990s to 32.2 per cent against 33.4 per cent for men in the 2000s. Lebanon is the only country in the region where women's participation in informal employment is higher than men's.

The characteristics we observe in North Africa are similar to those of West Asia, with 43.3 per cent of women working in informal employment, against 49.3 per cent for men. New data for transition countries in the 2000s show quite low, but probably increasing, levels of participation in informal employment, with the exception of Kyrgyzstan where levels are already high, with more than 40 per cent of both men and women in informal employment. These countries show lower levels for women, a typical characteristic for economies emerging from generalised wage employment with gender equality.

Table 2.4 shows that in sub-Saharan Africa and in Latin America after 2000, informal employment contributes more to total non-agricultural female employment than to male employment, as the figures are systematically higher for women. It is the contrary in North Africa and in West Asia, as well as in transition countries, but not for the same reasons. In North Africa and in West Asia, cultural reasons explain the relatively low share of women in total employment, be it formal or informal. In transition countries, on the contrary, there has always been a relatively high share of women within formal wage work, which led in the process of economic restructuring and privatisation to relatively high rates of women in informal paid employment, but to relatively lower rates compared with men in total informal employment.

With respect to the composition of informal employment, there are signs of a slight tendency of increasing involvement of women in self-employment in Latin America, as well as in South Africa and Turkey; in Egypt, and probably in poor African countries, an increase in informal paid employment is observed. It is however difficult to conclude definitely on the trends.

ISBN: 978-92-64-05923-8 - © OECD 2009

Figure 2.4. Share of Informal Employment in Total Non-Agricultural Employment by Country and Gender

(in percentages) latest available period

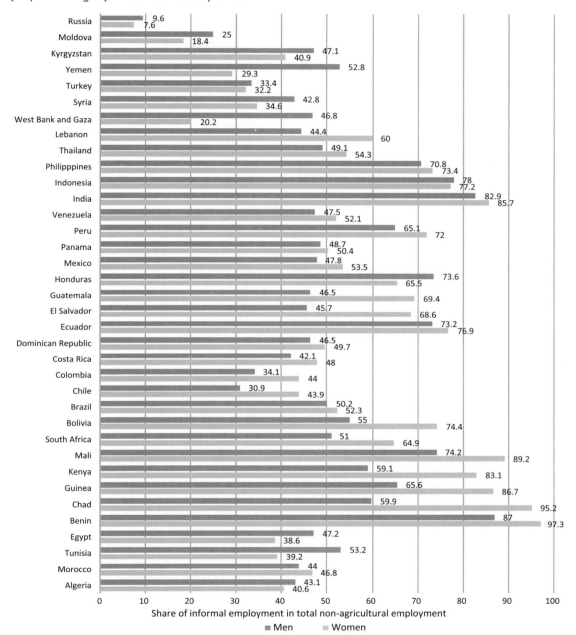

Share of informal employment in total non-agricultural employment

■ Men   ■ Women

Sources: Charmes (2002), for the ILO *Women and Men in the Informal Economy*, 2002. For the most recent period: Heintz and Chang (2007); and for West Asia: Charmes (2007, 2008). For detailed sources, see Annex 2.A4.

StatLink ᕯᔑᖁ http://dx.doi.org/10.1787/533180763815

41

ISBN: 978-92-64-05923-8 - © OECD 2009

Table 2.4. Informal Employment by Gender, Employment Status, Countries and Regions, 2000s

Regions/Countries	Years	Informal employment in % of non agricultural employment		Self-employed in % of informal employment		Paid employees in % of informal employment	
		Women	Men	Women	Men	Women	Men
North Africa							
Egypt	2006	38.6	46.5	46.7	33.2	53.3	76.7
Sub-Saharan Africa							
Mali	2004	89.2	74.2	85.4	69.0	14.6	31.0
South Africa	2004	64.9	51.0	21.9	19.8	78.0	80.2
Latin America		**59.5**	**55.4**	**55.3**	**57.0**	**44.7**	**43.0**
Brazil	2003	52.3	50.2	44.6	59.8	55.4	40.4
Ecuador	2004	76.9	73.2	53.6	38.8	46.6	61.2
Mexico	2005	53.5	47.8	54.0	50.6	46.0	49.4
Panama	2004	50.4	48.7	49.8	61.4	50.2	38.6
Peru	2004	72.0	65.1	57.1	61.1	43.1	38.9
Venezuela	2004	52.1	47.5	72.9	70.3	27.1	29.5
West Asia		**30.8**	**45.3**	**39.2**	**51.0**	**60.9**	**49.0**
Lebanon	2004	40.0	55.6	25.1	51.8	74.9	48.2
West Bank and Gaza	2004	20.2	46.8	63.4	61.9	36.6	38.1
Turkey	2004	32.2	33.4	29.2	39.2	71.1	60.8
Transition countries		**22.3**	**27.2**	**39.9**	**46.4**	**59.9**	**53.6**
Kyrgyzstan	2003	40.9	47.1	55.3	52.2	44.7	47.6
Moldova	2004	18.4	25.0	22.3	40.0	77.2	60.0
Russia	2004	7.6	9.6	42.1	46.9	57.9	53.1

Sources: based on tabulations by Heintz and Chang (2007) for the ILO. For West Asia: Charmes (2008). For detailed sources, see Annex 2.A4.

StatLink ⟶ http://dx.doi.org/10.1787/533505356887

The share of *self-employed women* in total female non-agricultural employment, as detailed in Table 2.3, has been generally higher than men's and on the rise over time. At the world level, the figure rose from 23.7 per cent (against 22.5 per cent for both sexes) in the 1970s, to 29 per cent (against 26.8 per cent for both sexes) in the 1980s to 32.2 per cent (against 31.3 per cent) in the 1990s. It seems, however, that this trend has stopped in the 2000s: the indicator is at 23.7 per cent (world level without Central and West Africa), against 24.4 per cent for both sexes.

For *Africa*, the share of self-employed women is also and very significantly higher than men's and on the rise for *North Africa,* where it characterises the new tendency of women to enter the labour markets through this employment status, especially in Egypt and Morocco (with an opposite trend for Tunisia where women's entry into the labour market passes through wage employment in the formal sector): at sub-regional level, the ratio increased from 16.1 per cent in the 1970s to 41.1 per cent in the 2000s (against 19.2 per cent and 35.1 per cent respectively for both sexes). Similar trends are observed in sub-Saharan Africa (with differences of 4 to 5 percentage points between women and men).

ISBN: 978-92-64-05923-8 - © OECD 2009

Latin America is also characterised by significantly higher female ratios in the 1990s, but they seem to be downward-oriented in the 2000s, especially in Central America.

As for *Asia*, female ratios have been upward-oriented since the 1980s (from 23.6 per cent to 33.5 per cent in the 2000s), especially in South Asia (from 37.7 per cent in the 1980s to 53.7 per cent and 53.8 per cent in the 1990s and 2000s) and in West Asia (from 6.4 per cent in the1980s to 20.1 per cent in the 2000s).

Finally, the observed trends in female self-employment have increased women's share in total non-agricultural self-employment which rose from 25.6 per cent in the 1970s to 40.5 per cent globally in the 2000s. This step toward more equality between women and men has been particularly rapid in developed countries (increasing from 29.1 per cent in the 1970s to 45.6 per cent in the 2000s), especially in Western Europe (26.5 per cent to 44.6 per cent) and in other developed countries (28.9 per cent to 45.1 per cent). This indicator has increased in North Africa (from 13.2 per cent to 22.8 per cent), in East Africa (from 13.8 per cent to 47.4 per cent), in Latin America (from 32.8 per cent to 44.7 per cent) and in Asia (from 17.8 per cent to 31 per cent. During the last period, however, it declined in all sub-regions of Asia except in West Asia (5.9 per cent to 19.0 per cent). The indicator can be interpreted in different ways: while in developed regions and transition countries it may mean more independence for women who get access to private businesses, it can be a sign, in developing countries, of more informality and more precariousness.

It is important to note that among the self-employed own-account workers represent 63.8 per cent of total self-employment globally (a ratio which drops down to 59.3 per cent for women). High ratios for own-account workers mean low ratios for contributing family workers, a status in employment which is one of dependency. The lowest ratios of own-account workers are observed in North Africa (37 per cent for women against 44.1 per cent for both sexes) and in West Asia (36.6 per cent for women against 47.2 per cent for both sexes), then in East Asia (respectively 42.9 per cent against 49.9 per cent), with gaps of more than 7 to 10 percentage points. The highest ratios are in Northern and Western Europe (respectively 85 per cent against 85.9 per cent, and 66.5 per cent against 66.1 per cent) and, more curiously, in Central America.

43

ISBN: 978-92-64-05923-8 - © OECD 2009

Figure 2.5. Share of Own-Account Workers among the Self-Employed, 2000s
(percentages)

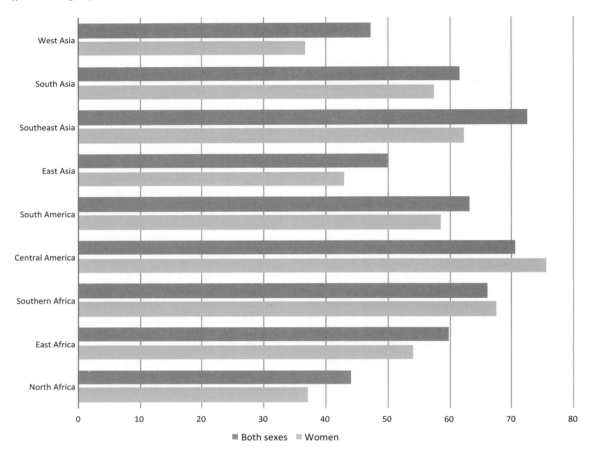

Source: See Table 2.3.
StatLink http://dx.doi.org/10.1787/533236024214

Income and Wages

Work in the informal sector was originally assumed not to be rewarding for its entrepreneurs and workers. However, more recently, empirical evidence (Charmes, 2002) has shown that small entrepreneurs in the informal sector are earning several times the legal minimum wage and even several times the average wage in the formal sector, while paid employees – in general younger than in the total population of wage workers – are earning approximately the equivalent of the legal minimum wage. Although these results cannot be generalised and also bearing in mind that profits and wages in the informal sector cannot be directly compared to wages in the formal sector, because they do not include social contributions and social benefits, it must be noted that the following Table 2.5 (and additional Tables 2.A3 and 2.A4 in Annex 2.A1) only cover the micro and small enterprises of the informal sector. Data on wages in informal employment in the formal sector are scarce and generally not representative because the sources that can be used are enterprise surveys, which omit to declare informal workers, or labour force surveys, which rarely identify informal wage earners separately. Moreover, informal sector surveys often publish data on income for the whole population of informal sector participants without distinguishing between owners, wage workers, contributing family workers or apprentices. They also most often cover urban areas or major cities or even only capital cities, rather than the whole country.

ISBN: 978-92-64-05923-8 - © OECD 2009

Table 2.5. Average Monthly Income and Wages paid by Small Entrepreneurs in the Informal Sector of Various Developing Countries at the end of the 1990s-beginning of the 2000s (in local currency and as multiples of the legal minimum wage)

Countries	Year	Local currency	Legal minimum salary (or average wage*)	Income		Wage [a]	
				In local currency	multiples of minimum salary (or average wage*)	In local currency	multiples of minimum salary (or average wage*)
North Africa							
Egypt	2004	EGP	825*	1 487	1.8	195	0.2*
Morocco	1997	MAD	1 510	2 492	1.7	1 556	1.0
Morocco	2003	MAD	1 826	7 843	4.3 (2.7*)	1 186	0.6
Tunisia	1997	TND	169.3	669.9	4.0 (2.2*)	186	1.1
Tunisia	2002	TND	206	617.6	3.0	219	1.1
Sub-Saharan Africa							
Benin	1992	FCFA	13 904	41 412	3.0	23 216	1.7
Street vendors				23 901	1.7		
Chad	1995-96	FCFA	25 600	40 987	1.6	16 408	0.6
Ethiopia (urban)	1996	ETB		105.5		51.4	
Kenya	1999	KES	2 363	6 158	2.6	6 496	2.7
Mauritania Three main towns	1992-93	MRO	5 312	17 208	3.2	8 046	1.5
Secondary towns				26 647	5.0	6 906	1.3
All urban				22 258	4.2	6 289	1.2
Mali	1996	FCFA	20 965	120 757	5.8	18 038	0.9
Niger	1995	FCFA	18 000	26 360	1.5		
Latin America							
Brazil (urban)	1997	BRL	612.5*	565[b]	(0.9)	240	(0.4)
				1 040[c]	(1.7)		
Colombia (urban)	1996				1.6[d]		1.5
					4.2[e]		
Mexico (urban)	1998	MXN	419.1			690.3	1.7
South and Southeast Asia							
India	1999-2000	INR	1 498	2 003[d]	1.3	1 413[d]	0.9
				8 035[e]	5.4	1 656[e]	1.1
				2 765[f]	1.8	1 642[f]	1.1
Indonesia	1998	IDR	281 038	843 114	3.0[g]		
West Asia							
Lebanon	2004	LBP	1 495 ±	1 486	1.0 ±	280	0.2 ±
Turkey (urban)	2000	TRL	114.3 million	197.1	1.7		
Turkey	2002	TRL	236 million	4 706	19.9	277	1.8

Notes:
* figure refers to average wage; ± figure refers to GDP per worker.
a) Apprentices and family workers excluded.
b) Main activity.
c) Main and secondary activities.
d) Own-account.
e) Employers of micro-enterprises (fewer than 10 workers).
f) Own account and employers combined.
g) In multiple of the average wage of production workers under supervisory level.

Sources: Charmes (2002), for the ILO *Women and Men in the Informal Economy*, 2002. For Western Asia: Charmes (2008). For detailed sources, see Annex 2.A4.

StatLink ᴟᴸᴪ http://dx.doi.org/10.1787/533507884373

ISBN: 978-92-64-05923-8 - © OECD 2009

Table 2.5 shows that the incomes of small entrepreneurs in the informal sector are systematically higher than the legal minimum wage: from 1.5 times in Niger (1995) to 4.3 times in Morocco (2003) and 5.8 times in Mali (1996), though an exception needs to be made for Turkey (19.9 times) which was experiencing very high inflation during this period. However, the legal minimum wage – where it exists – might have not followed the cost of living. A comparison with the average wage in the formal sector, or in the public sector, could be more valid and interesting. Unfortunately this information is rarely available in developing countries. Compared to the average wage in the formal sector, the entrepreneurs' incomes are still higher: from 1.8 times in Egypt (2004) to 2.7 times in Morocco (2003).

Two other observations can be derived from Table 2.5. First, secondary activities (or multiple jobs) allow informal sector operators to double their incomes, as shown in urban Brazil where the entrepreneurs' income represents 0.9 times the average salary, but this indicator rises to 1.7 times with the secondary activities. It should also be noted that the category of informal entrepreneurs is very heterogeneous, with own-account workers on the one hand, and small employers on the other. In India, for example, the informal sector entrepreneurs earned 1.8 times the legal minimum salary in 1999-2000, but the indicator dropped to 1.3 times for the own-account workers, and jumped to 5.4 times for the employers. The same gap is observed in urban Colombia (1.6 against 4.2 in 1996). This is confirmed by Table 2.A4 (Annex 2.A1), which refers to the survey carried out in seven capital cities of West Africa and shows that while employers are earning the equivalent of the average wage in the formal private sector, the own-account workers are only earning the equivalent of half this wage.

Looking now at wages (excluding apprentices and "unpaid" family workers), Table 2.5 shows that the legal minimum wage seems to be a reference in most countries in that the average wage in the informal sector is very often quite close to this minimum. It ranges from 0.6 times the minimum wage (in Morocco 2003) to 1.8 times in Turkey (2002), with many of the observations around 0.9, 1, 1.1 or 1.2. Not only are the paid employees in the informal sector younger than their counterparts in the formal sector (because they seek rapidly to open their own micro-enterprise), but also the tendency of employers is to declare their workforce at the minimum salary in order to pay the minimum social contributions (in case of controls).

Surprisingly, the paid employees of the informal sector in the capital cities of West Africa are earning the equivalent of 0.6 times the average wage of the formal private sector, which is more than own-account workers earn (0.5) while the informal sector employers earn the equivalent of this same average wage. See Table 2.A3 (Annex 2.A1) for further details.

CONCLUSION

Recent efforts to define and measure informal employment have yielded an increasing amount of data on the issue at the *national* level in all regions. However, the systematic compilation of data at the *world* level shows that there are still many obstacles to drawing up a statistical picture of the phenomenon and of its trends. Countries do not use harmonised definitions because it takes time to include new concepts and new questions in the regular statistical surveys and censuses.

In spite of these difficulties, the general perspective is that of an upward-oriented trend of informal employment, especially in poorer countries of sub-Saharan Africa, with an increase in informal employment in the formal sector of the economy. This latter trend indicates an expansion of the instability of wage work and a restriction of social protection, which faces obstacles in extending its benefits to workers.

The generalisation of regular labour force surveys in all developing countries with inclusion of a set of questions on informality (benefit of social protection, characteristics of economic units) will allow, in the years to come, a better and more comprehensive capture of informal employment: a phenomenon which has come to represent, in many countries, the normal situation of most workers and which constitutes for policy makers a dilemma and, increasingly in the future, a challenge.

ISBN: 978-92-64-05923-8 - © OECD 2009

ANNEX 2.A1. ADDITIONAL DATA TABLES

Table 2.A1. **Share of Informal Employment in Total Non-Agricultural Employment,**
by country, region and gender (in percentages), 1990s and 2000s

	1990-99		2000-07	
	Women	**Men**	**Women**	**Men**
North Africa	**43.3**	**49.3**		
Algeria	40.6	43.1		
Morocco	46.8	44		
Tunisia	39.2	53.2		
Egypt	46.5	56.9	38.6	47.2
Sub-Saharan Africa	**84.1**	**63.0**	**77.1**	**62.6**
Benin	97.3	87		
Chad	95.2	59.9		
Guinea	86.7	65.6		
Kenya	83.1	59.1		
Mali			89.2	74.2
South Africa	58.4	43.6	64.9	51
Latin America	**56.2**	**47.1**	**59.5**	**55.4**
Bolivia	74.4	55		
Brazil	67.3	54.7	52.3	50.2
Chile	43.9	30.9		
Colombia	44	34.1		
Costa Rica	48	42.1		
Dominican Republic	49.7	46.5		
Ecuador			76.9	73.2
El Salvador	68.6	45.7		
Guatemala	69.4	46.5		
Honduras	65.5	73.6		
Mexico	55	54.3	53.5	47.8
Panama	40.8	35.5	50.4	48.7
Peru			72	65.1
Venezuela	47.3	46.7	52.1	47.5
South and Southeast Asia	**72.7**	**70.2**		
India	85.7	82.9		
Indonesia	77.2	78		
Philippines	73.4	70.8		
Thailand	54.3	49.1		
West Asia	**31.1**	**43.4**	**35.4**	**44.4**
Lebanon			60	44.4
West Bank and Gaza Strip			20.2	46.8
Syria	34.6	42.8		
Turkey	19.1	29.1	32.2	33.4
Yemen	39.7	58.2	29.3	52.8
Transition countries			**22.3**	**27.2**
Kyrgyzstan			40.9	47.1
Moldova			18.4	25
Russia			7.6	9.6

47

Sources: Charmes (2002), for the ILO "Women and Men in the Informal Economy", 2002. For the most recent period: Heintz and Chang (2007), and for West Asia: Charmes (2007 and 2008). For detailed sources, see Annex 2.A4.

StatLink 🔗 http://dx.doi.org/10.1787/533525870513

ISBN: 978-92-64-05923-8 - © OECD 2009

Table 2.A2. **Female Informal Employment by Status in Employment,**
Countries and Regions, 1990s

Regions/Countries	Years	% informal employment in non agricultural	% self-employed in total informal	% paid employees in informal employment	Share of women in total informal employment
North Africa	**1994-98**	**42.2**	**71.7**	**28.3**	**19.7**
Algeria	1997		80.9	19.1	16.8
Morocco	1995	40.6	88.6	11.4	29.6
Tunisia	1994-95	46.8	50.6	49.4	18.5
Egypt	1998	39.2	66.8	33.2	14.0
Sub-Saharan Africa	**1992-2000**	**81.1**	**70.9**	**29.1**	**52.3**
Benin	1992	43.3	98.4	1.6	59.7
Chad	1993	97.3	99.0	1.0	52.7
Guinea	1991	95.2	97.5	2.5	35.7
Kenya	1999	86.7	32.6	67.4	60.3
South Africa	2000	83.1	26.8	73.2	53.2
Latin America	**1995-00**	**59.2**	**57.5**	**42.6**	**46.5**
Bolivia	1997	84.1	91.5	8.5	51.2
Brazil	1996	74.4	31.8	68.2	46.9
Chile	1996	67.3	38.7	61.3	46.1
Colombia	1996	43.9	36.4	63.6	49.7
Costa Rica	1997	44.0	48.6	51.4	39.6
Dominican Republic	1997	48.0	63.3	36.7	37.4
El Salvador	1997	49.7	71.0	29.0	57.9
Guatemala	1989	68.6	64.6	35.4	51.8
Honduras	1997	69.4	77.1	22.9	56.4
Mexico	2000	65.5	53.3	46.7	39.0
Panama	1997	55.0	46.9	53.1	43.8
Venezuela	1997	40.8	66.2	33.8	38.1
Asia	**1994-2000**	**19.1**	**53.4**	**46.6**	**28.6**
India	1999-2000	56.2	56.8	43.2	20.0
Indonesia	1998	85.7	69.6	30.4	37.6
Philippines	1995	77.2	63.2	36.8	46.3
Thailand	1994	73.4	67.8	32.2	47.4
Syria	1994	54.3	56.6	43.4	10.6
Turkey	1996	34.6	6.3	93.7	9.9

Sources: Charmes (2002), for the ILO *Women and Men in the Informal Economy*. 2002. For detailed sources, see Annex 2.A4.
StatLink ⟶ http://dx.doi.org/10.1787/533605336567

48

Table 2.A3. Income and Wages in the Informal Sector of Seven Capital Cities of West Africa, 2001-02

Countries	Workers' salaries in the private formal sector (1)	Informal sector employers' income (2)	Informal own-account workers' income (3)	Workers' salaries in the informal sector (4)	(2) in multiples of (1) = (5)	(3) in multiples of (1) = (6)	(4) in multiples of (1) = (7)
Cotonou (Benin)	49.9	56.9	32.3	29.6	1.1	0.6	0.6
Ouagadougou (Burkina Faso)	55.0	59.0	23.2	28.7	1.1	0.4	0.5
Abidjan (Côte d'Ivoire) (Economic capital)	91.8	83.7	41.6	54.5	0.9	0.5	0.6
Bamako (Mali)	52.4	77.0	40.2	39.5	1.5	0.8	0.8
Niamey (Niger)	48.7	102.2	32.5	40.7	2.1	0.7	0.8
Dakar (Senegal)	87.9	110.8	50.0	44.3	1.3	0.6	0.5
Lomé (Togo)	40.7	34.3	19.4	22.4	0.8	0.5	0.6
7 cities	**77.6**	**75.4**	**36.8**	**45.2**	**1.0**	**0.5**	**0.6**

Note: in thousands of FCFA.

Source: Afristat (2004).

StatLink http://dx.doi.org/10.1787/533610182123

Table 2.A4. Gender Gap in Income Levels from Enterprise and Wages in the Informal Sector

Countries	Entrepreneurs' income			Wages		
	Women	Men	Women/Men %	Women	Men	Women/Men %
Morocco (2002)	4 649	8 724	53.3	867	1 320	65.7
Tunisia (1997)	555	683	81.3	148	196	75.5
Tunisia (2002)	523	633	82.6	157	232	67.7
Ethiopia (1996 urban)				37.2	58.1	64.0
Kenya (1999)	4 452	7 817	57.0			
Brazil (1997 urban)	372[a]	664[a]	56.0[a]	218[c]	253	86.2[c]
Colombia (1996 urban)	660[b]	1 298[b]	50.8[b]	289[d]	306	94.4[d]
			63.2[c]			87.5
			75.6[d]			
Mexico (1994 urban)				538.1	741.2	72.6
Haiti (2000)			88.9			
Lebanon (2004)	1 019	1 522	67.0			
Turkey (2000 urban)	204 776	106 250	51.9			

Notes: Average monthly income and wages in national currency.
a) Main activity. b) Main and secondary activities. c) Own-account workers. d) Employers of micro-enterprises (fewer than ten workers).

Sources: Charmes (2002), for the ILO *Women and Men in the Informal Economy* 2002. For West Asia and North Africa: Charmes (2008). For detailed sources, see Annex 2.A4.

StatLink http://dx.doi.org/10.1787/534080466327

49

ANNEX 2.A2. METHODOLOGICAL NOTE ON TABLES ON INFORMAL EMPLOYMENT
BY COUNTRIES, REGIONS AND SUB-REGIONS (TABLES 2.1 AND 2.2)

Data on informal employment have been estimated with various methods and definitions according to the periods of time.

Informal employment being defined as the non-coverage by social protection, it is measured by the response to the question on coverage in labour force surveys. However, it is only recently that labour force surveys have included this type of question. Previously labour statisticians assumed that registered employment was equivalent to protected employment and the use of the "residual method" which consists of subtracting registered formal employment from total employment for the various industries was systematically implemented.

During the 1970s and the 1980s, and until recently for some countries, data on informal employment were obtained in this way. With progress and improvements in definitions and data collection, direct data have been obtained from labour force surveys, which have more often included appropriate questions for capturing informal employment, especially questions on social protection coverage.

Recently, the adoption of guidelines for the definition and measurement of informal employment by the 17th ICLS in 2003 has facilitated the compilation of harmonised data through labour force surveys and the response to the question of the benefit of social protection. In the most recent period, labour force surveys have come to include the criteria for defining informal employment (most Latin American countries, Thailand, Algeria), and some of them have simultaneously included the criteria for defining the informal sector (Algeria, Russia), which allows a more detailed knowledge of the composition of informal employment.

Before the approach to "informal sector" measurement was recommended through mixed household/establishment surveys (in the early 1990s) and through labour force surveys (in the early 2000s), the "residual method" was systematically implemented, subtracting formal registered employment from total non-agricultural employment: Algeria (1977, 1985), Tunisia (1975, 1980), Egypt (1976, 1986), Morocco (1982), Mali (1976), Niger (1977), Mauritania (1980, 1988), Senegal (1980), Burkina Faso (1985), Guinea (1984), Kenya (1990) and Iran (1986, 2004). Generally, the first estimate available in a country is the "residual" one, allowing policy makers and statisticians to become aware of the size of the segment of the labour force and to convince them of the necessity to implement a survey of the phenomenon.

In a second period, the first mixed household/establishment surveys become available: Mali (1989), Mexico (1989), Niger (1994), Kenya (1999), India (1999-2000), Morocco (1999-2000); in other countries, improvements of establishment surveys and micro-enterprise surveys are preferred, leading to improved residual estimates: Tunisia (1997, 2002).

In all cases, the elaboration of "labour inputs matrices" in the framework of national accounts allows a better assessment of all components of employment, because of imperfections of data collection due to incomplete geographical coverage, for instance.

For a detailed description of the labour input matrix (an improved "residual method"), see:

CHARMES J. (2006), *Measurement of the Contribution of Informal Sector and Informal Employment to GDP in Developing Countries: Some Conceptual and Methodological Issues*, Paper presented at the 9th meeting of the Delhi Group on Informal sector Statistics, New Delhi, 11-12 May.

and

CHARMES J. (2007), Use of data for National Accounts purposes, Chapter 10 of the *Handbook for Measurement of Informal Sector and Informal Employment,* ILO-WIEGO.

50

ANNEX 2.A3. METHODOLOGICAL NOTE ON TABLES ON NON-AGRICULTURAL SELF-EMPLOYMENT
BY COUNTRIES, REGIONS AND SUB-REGIONS (TABLE 2.1 AND TABLE 2.A1 IN ANNEX 2.A1)

At world level and for most countries, the only sources of data on self-employment have been the population censuses undertaken every ten years, and sometimes with longer intervals in African countries. For the 1970s and 1980s, they are therefore the main source of data on self-employment. In some countries it was years before the results were published, and in the particular case of data on employment it has frequently been the case that they were not published at all, because the results were not of good quality or because, at that time, the required tabulation was considered as not important enough to justify computation and analysis. Very often the data were collected, analysed and published, but not with the required cross-classification of employment status by industries and gender. This is why the information is not available for each country for at least one year in a decade. In particular, population censuses remain the main, if not the only, source for Central and West Africa, and consequently, the data have not yet been made available for the 2000s.

In the 1990s (and even in the 1980s), labour force surveys have started to be carried out on a yearly basis, and even on a quarterly basis in many emerging economies of Asia (India, Thailand), Latin America (Mexico, Chile, Argentina), North Africa and also in transition countries, so that several sources have existed for a decade.

In Tables 2.1 and 2.A1, the population censuses are the main sources for the decades of the 1970s and 1980s, based on the compilation of the various rounds of population censuses prepared by the ILO in 1990 and completed by the compilation of the UN Population Division in its *Demographic Yearbook* 1994. Labour force surveys became the main sources of data in the 1990s and 2000s. The ILO statistics bureau, as the institution in charge of the compilation of labour force statistics, has prepared and regularly updated the database LABORSTA, making the cross-tabulation of employment status by industries and gender available on line for the users. It has been the main source used for the 2000s. These various sources have been completed by national sources (for Algeria for example), because the data bases are not always updated on time or because the countries do not transmit rapidly their results to the UN institutions.

However, these various databases and sources do not provide the required indicators directly. Table 1C of LABORSTA for example usually deals with active population (or labour force) rather than employment, so that it has been necessary to calculate the figures for employment, especially for agricultural and non-agricultural employment, by adding up the various industries or by subtracting agriculture, forestry and fisheries from total employment. Similarly, it was necessary to add up the various categories of status in employment (or to subtract wage or paid employment from total) to generate the self-employment figures.

Finally, data are available in the 1970s (i.e. from 1970 to 1979, depending on the year of availability for each country) for 75 countries, for 73 countries in the 1980s (from 1980 to 1989), for 80 countries in the 1990s (from 1990 to 1999) and for 63 countries in the 2000s (from 2000 to 2006). One of the major difficulties is that the sample of countries by sub-region is not exactly the same from one decade to another. It is particularly the case for Africa where labour-force surveys are not yet generalised and where the results of the 2000 round of population censuses are still awaited.

There are two options for dealing with this issue:

— either to keep the same countries in the sample from decade to decade (with the necessity for the country to fulfil at least three out of four decades, or the two last decades, or the first and the last decades),

51

ISBN: 978-92-64-05923-8 - © OECD 2009

—   or to maintain the table as complete as possible and to delete or evacuate the figures that seem invalid (for instance, according to LABORSTA non-agricultural self-employment in Ecuador 2006 has jumped to 80 per cent, because the labour force survey covers only the main cities and is not comparable with the source for this country in the 1990s) and to note in italics the regional averages that should not be taken into account because of inconsistencies or insufficient number of countries in the sample.

This second option has been preferred, provided that many new data will be available for Africa in the next period.

Regional, sub-regional and world averages are non-weighted averages: each country has the same weight whatever the size of its labour force or of its population.

ISBN: 978-92-64-05923-8 - © OECD 2009

ANNEX 2.A4. SOURCES OF DATA FOR TABLES 2.1 TO 2.4 AND 2.A1, 2.A2 AND 2.A3

North Africa	
Algeria	CHARMES, J. (1988), *Emploi et secteur informel en Algérie. 1977-85.* UNDP - OPS, CENEAP. CHARMES, J. (2004), *Secteur Informel et emploi informel au Maghreb : un état des lieux et des connaissances par rapport à d'autres expériences dans le monde*, Centre de Recherche en Economie Appliquée pour le Développement (CREAD), Colloque international sur « La question de l'emploi en Afrique du Nord : Tendances récentes et perspectives 2020 », Algiers, 26, 27 and 28 June. MOHAMED, S. and J. CHARMES (eds.) (2006), *Informalisation des économies maghrébines: Une stratégie d'adaptation à la crise du travail ou une limite aux politiques actives ?,* Editions du CREAD, Algiers. CHARMES, J. (2008), "Statistics on Informal Employment in the Arab Region", Chapter 3 of *Gender Equality and Workers' Rights in the Informal Economies of Arab States*, ILO Regional Office for the Arab States and CAWTAR (Center of Arab Women for Training and Research), Beirut and Tunis, 116p. (pp. 54-72).
Morocco	ROYAUME DU MAROC, MINISTÈRE DE L'HABITAT, DE L'EMPLOI ET DE LA FORMATION PROFESSIONNELLE, (1997),*Enquête sur le secteur informel localisé en milieu urbain,* EDESA, Rabat. DIRECTION DE LA STATISTIQUE (2003), *Enquête nationale sur le secteur informel non agricole 1999-2000*, Rapport des premiers résultats, Rabat. CHARMES, J. (2008), "Micro and Small Enterprises in the Middle East and North Africa (MENA) in a Comparative Perspective. A Synthesis of the MSEs Surveys conducted in Turkey, Lebanon, Egypt and Morocco from 2001 to 2004", Economic Research Forum, Project "Promoting Competitiveness in the Micro and Small Enterprise Sector in the MENA Region", Cairo.
Tunisia	INSTITUT NATIONAL DE LA STATISTIQUE (2001), *Le secteur des micro-entreprises en Tunisie, Analyse des résultats de la seconde enquête nationale sur les activités économiques ENAE 1997*, Tunis. INSTITUT NATIONAL DE LA STATISTIQUE (2006), *Le secteur des micro-entreprises en Tunisie, Analyse des résultats de la seconde enquête nationale sur les activités économiques ENAE 2002*, Tunis.
Egypt	CHARMES, J. (2008), "Micro and Small Enterprises in the Middle East and North Africa (MENA) in a Comparative Perspective. A Synthesis of the MSEs Surveys conducted in Turkey, Lebanon, Egypt and Morocco from 2001 to 2004", Economic Research Forum, Project "Promoting Competitiveness in the Micro and Small Enterprise Sector in the MENA Region", Cairo.

53

ISBN: 978-92-64-05923-8 - © OECD 2009

Sub-Saharan Africa	
Benin	PEESI, BIT-PNUD-INSAE (1992), *Enquête sur le secteur informel urbain 1992*, BIT, Cotonou. MALDONADO, C. (1994), *Analyse des résultats du recensement national des établissements économiques urbains du Bénin,* BIT-PNUD-INSAE-PEESI, Geneva. MALDONADO, C., C. CASSEHOUIN and D. MUSTAPHA (1996), *Analyse des résultats de l'enquête des unités économiques du secteur informel urbain du Bénin,* BIT-PNUD-INSAE-PEESI, Geneva. INSAE (2000), *Analyse des résultats de l'enquête auprès des micro-entreprises du secteur informel, Cotonou.* INSAE (2002), *L'emploi, le chômage et les conditions d'activité dans l'agglomération de Cotonou. Premiers résultats de l'Enquête Emploi 2001,* INSAE. CHARMES, J. (2008), *Situation et perspectives de la population active et de l'emploi au Bénin: 1979-2002,* Ministère du Plan, de la Restructuration Economique et de la Promotion de l'Emploi, PNUD, Cotonou.
Burkina Faso	CHARMES, J. (1989), *Trente-cinq ans de comptabilité nationale du secteur informel au Burkina Faso (1954-89). Leçons d'une expérience et perspectives d'amélioration* (Thirty-five years of national accounts of the informal sector in Burkina Faso (1954-89). Lessons of an experiment and perspectives of improvement), Ministère du Plan et de la Coopération, PNUD-DTCD, Ouagadougou. CHARMES, J. (1996), *Le secteur informel au Burkina Faso. Evolution sur longue période et suivi conjoncturel.* Ministère de l'Economie, des Finances et du Plan, GTZ.
Chad	CHARMES, J. (1994), *Le secteur informel dans l'économie tchadienne. Premières estimations et programme d'enquêtes,* Ministère du Plan et de la Coopération, DSEED, N'Djamena. RÉPUBLIQUE DU TCHAD, DIRECTION DE LA STATISTIQUE DES ETUDES ECONOMIQUES ET DÉMOGRAPHIQUES (DSEED) (1998), *Enquête sur la Consommation et le Secteur Informel au Tchad ECOSIT 1995-96,* N'Djamena, PNUD-DAES, projet CHD/91/003.
Ethiopia	CENTRAL STATISTICAL AUTHORITY AND MINISTRY OF LABOUR AND SOCIAL AFFAIRS (1997), *Report on Urban Informal Sector Sample Survey, December 1996,* Addis Ababa, Statistical Bulletin No. 174. CENTRAL STATISTICAL AUTHORITY (1999), *Statistical Report on the 1999 National Labour Force Survey,* March 1999, Statistical Bulletin No. 225, Addis Ababa.
Guinea	MINISTÈRE DU PLAN ET DES FINANCES (1992), *Enquête sur les Informations Prioritaires (ESIP), Rapport Final + Annexes Statistiques,* Projet d'Appui au Développement Socio-Economique (PADSE), Enquête Permanente auprès des Ménages, Conakry. CHARMES, J. and Y. WILLAERT (1994), *Pauvreté et vulnérabilité en Guinée. Etat des connaissances, programmes d'action, instruments de suivi et d'évaluation,* Ministère du Plan et des Finances, Projet d'Appui au Développement Socio-Economique (PADSE). DIRECTION NATIONALE DE LA STATISTIQUE (1996), *Enquête intégrale sur les conditions de vie des ménages avec module budget et consommation), Rapport Final,* Projet d'Appui au Développement Socio-Economique (PADSE), Conakry.

■**54**

ISBN: 978-92-64-05923-8 - © OECD 2009

Kenya	CBS-ICEG-K-Rᴇᴘ (1999), *National Micro and Small Enterprise Baseline Survey 1999, Survey results,* Nairobi.
Mali	Rᴇ́ᴘᴜʙʟɪQᴜᴇ ᴅᴜ Mᴀʟɪ, Dɪʀᴇᴄᴛɪᴏɴ Nᴀᴛɪᴏɴᴀʟᴇ ᴅᴇ ʟᴀ SᴛᴀᴛɪsᴛɪQᴜᴇ ᴇᴛ ᴅᴇ ʟ'IɴғᴏʀᴍᴀᴛɪQᴜᴇ (DNSI), (1994), *Enquête nationale sur les activités économiques des ménages (enquête secteur informel) 1989,* Bamako, projet PADEM MLI/90/007. Oʙsᴇʀᴠᴀᴛᴏɪʀᴇ ᴅᴇ ʟ'ᴇᴍᴘʟᴏɪ ᴇᴛ ᴅᴇ ʟᴀ ғᴏʀᴍᴀᴛɪᴏɴ (1997), *Enquête nationale sur le secteur informel, Mali 1996,* Bamako. Cʜᴀʀᴍᴇs, J. (1998*), Emploi et qualifications au Mali. Principales sources d'information, connaissances actuelles, besoins des utilisateurs et projets de suivi.* Rapport pour l'Observatoire de l'Emploi et de la Formation (OEF) du Mali. Communication aux journées sur l'emploi et la formation, Ministère de l'Emploi, de la Fonction Publique et du Travail, Office National de la Main d'Oeuvre et de l'Emploi, Observatoire de l'Emploi et de la Formation, Bamako, 23-25 March.
Mauritania	Cʜᴀʀᴍᴇs, J. (1992), *La contribution du secteur informel à l'emploi et au produit national en Mauritanie, 1977-92,* Ministère du Plan, projet DSA, Nouakchott. Oғғɪᴄᴇ Nᴀᴛɪᴏɴᴀʟ ᴅᴇ ʟᴀ SᴛᴀᴛɪsᴛɪQᴜᴇ (1994), *Enquête sur le secteur informel à Nouakchott, Nouadhibou et Kaédi, 1992, Résultats,* Vol. 2: Emploi dans les secteurs Commerce, Services et Artisanat, Nouakchott. Oғғɪᴄᴇ Nᴀᴛɪᴏɴᴀʟ ᴅᴇ ʟᴀ SᴛᴀᴛɪsᴛɪQᴜᴇ (1996), *Enquête sur le secteur informel à Nouakchott, Nouadhibou et Kaédi, Résultats,* Vol. 3: Facteurs d'exploitation, recettes et consommations intermédiaires, Nouakchott. Oғғɪᴄᴇ Nᴀᴛɪᴏɴᴀʟ ᴅᴇ ʟᴀ SᴛᴀᴛɪsᴛɪQᴜᴇ (1997), *Enquête sur le secteur informel en mileu urbain (2ème phase), Résultats,* Vol. 4: Caractéristiques des secteurs Commerce, Services et Artisanat, Nouakchott. Oғғɪᴄᴇ Nᴀᴛɪᴏɴᴀʟ ᴅᴇ ʟᴀ SᴛᴀᴛɪsᴛɪQᴜᴇ (1997), *Enquête sur le secteur informel en milieu urbain (2ème phase), Résultats,* Vol. 5: Emploi dans les secteurs Commerce, Services et Artisanat, Nouakchott. Oғғɪᴄᴇ Nᴀᴛɪᴏɴᴀʟ ᴅᴇ ʟᴀ SᴛᴀᴛɪsᴛɪQᴜᴇ (1999), *Enquête sur le secteur informel en milieu urbain (2ème phase), Résultats,* Vol. 6 : Valeur ajoutée des établissements informels, Nouakchott.
Mozambique	Aʀᴅᴇɴɪ, P.(1997), "The Informal Sector and Economic Policy in Mozambique", in AFRISTAT (1997), *Le secteur informel et la politique économique en Afrique subsaharienne,* Vol. 3 (pp. 153-171).
Niger	Cʜᴀʀᴍᴇs, J. (1987), *Contribution du secteur informel à l'emploi et à la production au Niger. Essais d'estimation et perspectives,* Ministère du Plan, Direction de la Statistique et de l'Informatique, Niamey. Rᴇ́ᴘᴜʙʟɪQᴜᴇ ᴅᴜ Nɪɢᴇʀ, Dɪʀᴇᴄᴛɪᴏɴ ᴅᴇ ʟᴀ SᴛᴀᴛɪsᴛɪQᴜᴇ ᴇᴛ ᴅᴇs Cᴏᴍᴘᴛᴇs Nᴀᴛɪᴏɴᴀᴜx (1997), Enquête Nationale sur le secteur informel, 1995, Niamey, projet PADEM NER/89/011.
Senegal	Cʜᴀʀᴍᴇs, J. (1989), *Economie non enregistrée, secteur informel et comptabilité nationale au Sénégal : 1977-88,* Direction de la Statistique, PAGD, Dakar.
South Africa	Sᴛᴀᴛɪsᴛɪᴄs Sᴏᴜᴛʜ Aғʀɪᴄᴀ (2002), *The Contribution of Small and Micro Enterprises to the Economy of the Country: a Survey of Non-VAT-Registered Businesses in South Africa,* Pretoria.
Zaire (now Democratic Republic of Congo)	Cʜᴀʀᴍᴇs, J. (1989) with D. Naudet, *Secteur artisanal et Comptabilité Nationale au Zaïre, Résultats de l'enquête légère sur le secteur informel urbain de la production et des services.* 1989. Institut National de Statistique, PNUD - PRAIGEFI.

55

ISBN: 978-92-64-05923-8 - © OECD 2009

Latin America	
Argentina	OIT (various years), *Panorama Laboral, America Latina y el Caribe,* Lima.
Bolivia	OIT (various years), *Panorama Laboral, America Latina y el Caribe,* Lima.
Brazil	IBGE (1999), *Economia Informal Urbana 1997, Brasil,* Rio de Janeiro, Vol 1, 345p.
	OIT (various years), *Panorama Laboral, America Latina y el Caribe,* Lima.
Chile	OIT (various years), *Panorama Laboral, America Latina y el Caribe,* Lima.
Colombia	OIT (various years), *Panorama Laboral, America Latina y el Caribe,* Lima.
Costa Rica	OIT (various years), *Panorama Laboral, America Latina y el Caribe,* Lima.
Dominican Republic	OIT (various years), *Panorama Laboral, America Latina y el Caribe,* Lima.
Ecuador	OIT (various years), *Panorama Laboral, America Latina y el Caribe,* Lima.
El Salvador	OIT (various years), *Panorama Laboral, America Latina y el Caribe,* Lima.
Guatemala	OIT (various years), *Panorama Laboral, America Latina y el Caribe,* Lima.
Haiti	OIT (various years), *Panorama Laboral, America Latina y el Caribe,* Lima.
Honduras	OIT (various years), *Panorama Laboral, America Latina y el Caribe,* Lima.
Mexico	INEGI (2000), *El Empleo en el Sector Informal Urbano en Mexico en la Decada de los Noventa,* Aguas Calientes.
	INEGI (2000), *Cuenta Satélite del Subsector Informal de los Hogares, 1993-1998,* Mexico.
	INEGI (2002), *Encuesta Nacional de Empleo 2000,* INEGI , Secretaria del Trabajo y Prevision Social, Mexico.
	OIT (various years), *Panorama Laboral, America Latina y el Caribe,* Lima.
Panama	OIT (various years), *Panorama Laboral, America Latina y el Caribe,* Lima.
Paraguay	OIT (various years), *Panorama Laboral, America Latina y el Caribe,* Lima.
Peru	OIT (various years), *Panorama Laboral, America Latina y el Caribe,* Lima.
Venezuela	OIT (various years), *Panorama Laboral, America Latina y el Caribe,* Lima.

56

ISBN: 978-92-64-05923-8 - © OECD 2009

South and Southeast Asia	
India	GOVERNMENT OF INDIA, NATIONAL SAMPLE SURVEY ORGANISATION (NSSO) (2001), *Informal sector in India 1999-2000, Salient Features,* NSS 55th round July 1999-June 2000, New Delhi. NATIONAL SAMPLE SURVEY ORGANISATION (2001), *Non-agricultural Workers in Informal Sector based on Employment-Unemployment Survey 1999-2000,* NSS 55th round July 1999-June 2000, New Delhi.
Indonesia	BADAN PUSAT STATISTIK, (1999), *Contribution of the Small Scale, Medium and Large Enterprises to GDP and Labour Absorption* (in Indonesian). Final report, BPS, Jakarta. CHARMES, J. (2001), *The Informal Sector, an Engine for Growth or a Social Insurance for the Poor? Its Role in Economic Growth and During the Recent Financial Crisis in East Asia, in the Light of Some European Views on the Informal Sector,* ASEM/Asian Development Bank/World Bank, Conference on Social exclusion, social capital and the East Asian crisis, Manila, 5-7 November 2001, published under the title "Social Policy and the Informal Sector" in MARSHALL, K. and O. BUTZBACH (eds.) (2003), *New Social Policy Agendas for Europe and Asia: Challenges, Experience and lessons*, The World Bank, Washington, D.C., pp. 307-313.
Philippines	CHARMES, J. (2001), *The Informal Sector, an Engine for Growth or a Social Insurance for the Poor? Its Role in Economic Growth and During the Recent Financial Crisis in East Asia, in the Light of Some European Views on the Informal Sector,* ASEM/Asian Development Bank/World Bank, Conference on Social exclusion, social capital and the East Asian crisis, Manila, 5-7 November 2001, published under the title "Social Policy and the Informal Sector" in MARSHALL, K. and O.BUTZBACH (eds). (2003), *New Social Policy Agendas for Europe and Asia, Challenges, Experience and lessons*, World Bank, Washington D.C. pp. 307-313.
Thailand	NATIONAL STATISTICAL OFFICE (1996), *Formal and Informal Labor Force Market, 1994 Labor Force Survey,* NSO, Bangkok. CHARMES, J. (2001), *The Informal Sector, an Engine for Growth or a Social Insurance for the Poor? Its Role in Economic Growth and During the Recent Financial Crisis in East Asia, in the Light of Some European Views on the Informal Sector,* ASEM/Asian Development Bank/World Bank, Conference on Social exclusion, social capital and the East Asian crisis, Manila, 5-7 November, 2001, published under the title "Social Policy and the Informal Sector" in MARSHALL, K. and O.BUTZBACH (eds.) (2003), World Bank, Washington D.C., pp. 307-313.

57

West Asia	
Iran	HEDAYAT, M. (1988), *L'emploi dans le secteur non structuré en Iran*, INSEE, Service de Coopération, Paris. CHARMES, J. (2008), *Informal Employment in Iran: Size and Contribution to GDP,* World Bank, Washington, D.C.
Lebanon	CHARMES, J. (2008), "Micro and Small Enterprises in the Middle East and North Africa (MENA) in a Comparative Perspective. A Synthesis of the MSEs Surveys Conducted in Turkey, Lebanon, Egypt and Morocco from 2001 to 2004", Economic Research Forum, Project "Promoting Competitiveness in the Micro and Small Enterprise Sector in the MENA region", Cairo.
West Bank and Gaza	CHARMES, J. (2008), "Statistics on Informal Employment in the Arab Region", Chapter 3 of *Gender Equality and Workers' Rights in the Informal Economies of Arab States*, ILO Regional Office for the Arab States and CAWTAR (Center of Arab Women for Training and Research, Beirut and Tunis (pp. 54-72).
Syria	CHARMES, J. (2008), "Statistics on Informal Employment in the Arab Region", Chapter 3 of *Gender Equality and Workers' Rights in the Informal Economies of Arab States*, ILO Regional Office for the Arab States and CAWTAR (Center of Arab Women for Training and Research, Beirut and Tunis (pp.54-72).
Turkey	STATE INSTITUTE OF STATISTICS (2001), *Urban Informal Sector Survey 2000, Preliminary Results* (in Turkish), Haber Bülteni, Statistics Bulletin, Ankara. STATE INSTITUTE OF STATISTICS (2003), *Employment in Small and Unincorporated Enterprises 2000*, Ankara. CHARMES, J. (2008), "Micro and Small Enterprises in the Middle East and North Africa (MENA) in a Comparative Perspective. A Synthesis of the MSEs Surveys conducted in Turkey, Lebanon, Egypt and Morocco from 2001 to 2004", Economic Research Forum, Project "Promoting Competitiveness in the Micro and Small Enterprise Sector in the MENA region", Cairo.
Yemen	CHARMES, J. (2008), "Statistics on Informal Employment in the Arab Region", Chapter 3 of *Gender Equality and Workers' Rights in the Informal Economies of Arab States*, ILO Regional Office for the Arab States and CAWTAR (Center of Arab Women for Training and Research, Beirut and Tunis (pp.54-72).

ISBN: 978-92-64-05923-8 – © OECD 2009

Transition countries	
Kyrgyzstan	HEINTZ, J. and G. CHANG (2007), *Statistics on Employment in the Informal Sector and Informal Employment: a summary of updated estimates from the ILO Bureau of Statistics database*, Paper prepared for the ILO, Employment sector, Geneva.
Moldova	CHARMES, J. (2002), *Informal Employment, Informal Sector and the Non-Observed Economy in Moldova. A Tentative Assessment of their Size, Contribution and Trends in 2000.* Report of a mission at the Department of Statistics and Sociology, ILO, for Eurostat and INSEE (TACIS programme), DSS-INSEE. CHARMES, J. (2003), co-author *Employment in the Informal Economy in the Republic of Moldova,* Department for Statistics and Sociology, ILO, TACIS-EU, Chisinau (in English and Romanian). CHARMES, J. (2004), *Secteur informel, emploi informel, économie non observée: méthodes de mesure et d'estimation appliquées aux économies en transition. L'exemple de la Moldavie,* séminaire du ROSES, Paris I.
Romania	STĂNCULESCU, M. (2006), "Informal Economy and Unregistered Work in Romania", paper presented at the *EU-ILO Project on Social Dialogue as a Tool to Address Unregistered Work in Turkey*, 4 November. PARLEVLIET J. and T. XENOGIANI (2008), "Report on Informal Employment in Romania", *OECD Development Centre Working Paper* No. 271, Paris.
Russia	GOSKOMSTAT (2002), *Employment in the Informal Sector in the Russian Federation, 2001* (in Russian).

59

ANNEX 2.A5. REGIONAL GROUPINGS USED FOR DATA ON SELF-EMPLOYMENT

Eastern Europe	Bulgaria, Croatia, Czech Republic, Hungary, Lithuania, Poland, Romania, Russia, Slovakia, Slovenia.
Northern Europe	Denmark, Finland, Netherlands, Norway, Sweden.
Southern Europe	Greece, Italy, Portugal, Spain.
Rest of Western Europe	Austria, Belgium, France, Germany, Ireland, United Kingdom.
Other developed countries	Australia, Canada, Japan, New Zealand, United States.
Northern Africa	Algeria, Egypt, Libya, Morocco, Tunisia.
Eastern Africa	Comoros, Ethiopia, Kenya, Mauritius, Mozambique, Tanzania.
Central Africa	Burundi, Central African Republic, Cameroon, Congo, Chad, Democratic Republic of Congo Rwanda, Sudan.
Southern Africa	Botswana, Lesotho, Madagascar, Malawi, South Africa, Zambia.
West Africa	Benin, Burkina Faso, Gambia, Ghana, Guinea, Guinea Bissau, Liberia, Mali, Niger, Togo.
Central America	Costa Rica, El Salvador, Guatemala, Honduras, Mexico, Nicaragua, Panama.
South America	Argentina, Bolivia, Brazil, Chile, Colombia, Ecuador, Paraguay, Peru, Uruguay, Venezuela.
Caribbean	Cuba, Dominican Republic, Haiti.
East Asia	China; Hong Kong, China; Korea.
Southeast Asia	Cambodia, Indonesia, Malaysia, Philippines, Singapore, Thailand.
South Asia	Bangladesh, India, Iran, Nepal, Pakistan, Sri Lanka.
West Asia	Bahrain, Kuwait, Iraq, Jordan, Lebanon, Oman, Qatar, Syria, Turkey, United Arab Emirates, Yemen.

ISBN: 978-92-64-05923-8 - © OECD 2009

NOTE

1. International definitions of the *informal sector* and of *informal employment* have been adopted respectively as resolutions and guidelines by the International Conference of Labor Statisticians (ICLS) in 1993*a*, 1993*b* 2002 and 2003. The reports of these three conferences as well as the discussions and recommendations of the International Expert Group on Informal Sector Statistics (also known as the Delhi Group) are the main sources for recent knowledge on the subject and for applying the most up-to-date international definitions of informal employment and its components.

ISBN: 978-92-64-05923-8 - © OECD 2009

REFERENCES

AFRISTAT (2004), *"L'emploi, le chômage et les conditions d'activité dans la principale agglomération de sept Etats membres de l'UEMOA"*. Principaux résultats de l'enquête 1-2-3 de 2001-2002, Bamako.

CHARMES, J. (2002), "Self-employment, Informal Employment, Informal Sector Employment: Trends and Characteristics. A Tentative Assessment of their Statistical Knowledge", contribution to the ILO/WIEGO report on informal employment for the International Labour Conference 2002 and to *Women and Men in the Informal Economy: a Statistical Picture*.

CHARMES, J. (2004), *Data Collection on the Informal Sector: a Review of Concepts and Methods Used since the Adoption of an International Definition Towards a Better Comparability of Available Statistics*, ILO, Bureau of Statistics, Geneva.

CHARMES, J. (2007), *Informal Employment in Iran: Size and Contribution to GDP*, Paper prepared for the World Bank, Washington D.C.

CHARMES, J. (2008), "Statistics on Informal Employment in the Arab Region", Chapter 3 of *Gender Equality and Workers' Rights in the Informal Economies of Arab States*, ILO Regional Office for the Arab States and CAWTAR (Center of Arab Women for Training and Research, Beirut and Tunis), pp.54-72.

HART, K. (1973), "Informal Income Opportunities and Urban Employment in Ghana", *Journal of Modern African Studies*, Vol. II.

HEINTZ, J. and G. CHANG (2007), *Statistics on Employment in the Informal Sector and Informal Employment: a Summary of Updated Estimates from the ILO Bureau of Statistics Database*, paper prepared for the ILO, Employment Sector, Geneva.

HUSSMANNS, R. (2001), *Informal Sector and Informal Employment: Elements for a Conceptual Framework*, paper presented at the Fifth Meeting of the Expert Group on Informal Sector Statistics (Delhi Group), New Delhi, 19-21 September.

ILO (1972), *Employment, Incomes and Equality. A Strategy for Increasing Productive Employment in Kenya*, Geneva.

ILO (1990), *"Retrospective Edition on Population Censuses, 1945-89"*, *Yearbook of Labour Statistics*, ILO, Geneva.

ILO (1993a), *Statistics of Employment in the Informal Sector*, Report for the Fifteenth International Conference of Labour Statisticians, Geneva, 19-28 January.

ILO (1993b), *Report of the Conference*, Report of the Fifteenth International Conference of Labour Statisticians, Geneva, 19-28 January.

ILO (2002), *Women and Men in the Informal Economy, A Statistical Picture*, ILO, Employment sector, Geneva.

ILO (2003), *Report 1, General Report*, Seventeenth International Conference of Labour Statisticians, ILO, Geneva, 24 November-3 December.

UNITED NATIONS (1994), *Demographic Yearbook 1994*, 46th edition, Population Census Statistics, Special Topic, Active Population, Department of Economic and Social Affairs, Population Division, New York, NY.

ISBN: 978-92-64-05923-8 - © OECD 2009

Persisting Informal Employment: What Explains It?

David Kucera and Theodora Xenogiani

ABSTRACT

Why do informal employment and its associated poverty persist? It might be thought that economic growth would bring a switch into more formal and therefore secure jobs but it is far from clear that this is necessarily the case. Some observers suggest that there are not enough formal jobs to go round; others that the informal sector is more dynamic; yet others that regulations and bureaucracy are disincentives to a move into the formal sector. Part of the answer may lie in the existence of two distinct informal labour markets with some workers voluntarily opting for the informal sector. The relationships between growth, poverty and informal employment are complex and becoming more so with the emergence of global commodity chains. Does growth encourage informality or does informality spur growth? There are reasons to believe that growth may not be enough to reduce informal employment.

63

ISBN: 978-92-64-05923-8 - © OECD 2009

INTRODUCTION

Informal employment presents policy makers with a challenge. It is associated with poverty and with a lack of social and labour law protection yet at the same time it is emerging in forms that are complementary with economic growth. This chapter seeks better to understand the determinants of informal employment, something that is indispensible for policy guidance. In spite of the strong relationship across countries between higher per capita incomes and lower shares of informal employment in richer countries, the chapter argues that economic growth by itself is insufficient to achieve a substantial reduction in informal employment.

Theories used to explain informal employment can be classified into two sets: those that emphasise growth performance and patterns and those that concentrate on institutions. For the first set, output growth in the formal sector has been inadequate, with the consequence that employment has grown in the informal sector as the labour force has expanded (what Betcherman [2002] refers to as the "no-growth" hypothesis). Alternatively, growth in the formal sector might generate low levels of employment because of the technology used within an industry or because that growth is being driven by more capital-intensive industries. Finally, it may simply be that the informal sector is more dynamic than the formal, leading to a disproportionate increase in informal employment.

The second set of hypotheses focuses on institutions. These include labour market institutions and regulations and the protection and formalisation of property rights. It includes, in addition, emerging forms of informal employment, such as those within formal establishments and global supply chains. If the persistence of informal employment is to be understood, both its extent and composition need to be accounted for.

64

WHAT DO THE DATA SAY? PERSISTING INFORMAL EMPLOYMENT, GROWTH AND POVERTY LINKAGES

There is a strong negative relationship across countries between per capita incomes and proportions of non-agricultural informal employment (Figure 3.1): that is, poorer countries generally have more informal unemployment.

ISBN: 978-92-64-05923-8 - © OECD 2009

Figure 3.1. Informal Employment is Negatively Related to GDP Per Capita
(most recent data available)

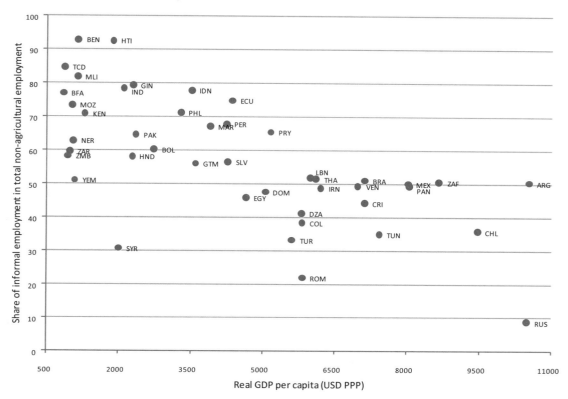

Source: Table 2.1 and Penn World Tables (Heston *et al.,* 2006).
StatLink http://dx.doi.org/10.1787/533243376536

Though historical data on informal employment are lacking, such data are available for shares of self-employment (one of the main components of informal employment), which show the same negative relationship with per capita incomes going back to the 1970s (Figure 3.2). As can be seen in the figure, the relationship has been quite stable over recent decades. The negative relationships shown in Figures 3.1 and 3.2 are consistent with the view that over time economic growth leads to less informal employment. The basic underlying dynamic is that economic growth, and economic development more broadly, are characterised by the growth of formal jobs, with workers shifting to formal employment from informal employment (both agricultural and non-agricultural).

ISBN: 978-92-64-05923-8 - © OECD 2009

Figure 3.2. A Stable Cross-Sectional Relationship between Self-Employment and GDP Per Capita

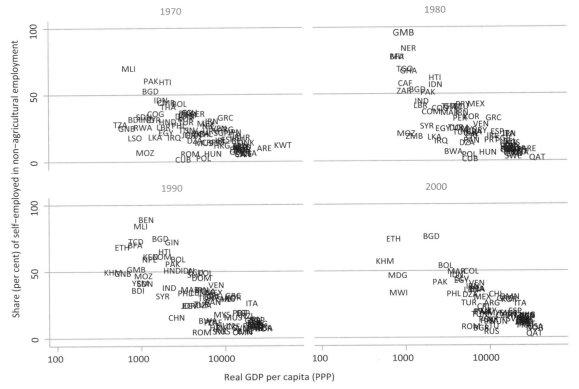

Source: Chapter 2 and Penn World Tables (Heston *et al.*, 2006).
StatLink http://dx.doi.org/10.1787/533247388504

Yet regional trends in shares of informal employment tell a more nuanced story (Figure 3.3). In none of the regions considered has there been a marked trend decline in shares of informal employment. Similar patterns hold for individual countries such as India, where the solid economic growth of the 1990s was accompanied by a rising share of informal employment.

ISBN: 978-92-64-05923-8 - © OECD 2009

Figure 3.3. **Informal Employment and Growth Across Regions**

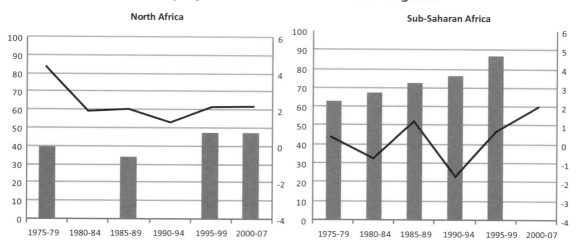

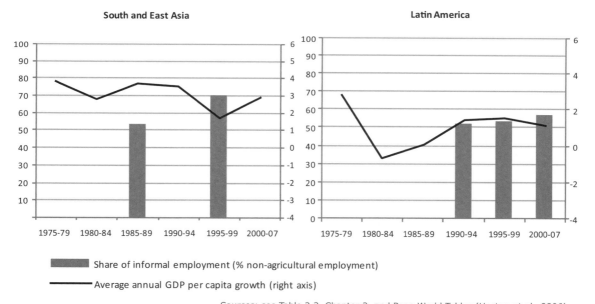

Share of informal employment (% non-agricultural employment)

Average annual GDP per capita growth (right axis)

Sources: see Table 2.3, Chapter 2, and Penn World Tables (Heston *et al.*, 2006).
StatLink http://dx.doi.org/10.1787/533256318717

This evidence suggests that, at least in the medium term, economic growth does not necessarily lead to a fall in informal employment.

Mirroring the negative relationship across countries between per capita incomes and shares of informal employment is a positive relationship between poverty and shares of informal employment (Figure 3.4).

Figure 3.4. **Poverty and Informal Employment**

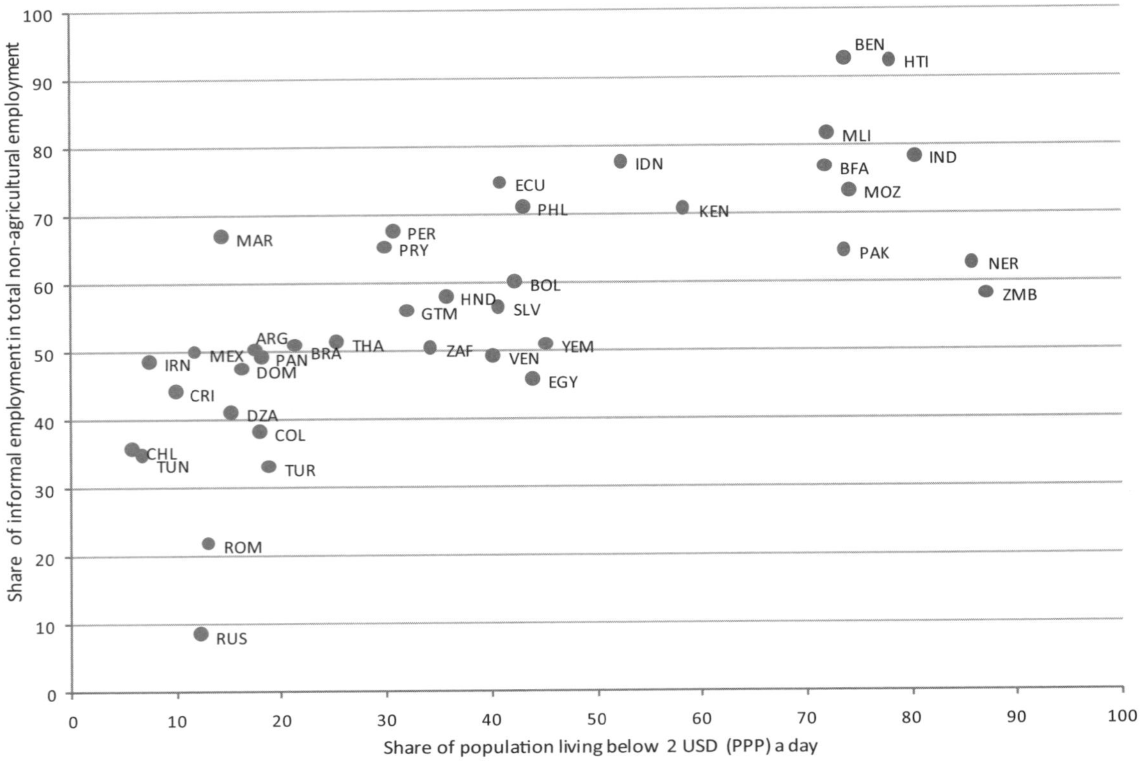

Source: Table 2.1 and World Bank (2007*a*).
StatLink ⬛⬛⬛ http://dx.doi.org/10.1787/533307807050

That latter relationship is also suggested by a consideration of the two poorest regions of the world, sub-Saharan Africa and South Asia. In these regions, the vast majority of workers are in informal employment and the vast majority of people live in extreme poverty, to the point where there is inevitably a very substantial overlap between the two. Indeed, a key reason why persistent informal employment is so troubling is that it is so commonly associated with poverty.

Why, then, is informal employment so extensive and persistent, and how does this tie in with poverty and economic development more generally? Theories providing fundamental insights into these questions are considered next.

DUAL LABOUR MARKETS

Theoretical Underpinnings

Lewis's seminal paper on the "dual economy" (1954) addresses employment dynamics between what he referred to as the "capitalist" and "subsistence" sectors of the economy. Particularly relevant here is the argument that the expansion of the capitalist sector is made possible by the shift of unskilled workers from the subsistence to the capitalist sector in the context of the "unlimited" supply of unskilled workers in the subsistence sector. In respect of constraints on the expansion of employment in the capitalist sector, limiting its capacity to absorb workers from the subsistence sector, Lewis writes that: "The real bottlenecks to expansion are … capital and natural resources."

ISBN: 978-92-64-05923-8 - © OECD 2009

Though much of Lewis's discussion of the subsistence sector addresses agriculture, he also presents a familiar picture of urban informal employment, even though the paper predated such terminology:

> "The phenomenon [of "disguised" unemployment] is not, however, by any means confined to the countryside. Another large sector to which it applies is the whole range of casual jobs – the workers on the docks, the young men who rush forward asking to carry your bags as you appear, the jobbing gardener … petty retail trading."

These are Lewis's examples for the urban self-employed, whereas for urban wage earners, Lewis wrote, "most important… is domestic service." The Lewis model is relevant, in this sense, for thinking about formal and informal employment, equating capitalist with formal and subsistence with informal.

Drawing on their research in sub-Saharan Africa, Harris and Todaro (1970) developed a formal (in the theoretical sense) model of labour market dualism. The Harris-Todaro model provides an account of why the number of rural-to-urban migrants could exceed the number of available urban jobs, resulting in open urban unemployment. In this model, entry-level urban wages are hypothesised to be above both agricultural earnings and a hypothesised market-clearing level. Discussing policies to reduce urban unemployment, Harris and Todaro proposed a two-fold policy package combining restrictions on rural-urban migration with limited wage subsidies or direct employment by governments.

Though the Harris-Todaro model did not explicitly address informal employment, it nonetheless provided the foundation for subsequent theories about it. Fields (1975) extended the Harris-Todaro model in several directions, most relevantly by incorporating an urban informal sector. Fields (2005a) used the Harris-Todaro model to evaluate the effects of three policies – "modern sector job creation", "modern sector wage restraint" and "rural development" – on unemployment and, by implication, on informal employment. In this context, Fields finds that modern sector wage restraint can result in either higher or lower unemployment, depending on whether the demand for labour is sufficiently elastic or inelastic. Modern sector job creation results in higher unemployment and rural development in lower unemployment.

There is, then, a striking contrast between the policy implications of the Lewis and the Harris-Todaro models: in the Lewis model, the expansion of formal employment results in less informal employment; in the Harris-Todaro model, the expansion of formal (non-governmental) employment results in more informal employment. In the Lewis model, in other words, the cause of persisting informal employment is too few formal jobs and the cause of too few formal jobs is the lack of capital.

An important insight resulting from the Harris-Todaro model is that rural development matters not just because it can reduce urban informal employment (restricting rural-urban migration could do the same) but because it does so by reducing rural poverty. Yet broader economic growth and development are historically characterised by both urbanisation and industrialisation, with productivity increases in industry driving productivity increases and employment growth in the economy as a whole (Pieper, 2000). Because of agglomeration economies, where economies of scale and networks lead to geographical clustering, industry is concentrated in urban areas[1]. Economic growth and development have also been associated, historically at least, with a rising share of formal employment.

Taken together, these points suggest that the Lewis model may provide a more useful foundation for addressing the dynamics between formal and informal employment in many developing country contexts. The experience of the East Asian Tigers comes to mind in this regard, where the number of formal jobs created largely offset the number of rural-urban migrants. It is not surprising that research on informal employment is most extensive in developing regions where informal employment itself is most extensive. Yet a deeper understanding of the persistence of informal employment may require greater attention to the labour market dynamics of developing regions that were better able to combine urbanisation and industrialisation with low levels of urban unemployment and informal employment.

69

Lewis focused on the demand side, but what about supply side considerations, such as levels of educational attainment? On this point, Lewis (1954) wrote that "if the capital is available for development, the capitalists or government will soon provide the facilities for training more skilled people." His view is worth bearing in mind, but at the same time increasing educational attainment can itself affect the demand side, for example by attracting foreign direct investment in an open economy context.

Dualism Within the Informal Sector

The contributions noted in the previous section share the assumption that informal employment is undesirable and that reducing it is an important policy objective. At the same time, the fact that informal employment has many faces was not just recognised but indeed emphasised in the earliest studies referring explicitly to an "informal sector" (e.g. Hart, 1973).

An essential work on voluntary informal employment is Fields (1990), but the issue has received renewed attention with the work of Maloney and others (e.g. Maloney, 2004; Bosch *et al.*, 2007). Fields developed the idea of dualism within urban informal employment characterised by "easy-entry", or "lower-tier", and "upper-tier" informal employment, based on his research in urban Costa Rica and Malaysia. Fields found that many upper-tier informal workers previously worked in formal employment, where they gained the skills and savings to set up their own informal enterprises. Though Fields emphasised that upper-tier informal employment is "voluntary", he also refers to its "constrained voluntary nature", explaining that "given the constrained choices available to them, a great many of informal sector workers are in that sector voluntarily".

Maloney's (2004) description of voluntary informal employment is similar to that of Fields in many respects, but differs in emphasising formal social protection both as a defining characteristic of formal employment and for its role in creating incentives to work informally. For example, in a scenario in which an entire family is eligible for medical benefits as long as one member is formally employed, there is less incentive for additional members to be formally employed. That assumes workers pay for these benefits in some form and that the formal and informal jobs in question are broadly comparable. Another scenario is that workers may eschew mandatory contributions to pension schemes because of their upfront cost relative to an uncertain future return. More generally, the less efficient the delivery of formal social protection, the weaker is the incentive to participate.

Voluntary informal employment poses a challenge to conceptions concentrating on "easy-entry" informal employment. Maloney (2004) suggests that it also poses a challenge to the ILO's definition of "decent work". He writes:

> "This view of the voluntary informal entrepreneur has important implications for how we think about good vs. bad jobs, 'unprotectedness' and precariousness. The International Labour Organization, for instance, defines 'decent' work as jobs covered and protected by formal labour institutions."

Yet in its last major report on informal employment, the ILO (2002) also emphasised the heterogeneity of informal employment in a manner consistent with the notion of voluntary informal employment, saying there was "no simple relationship between working informally and being poor, and working formally and escaping poverty." The implication is that some informal workers are not in poverty and that some formal workers are, and therefore that some informal jobs are better paid than some formal jobs. So it is unsurprising that some workers might prefer informal to formal work: and that is what is meant in these debates by voluntary informal employment. The question is not whether there exists some voluntary informal employment in developing countries but rather how widespread it is and how this might vary for countries at different levels of development.

Much of the evidence on voluntary informal employment comes from Latin America, in particular from Argentina, Brazil and especially Mexico. These three countries have micro-panel data, making it possible to trace the movement of workers between formal and informal employment.

70

ISBN: 978-92-64-05923-8 - © OECD 2009

Yet these are among the most developed of developing countries, raising the question of how meaningful their findings are for poorer developing countries and regions. Fields (2005b) makes this point, writing that "perhaps most informal entrepreneurs are in the upper-tier in Mexico, but I doubt this is the case in India, Bolivia and Kenya[2]."

Indeed there are several reasons to suspect that there might be a generally positive relationship between the ratio of voluntary to involuntary informal employment and levels of economic development. In other words the poorer the country, the lower the proportion of voluntary informal employment.

More developed countries generally have stronger unemployment insurance systems, and thus open unemployment can more readily provide an alternative to involuntary informal employment when jobs are lost. It should be remembered, too, that the share of informal employment is highest in the poorest developing regions, particularly in sub-Saharan Africa and South Asia. In India, for example, the share of informal non-agricultural employment was 83 per cent for the late 1990s, as noted in Chapter 2. Similarly, the share of employment in the "unorganised sector" was 77 per cent in urban areas and 95 per cent in rural areas in 1999-2000 (Sakthivel and Joddar, 2006)[3]. In sub-Saharan Africa and South Asia, it is less likely that a family member will be in formal employment and so the possibilities for other members to opt out of formal employment while receiving formal social protection (in cases of extension to family members) are more limited.

More fundamentally, voluntary informal employment implies a choice: namely that purportedly voluntary informal workers could work in formal employment if they so wished. Clearly the possibilities for this are exceedingly limited when the share of formal employment is very low. Even in countries where the share of formal employment is higher, while any given ostensibly voluntary informal worker might be able to work in formal employment individually, not all could do so at the same time. In this sense, estimates of the share of voluntary informal employment can be illusory.

Poorer developing countries and regions also have such high shares of informal employment and rates of poverty that there is necessarily much overlap between the two. In 2004, the USD 2 a day poverty headcount ratio was 22 per cent in Latin America and the Caribbean, compared to 72 per cent in sub-Saharan Africa and 77 per cent in South Asia (World Bank, 2007b). It is problematic to regard informal workers in poverty as voluntary. From these considerations it follows that the concept of voluntary informal employment may be least relevant where informal employment is most pervasive.

This brings the discussion back to the "constrained voluntary nature" of purportedly voluntary informal employment. For voluntary informal employment to be a meaningful notion, it is important to consider the quality of this employment as well as formal employment alternatives in an absolute, not just relative, sense. There are good and bad jobs within the formal sector, dualism within both formal and informal sectors. Indeed, it was just such concerns that motivated the ILO's 2003 definition of informal employment (Hussmanns, 2005).

These points are illustrated in Figure 3.5, showing hypothetical distributions of formal and informal workers by the quality of their jobs and assuming commensurability among the full range of job quality characteristics, including social protection. At both points 1 and 2, the equivalent quality of job is available to formal and informal workers, who therefore may be indifferent as to whether they are in formal or informal employment. At point 1, however, formal and informal workers are below the poverty line, whereas at point 2 they are above it. The difference between points 1 and 2 should be central to discussions of purportedly voluntary informal employment. This holds for decent work more generally, many aspects of which are defined in an absolute rather than relative sense, for example, regarding minimum working age and maximum working hours (cf. Anker et al., 2002).

71

Figure 3.5. **Job Quality Distribution for Formal and Informal Workers**

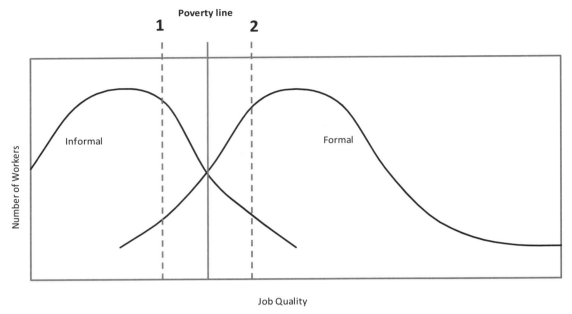

Source: Authors' own illustration.
StatLink http://dx.doi.org/10.1787/533376445435

Dualism within the informal sector is also addressed by Ranis and Stewart (1999), who develop a formal model of "traditional" (or "stagnant") versus "modernising" (or "dynamic") components of the informal sector as well as estimates of the size of these components in the Philippines and Thailand. The two components overlap to some extent with Fields' upper-tier and easy-entry informal employment, but Ranis and Stewart also emphasise possible production linkages between the modernising component of the informal sector and the formal sector.

In this approach, the relative size of the modernising versus traditional components of the informal sector is determined by the growth and organisation of the formal sector and economic growth more generally. For the Philippines in the 1980s, for instance, the authors observe a growth in the traditional and a decline in the modernising components; for Thailand, they observe the opposite. They attribute this divergence to the contrasting macroeconomic performance of the countries, as well as the organisation of the formal sector in Thailand that lent itself to the establishment of production linkages with the modernising component of the informal sector.

The approach taken by Ranis and Stewart usefully illustrates how economic growth can affect the composition of informal employment – that is, the relative share of traditional and modernising informal employment. It also helps consideration of how informal employment can persist and even grow in the face of economic growth, given the production linkages between formal and informal establishments. In this sense, the modernising component of the informal sector is akin to informal employment in formal establishments and global commodity chains. Yet economic growth might also cause an expansion of the traditional component of the informal sector, as here too there are production linkages with global commodity chains, typified by household production in the lower tiers of chains (Carr and Chen, 2001). In other words, both traditional and modernising informal employment can be complementary to economic growth and so account for the persistence of informal employment in the face of economic growth.

ISBN: 978-92-64-05923-8 - © OECD 2009

Formal Property Rights and Cultures of Evasion and Compliance

De Soto (2000) takes the view that informal employment persists in developing countries because informal workers generally do not have a legal title to their *de facto* property, particularly land and housing. Put another way, the system of formal property rights is weak in developing countries. It is argued that if informal workers were granted a legal title to their property, they could use this as collateral to obtain formal loans for investment in their businesses. As with Lewis, the lack of capital is seen as a key constraint in the expansion of formal employment. But where Lewis looked to capitalists' profits as a source of investment, de Soto looks to the potential of informal workers themselves. Elaborating his views, de Soto (2000) refers to six beneficial effects of a system of formal property rights.

— fixing the economic potential of assets;

— integrating dispersed information into one system;

— making people accountable;

— making assets fungible;

— networking people;

— protecting transactions.

There are a number of counter-arguments to de Soto's views on the benefits of a system of formal property rights. It is argued, for instance, that de Soto overstates the potential of legal titles on property to generate new investment. Moreover, property rights are often contested, and many informal workers are largely without assets, either land or property (Woodruff, 2001; Culpeper, 2002). Concluding his critique of de Soto's views on formal property rights, Woodruff (2001) writes: "There is almost certainly something to what de Soto says … The question is, How much? The answer awaits better data, and better analysis of the data."

While de Soto's approach may be faulted for its emphasis on formal property rights, it nevertheless provides a useful complement to Lewis's approach in allowing that the informal as well as the formal sector may be a source of investment that drives economic growth and the growth of formal employment. The point is well made by Fields (2004), who writes:

> "Lewis…assumed that the link from savings through investment through capital formation through economic growth took place only in the capitalistic sector and only via profits. What if capitalists use their profits for conspicuous consumption, investments in Swiss bank accounts and purchases of Florida real estate? And on the other hand, what if the poor use their surplus to add fertiliser to the family farm, put a proper roof on the family house and invest in the human capital of their children? For whom is the marginal propensity to form growth-producing capital higher? The answer is by no means evident, at least to me."

De Soto (1989*a*) also argues that informal employment persists in developing countries because of the time-consuming legal steps required to create a formal establishment. This view receives support from an empirical study described in the section on formal labour market institutions and regulations (Djankov *et al.*, 2002).

In motivating his own theories on the causes of informality in Latin America, de Soto (1989*b*) wrote, "Many outsiders look at the economies of Latin America and assume that social or cultural attitudes unique to the region account for the fact that so many people do not participate in the formal economy". His views are in a sense a reaction against cultural explanations of informality and an endeavour to provide a more concrete account. Yet explanations based on cultures of evasion and compliance persist and merit consideration.

One account is provided by Levi (1988), who argues that voluntary compliance is a form of implicit social contract that depends on two factors: first, the quality and quantity of public goods provided by governments in return for payments made by citizens; and, second, the extent to

73

which fellow citizens comply with regulations. The first of these factors is clear enough, but the second begs the question of what determines the extent to which fellow citizens comply.

Similarly, Fugazza and Jacques (2003) argue that there are "objective" and "subjective" costs of being in the informal economy. Objective costs are determined by the probability of being caught and punished. Subjective costs are more nebulous, described as the "psychic costs" of being in the informal economy that differ from individual to individual. In order to inform policy, it is important to know what determines these "psychic costs", just as it is important to know why fellow citizens comply with tax regulations.

One way of thinking about the limitations of the cultural approach is to imagine that in regions with high shares of informal employment a culture of compliance became universal. It is not evident that such a change could plausibly result in substantially higher shares of formal employment, suggesting that the causes of persistent informal employment are of a more tangible nature. As with "voluntary" informal employment, the cultures of evasion and compliance line of argument may be least relevant where informal employment is most prevalent and exists not evasively, but openly and indeed inescapably.

By contrast, de Soto's emphasis on the lack of capital provides a concrete account of persisting informal employment that usefully complements Lewis's approach in looking to the informal sector as an additional source of investment. Both provide demand side explanations, for which the cause of persistent informal employment is too few formal jobs caused in turn by a lack of investment.

FORMAL LABOUR INSTITUTIONS AND REGULATIONS AND INFORMAL EMPLOYMENT

Labour institutions and regulations are often identified as the cause of poor employment performance in both developed and developing countries. This view, focusing on negative unintended consequences, holds that labour institutions and regulations are no more than sand in the workings of labour markets. In a survey addressing key studies for developing countries, Freeman (2005) argues that the debate surrounding this claim is inconclusive for two reasons. First, he writes that "many adherents to this claim hold strong priors that labour markets operate nearly perfectly in the absence of institutions and let their priors dictate their modelling choices and interpretation of empirical results." Second, the evidence itself, mostly based on cross-country statistical analysis, is inconclusive.

What follows is a necessarily selective survey of a large literature on formal labour institutions and regulations and informal employment. To ensure that the selection is not itself the result of "priors", it is based largely on the World Bank's *Informality: Exit and Exclusion* (2007b). Though the World Bank report focuses on Latin America and the Caribbean, it contains a wide-ranging survey of the relevant empirical literature and so provides a useful point of comparison for the reading of this literature. Though some of these studies treat different aspects of labour institutions and regulations together, as far as possible studies on job security costs, union effects, general regulations on firms and firm entry, and minimum wages are addressed in order.

Institutions and Regulations

Law and Employment (2004), edited by Heckman and Pagés, surveys and compiles a number of studies on the impact of labour regulations in Latin America and the Caribbean. The volume is noteworthy for its emphasis on studies analysing micro-data (representing individuals). Most relevant are studies evaluating the effect of "job security costs" (cost of dismissing a worker) on formal employment in Argentina, Barbados, Brazil, Chile, Jamaica, Peru, and Trinidad and Tobago.

ISBN: 978-92-64-05923-8 - © OECD 2009

For these seven countries, statistically significant relationships between higher job security costs and fewer jobs are found only in Argentina and Peru. But what are the implications of job security costs for informal employment? For Argentina, the answer is ambiguous, as different definitions of informal employment show movements in opposite directions: defined as workers in informal establishments, the share of urban informal employment decreased in the 1990s; defined as workers without social security coverage, the share increased[4]. The case of Peru is more straightforward. In the 1990s, job security costs fell while formal employment increased (Saavedra and Torero, 2004). Yet by all measures urban informal employment increased even more rapidly, meaning that falling job security costs occurred alongside a rising share of informal employment[5].

Rather than being anomalous, Peru typifies the relationship between changes in job security costs and shares of informal employment in Latin American and Caribbean countries as well as OECD countries. The relevant study is Heckman and Pagés-Serra (2000). This estimates the effects on shares of self-employment (non-agricultural) of job security costs, measured as the cost of dismissing a worker according to law, expressed in multiples of monthly wages. This is a cross-country panel data analysis evaluating samples of Latin American-Caribbean and OECD countries from 1990 to 1999. Regressions driven mainly by variation across countries (OLS) show a positive relationship between job security costs and shares of self-employment. In contrast, regressions driven by change over time (fixed effects) show the opposite, and such longitudinal evidence provides the better test of policy impact. The longitudinal evidence is also stronger in terms of both the estimated strength and statistical significance of the relationship (Table 3.1). As with Peru, changes in job security costs in Latin American-Caribbean and OECD countries are associated with opposite changes in shares of informal employment: that is, reducing firing costs is associated with a higher share of informal employment.

Table 3.1. Estimated Effect of Jobs Security Costs on Shares of Self-Employment

	OLS	Fixed effects
OECD plus LAC	1.37 (5%)	-8.43 (1%)
LAC	1.09 (10%)	-8.34 (1%)

Source: Heckman and Pagés-Serra (2000).
StatLink http://dx.doi.org/10.1787/533623165325

Union Power

Galli and Kucera (2004) estimate the effects of trade union rights on shares of employment in formal and informal establishments in a cross-country panel data analysis evaluating a sample of Latin American countries from 1990 to 1999 according to the 1993 ILO definition. They find that countries with stronger "civic rights" for workers tend to have lower shares of informal employment.

In addition to the study in *Law and Employment* (Paes de Barros and Corseuil, 2004), Brazil is also the subject of a study by Bosch *et al.* (2007) that endeavours to determine the causes of the increase in the share of informal employment in the 1990s, particularly in light of trade liberalisation and the constitutional reform of 1988[6]. The study estimates the effects of "union power" on the share of urban formal employment, job creation and job destruction in a cross-industry panel data analysis (with time and industry fixed effects) for Brazil from 1983 to 2002, with union power measured by union enrolment rate in an industry. The study also evaluates the effects of overtime costs and "firing costs[7]". Results from the authors' "preferred specification" show that higher union enrolment is associated with higher shares of formal employment (p. 20). Moreover, the estimated positive and negative effects of union enrolment, overtime costs and firing costs on formal job creation and destruction cancel each other out over time[8].

In spite of these findings, the authors write that: "We establish that trade liberalisation played a relatively small part in this increase [in shares of informal employment], but find suggestive evidence that several dimensions of Constitutional reform, in particular regulations relating to firing costs, overtime and union power, explain much more."

Similarly, the authors write that: "A small fraction of this [rise in informality] is driven by trade liberalisation, and the remainder seems driven by rising labour costs and reduced flexibility arising from Constitutional reform."

Figures 3.6 and 3.7 show union enrolment rates and real manufacturing wages in Brazil during this period[9]. Hourly compensation costs in manufacturing (including non-wage labour costs) also declined markedly in Brazil during this period, as did aggregate real wages in both rural and urban areas after the mid-1990s (ILO, 2007; Instituto de Pesquisa Econômica Aplicada [IPEA] 2006). It is not evident how to reconcile the authors' conclusions with the sharp downward declines in these measures.

Figure 3.6. **Union Enrolment Rate, Brazil, 1986-99 (%)**

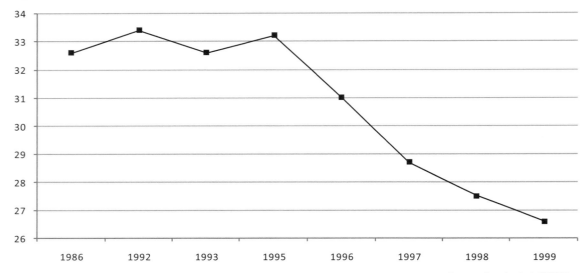

Source: Bosch et al. (2007).
StatLink ⌗ http://dx.doi.org/10.1787/533412258341

ISBN: 978-92-64-05923-8 - © OECD 2009

Figure 3.7. Real Manufacturing Wage Index, Brazil, 1994-2002 (2000 = 100)

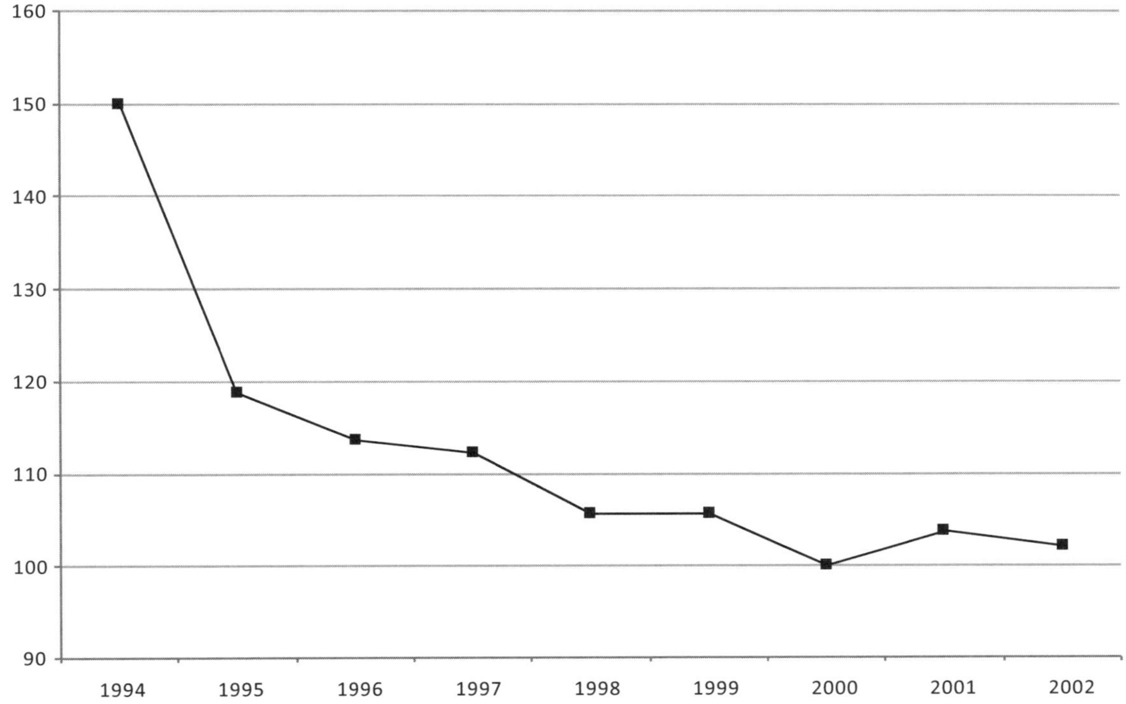

Source: ILO (2007).

StatLink http://dx.doi.org/ 10.1787/533424804624

77

Regulation Effects

The economic effects of labour regulations in India are addressed by Besley and Burgess (2004). The authors construct an indicator, equal to plus or minus one, of changes in labour market regulations related to the Industrial Disputes Act (IDA) and employ it in a cross-state panel data analysis for the 1958 to 1992 period. The authors find that "pro-worker" amendments to the IDA were associated with lower output and employment in formal manufacturing firms and higher output in informal manufacturing firms[10]. The study (and others using the Besley and Burgess indicator) has come under a number of criticisms, most extensively from Bhattacharjea (2006). Regarding problems with the indicator, for example, Bhattacharjea writes of "inappropriate classification of individual amendments, summary coding of incommensurable changes as either +1 or -1, and misleading cumulation over time" and also notes that the indicator does not account for judicial interpretation of the IDA and that the IDA is only one of at least 45 Acts addressing labour at the national level. In addition, Bhattacharjea writes that "the results of their [Besley and Burgess'] econometric analysis are extremely fragile", for instance with regard to model specification.

Loayza and Rigolini (2006) estimate the effects of "credit, labour and business" regulations on shares of self-employment (urban and rural) in a cross-country panel data analysis for the mid-1980s to 2004, evaluating samples of both developed and developing countries[11]. For the full sample of 42 countries, the study finds a borderline statistically significant relationship (10 per cent) between stronger regulations and more self-employment. However, for samples of only developing countries or only countries in Latin America and the Caribbean, the relationship is the opposite, though not statistically significant. In short, weak as the relationship is for the full sample of countries, for samples of developing countries it is non-existent. That is, this study does not provide solid evidence that stronger regulations lead to more informal employment.

ISBN: 978-92-64-05923-8 - © OECD 2009

The World Bank report (2007b) refers to Djankov et al. (2002) along with Friedman et al. (2000) as regards the statement that: "A substantial body of literature sees the size of the informal sector to be determined substantially by regulatory distortions or corruption". Yet Djankov et al. can be read as an example of the potentially negative repercussions of badly designed and implemented regulations rather than "regulatory distortions" as such. Across 85 developed and developing countries for 1999, the study finds a strong positive correlation between the number of procedures (including labour and social security-related procedures) required to start a company and the size of the "unofficial economy", measured as a share of GDP and a share of the labour force[12]. However, the number of such procedures indicates the extent to which states endeavour to regulate labour through firm entry (that is, how it regulates labour) rather than either the overall strength of labour regulations or de facto working conditions in a country. Canada and China provide a telling comparison, for Canada requires only two procedures to start a company – zero for labour and social security-related procedures – whereas China requires 12 – five for labour and social security-related procedures.

Friedman et al.'s (2000) main findings refer to corruption and taxes, which they summarise as follows: "Across 69 countries [developed and developing for the 1990s], higher tax rates are associated with less unofficial activity as a percentage of GDP but corruption is associated with more unofficial activity[13]". Friedman et al.'s findings leave open the possibility that higher taxes might be associated with stronger regulations – on the hypothesis that associated costs of regulations are paid for from taxes – and thus stronger regulations with less "unofficial" activity. The findings are also at odds with the cultures of evasion and compliance approach, for which one would expect higher taxes to be associated with more unofficial activity, not less.

Minimum Wages

Both Maloney and Nuñez Mendez (2003) and Arango and Pachón (2004) use micro-data for Colombia and find that higher minimum wages are associated with less employment and more unemployment. While these studies do not focus on the distinction between formal and informal employment, they nonetheless estimate weaker effects on self-employment than other forms of employment, consistent with the view that minimum wage increases lead to higher shares of self-employment.

Colombia provides a useful warning that badly designed and implemented labour regulations can have negative repercussions. For example, the minimum wage in Colombia was already among the highest in the region when it was further raised in the midst of the deep recession of the late 1990s, during which the unemployment rate more than doubled to a historical high of 20 per cent. But the case of Colombia is not representative. A study on Brazil by Lemos (2007), for example, provides evidence that higher minimum wages had the intended consequence of reducing earnings inequality without the unintended consequence of reducing employment, either for workers in general or for vulnerable workers. More generally, the effect of minimum wages on formal employment depends on a range of factors in addition to the state of the economy, including the difference between minimum and prevailing wages[14].

This empirical evidence is recapitulated in Table 3.2. Some of the statistically strongest results in the literature show a positive relationship between the strength of labour institutions and regulations and shares of formal employment. Most of the studies show essentially no relationship. In short, the empirical evidence does not support the view that formal labour institutions and regulations are a cause of persisting informal employment.

ISBN: 978-92-64-05923-8 - © OECD 2009

Table 3.2. Empirical Studies on Formal Labour Regulations and Informal Employment

Citations	Overview
Heckman and Pagés (2004)	Statistically significant relationships between higher job security costs and less formal employment are found in only two of seven Latin American and Caribbean countries evaluated, Argentina and Peru. Yet these findings do not have clear-cut implications for informal employment. For Argentina in this period, the share of informal employment diverged by different measures; for Peru, the share of informal employment increased by all measures, even though job security costs fell.
Heckman and Pagés-Serra (2000)	For samples of OECD and Latin American-Caribbean countries, OLS results (driven mainly by cross-country variation) show a positive relationship between job security costs and shares of self-employment; fixed effects results (driven by change over time) show a stronger negative relationship between job security costs and shares of self-employment, consistent with the case of Peru noted above.
Galli and Kucera (2004)	For a sample of Latin American countries, stronger "civic rights" for workers are associated with higher shares of formal employment.
Bosch et al. (2007)	The authors attribute the rising share of informal employment in Brazil in the 1990s to "rising labour costs" and "regulations relating to firing costs, overtime and union power". Yet this conclusion is not supported by the study's econometric analysis nor by the patterns of declining union enrolment rates and labour costs.
Besley and Burgess (2004) and Bhattacharjea (2006)	Besley and Burgess (2004) find that "pro-worker" amendments to India's Industrial Disputes Act are associated with less formal manufacturing output and employment and more informal manufacturing output, but their indicators and analysis have been extensively critiqued by Bhattacharjea (2006) and others.
Loayza and Rigolini (2006)	For a sample of developed and developing countries, stronger "credit, labour and business" regulations are associated with more self-employment (10 per cent statistical significance), but not in samples of developing countries only, where the relevant coefficient estimates are of opposite sign (though statistically insignificant).
Djankov et al. (2002)	For a sample of developed and developing countries, the number of procedures required to start a company is associated with a larger "unofficial" economy, measured as a share of GDP and a share of the labour force. Yet the number of procedures is more indicative of the means by which a country regulates rather than the strength of regulations or de facto conditions; e.g. while China requires five labour and social security-related procedures to start a company, Canada requires none.
Friedman et al. (2000)	For a sample of developed and developing countries, higher taxes and less corruption are associated with a smaller "unofficial" economy, measured as a share of GDP. Yet stronger regulations may be associated with a smaller "unofficial" economy on the hypothesis that the associated costs of regulations are paid for from taxes.
Maloney and Nuñez Mendez (2003) and Arango and Pachón (2004)	In the midst of the historically deep recession of the late-1990s, minimum wages in Colombia were increased, which was associated with more unemployment and less employment, with weaker effects on self-employment than other forms of employment.
Lemos (2007)	Higher minimum wages in Brazil are associated with reduced earnings inequality but not with lower employment, either for workers in general or for vulnerable workers.

79

GLOBALISATION, PRECARIOUS JOBS AND INFORMAL EMPLOYMENT

There are many possible causal channels linking globalisation and informal employment. Following the distinction made by Ranis and Stewart (1999) between traditional and modernising components of the informal sector, globalisation can increase production linkages between formal and informal establishments, for example through subcontracting in global supply chains. This could cause an expansion of modernising informal employment. Yet it might also cause an expansion of traditional informal employment, in that a sizeable share of employment in labour-intensive export-oriented industries is in households (as well as being disproportionately female) (Carr and Chen, 2001).

Carr and Chen (2001) refer to several possible linkages between globalisation and informal employment. They argue that globalisation has resulted in intensified competition, leading firms to rely increasingly on lower-cost informal workers, whether through the subcontracting arrangements of multinational corporations (MNCs) or through informal employment relationships within formal establishments. On the other hand, MNC establishments in developing countries tend to pay better wages and have better working conditions than local firms (Brown *et al.*, 2003). Moreover, the presence of MNCs may facilitate access to international markets for locally based firms (Hanson, 2001). In this sense, globalisation could be associated both with the growth of formal wage employment and improved prospects for local export-oriented firms, whether formal or informal.

Foreign direct investment represents the activities of MNCs, yet Carr and Chen (2001) also address short-term capital flows. They argue that financial crises resulting from volatile short-term capital flows have resulted in a decline in formal employment, as least in the immediate aftermath of these crises. Consistent with this viewpoint are the findings of a study on Korea showing a large increase in non-regular employment (much of it informal) in the wake of the late-1990s financial crisis, which persists to the present (Lee and Lee, 2007).

Global economic growth has slowed in recent decades compared with the immediate post-World War II decades, including in much of the developing world. The current global financial crisis greatly exacerbates this concern, with many countries facing the prospect of flat or even negative growth for the foreseeable future. On top of this, informal employment is emerging in different forms, such as within formal establishments and global commodity chains. These developments are associated with the broader growth of various forms of irregular employment, involving casual, contract and temporary workers as well as workers in disguised employment relationships.

The concern that these forms of informal employment are growing led the ILO in 2003 to adopt a new definition of informal employment (Hussmanns, 2005)[15]. Updating its prior definition based on employment in informal establishments, a particular concern of the 2003 definition is informal employment in the formal establishments. Though working in formal establishments, such workers may lack social protection and protection from national labour legislation and may not enjoy the employment benefits received by regular workers.

Because the ILO's definition was only recently adopted, there are insufficient data at present to assess the overall extent and growth of informal employment in formal establishments. Yet the more anecdotal observations that motivated the definition suggest that this may be an important cause of persisting informal employment. There is the possibility, in this sense, that even when the share of employment in formal establishments increases, the share of informal employment may remain stagnant.

Global commodity chains are distinguished between buyer-driven and producer-driven chains, the former in such industries as apparel and footwear and the latter in automobiles and electronics (Gereffi, 1994). Global commodity chains have also become important in agriculture, including in non-traditional agricultural exports. Because of their far-flung, decentralised nature it is difficult to assess the number of workers in global supply chains, particularly informal workers. By all accounts, though, the number is large and growing (e.g. Carr and Chen, 2001; Barrientos. 2009 forthcoming; Posthuma, 2009 forthcoming). Gereffi (2005), for example, refers to the employment aspects of the off-shoring of production as "the great global jobs shift".

Case studies of employment in global commodity chains find that informal workers are found throughout the chains, ranging from the upper tiers, where companies often complement a core of formal workers with contract labour and outsourced production, down to the lower tiers, where informal workers are especially prevalent (Barrientos, 2009). These studies also found that efforts to improve working conditions through "voluntary" initiatives organised by non-governmental organisations (NGOs) and trade union campaigns have been largely ineffective in reaching informal workers. Governments, too, have been challenged in this regard, both as regards enforcement and labour legislation that may not provide protection to informal workers, leading to "important regulatory gaps" (Posthuma, 2009). Not only are informal workers pervasive throughout global commodity chains and prospects for improving their working conditions uncertain, but possibilities for upgrading into higher value-added activities also appear limited (Posthuma, 2009).

Global commodity chains provide upper-tier firms with cost, flexibility and risk-shifting competitive advantages. Because of this, these chains are likely to continue to spread, along with informal employment within them. The growth of such informal employment will thus likely prove an ever more pressing policy challenge in coming years, for which economic growth does not appear to provide a ready answer.

CONCLUSION

A central concern of this chapter is the linkage between economic growth and the reduction of informal employment. Historically, economic growth and economic development more broadly have been associated with more formal and less informal employment. In recent decades, however, global economic growth has slowed. More than that, the linkage appears to have weakened in recent years as a result of the emergence of new forms of informal employment, such as that within formal establishments and global commodity chains.

As the literature on dualism within the informal sector makes clear, informal employment has many different faces. Yet many types of informal employment (upper-tier and easy entry, modernising and traditional) may be linked to formal establishments through global supply chains. Rather than being supplanted in the face of economic growth, these forms of informal employment can be complementary with economic growth. This holds for informal employment in formal establishments as well.

To what extent have these developments weakened the linkage between economic growth and the reduction of informal employment: that is, to what extent will informal employment persist even in the face of solid economic growth? These are clearly questions of degree, and there is at present a dearth of systematic evidence on the extent and growth of emerging forms of informal employment. The anecdotal evidence suggests, however, that these developments may pose serious challenges to growth-oriented policies for reducing informal employment. Though necessary, growth seems not to be sufficient.

The chapter situates these developments among a number of the more prevalent explanations of informal employment. It is argued that Lewis (1954) continues to be useful for thinking about why informal employment persists. In Lewis's approach, the fundamental problem is too few jobs in the formal sector (capitalist sector, in his terminology), caused in turn by too little investment by the formal sector. We argue too that his approach is usefully complemented by de Soto's (2000), particularly regarding the latter's emphasis on the informal sector as a source of investment.

81

The chapter also surveys empirical evidence on the effects of formal labour institutions and regulations on informal employment. The predominant direction of this evidence is clear, suggesting the coherence of simultaneously endeavouring to reduce informal employment and improve the quality of formal employment through labour institutions and regulations. But the exceptions – raising minimum wages in the midst of a deep recession, requiring a large number of procedures to start a new company – are instructive. Taken as a whole, the evidence suggests that the debate should be not about regulation versus deregulation as such, but rather about the optimal design and implementation of labour regulations in country and time-specific contexts.

82

ISBN: 978-92-64-05923-8 - © OECD 2009

NOTES

1. Agglomeration economies are also relevant for services, so economic development based more on services does not necessarily resolve the problem.

2. Supporting this view, for example, are the findings of a study on Côte d'Ivoire, estimating that about twice as many urban workers want to work in formal employment than actually do and that about three times as many urban workers are in the lower tier of informal employment than want to be (Günther and Launov, 2006). Even the case of Mexico remains unsettled, as a study by Duval Hernández (2006) takes a different approach to analysing the micro-data and finds evidence that a large majority of urban informal workers in Mexico are involuntary.

3. In defining employment in the "unorganised sector", Sakthivel and Joddar (2006) write that this is: "essentially based on the following variables: *a)* employment status of workers: salaried/regular labourers, casual wage workers and self-employed workers; *b)* type of enterprise; *c)* number of workers; *d)* type of job: part-time/temporary, etc; and *e)* coverage of provident fund".

4. This resulted from a compositional shift in employment from informal to formal establishments alongside declines in social security coverage in both informal and formal establishments (Galli and Kucera, 2008). Employment in informal establishments is defined along the lines of the 1993 ILO definition, including employees in small firms, the (non-professional) self-employed, and workers in domestic service. The index of job security costs constructed by Heckman and Pagés-Serra (2000) shows no change for Argentina over the 1990s.

5. Saavedra and Torero's data refer to Lima. See Heckman and Pagés-Serra (2000) and Galli and Kucera (2008) for corroborating evidence.

6. Data from Bosch *et al.* show an overall increase in the share of urban informal employment (self-employed and informal salaried workers) of about 10 percentage points from 1990 to 2002, with a slight decline from 2000 to 2002. Based on alternative definitions of informal employment, Gasparini and Tornarolli (2007) and Ernst (2008) present different trends in informal employment in Brazil. From 1990 to 2003, Gasparini and Tornarolli show a peak in the share of urban informal employment in 1996 by a "social protection" definition (workers with pensions linked to employment), with an overall increase of about 7 percentage points over the period, and a peak in 1999 by a "productive" definition (unskilled self-employed, unpaid, and salaried workers in small private firms), with an overall increase of about 2 percentage points. From 1992 to 2004, Ernst shows a peak in 1999 in the share of non-agricultural informal employment by an employment status definition (self-employed, unregistered, unpaid, and subsistence workers), with an overall increase of about 2 percentage points over the period.

7. Proxied respectively by the share of employees working more than the post-reform legal limit of 44 hours and the average job tenure of fired workers. Along with the union enrolment rate, these variables are constructed as industry annual averages for the pre-1988 period multiplied by a dummy variable with a break at 1988/1989.

8. That is, coefficient estimates on contemporaneous and lagged (one year) variables are close in magnitude and of opposite sign. This holds most strongly for coefficient estimates on formal job creation but also for the estimated effects of overtime and firing costs on shares of formal employment.

9. Bosch *et al.*'s union enrolment data are constructed from the Brazilian National Household Survey for "individuals of 18 to 65 years of age, economically active in the formal sector, and earning a positive wage". For all wage earners based on this same survey, the union enrolment rate declined much less, from 22 per cent in 1988 to 20 per cent in 2002 (Cardoso, 2004).

83

10. The authors define formal firms as registered firms, writing that "firms are required to register if either *i)* they have more than ten employees and electric power; or *ii)* they have more than 20 employees and do not use electric power".

11. The study uses an index developed by the Fraser Institute that addresses in one bundle the "regulation of credit, labour and business". The five labour regulation components of the index address "impact of minimum wage", "hiring and firing practices", "centralised collective bargaining", "unemployment benefits" and "use of conscripts to obtain military personnel". Note that 10 of the 15 components of the "credit, labour and business" index are not based on coding of regulations but rather on survey responses (Fraser Institute, 2008).

12. The authors define these as "Size of the shadow economy as a percentage of GDP," based largely on data from Schneider and Enste (2000) and "Share of the labour force employed in the unofficial economy in the capital city of each country", with data from Schneider (2000) and the Global Urban Indicators Database (2000) (Djankov *et al*., 2002).

13. Similarly with Djankov *et al*. (2002), data on "unofficial" activity come from Schneider and Enste (1998).

14. For comprehensive discussions of the workings and impacts of minimum wages in developing countries, see Saget (2006) and Eyraud and Saget (2008).

15. Similar concerns about "the increasingly widespread phenomenon of dependent workers who lack protection" led to the adoption in 2006 of the ILO's Employment Relationship Recommendation (R198), which provides guidelines on what constitutes an employment relationship (ILO, 2008).

ISBN: 978-92-64-05923-8 - © OECD 2009

REFERENCES

ANKER, R., I. CHERNYSHEV, P. EGGER, F. MEHRAN and J. RITTER (2002), "Measuring Decent Work with Statistical Indicators", *Policy Integration Department Working Paper* No. 2, ILO, Geneva.

ARANGO, C. and A. PACHON (2004), "Minimum Wages in Colombia: Holding the Middle with a Bite on the Poor", *Borradores de Economía 280*, Banco de la República, Bogotá.

BARRIENTOS, S. (2009), "Decent Work in Global Production Networks – Challenge for Vulnerable Workers", *in* A. POSTHUMA and D. NATHAN (eds.), *Labour in Global Production Networks,* Oxford University Press, New Delhi, forthcoming.

BESLEY, T. and R. BURGESS (2004), "Can Labor Regulation Hinder Higher Economic Performance? Evidence from India", *The Quarterly Journal of Economics,* Vol. 119, No. 1, pp. 91-134.

BETCHERMAN, G. (2002), *An Overview of Labor Markets World-wide: Key Trends And Major Policy Issues,* Social Protection Unit, World Bank, Washington, D.C.

BHATTACHARJEA, A. (2006), "Labour Market Regulation and Industrial Performance in India: A Critical Review of the Empirical Evidence", *The Indian Journal of Labour Economics,* Vol. 49, No. 2, pp. 211-232.

BOSCH, M., E. GONI and W. MALONEY (2007), "The Determinants of Rising Informality in Brazil: Evidence from Gross Worker Flows", *IZA Discussion Paper* No. 2970, Institute for the Study of Labour, Bonn.

BROWN, D., A. DEARDORFF and R.STERN (2003), "The Effects of Multinational Production on Wages and Working Conditions in Developing Countries", *NBER Working Papers* No. 9669, National Bureau of Economic Research, Cambridge, MA.

CARDOSO, A. (2004), "Industrial Relations, Social Dialogue and Employment in Argentina, Brazil and Mexico", *Employment Strategy Department Working Paper* No. 7, ILO, Geneva.

CARR, M. and M. CHEN (2001), "Globalization and the Informal Economy: How Global Trade and Investment Impact on the Working Poor", *WIEGO Working Paper,* WIEGO, Cambridge, MA.

CULPEPER, R. (2002), "Demystifying Hernando de Soto: A Review of The Mystery of Capital", prepared for a presentation to the Administrators` Colloquium, Ottawa, 26 March.

DJANKOV, S., R. LA PORTA, F. LOPEZ-DE-SILANES and A. SHLEIFER (2002), "The Regulation of Entry", *The Quarterly Journal of Economics,* Vol. 117, No. 1, pp. 1-37.

DUVAL HERNANDEZ, R. (2006), "Informality, Segmentation and Earnings in Urban Mexico", mimeo, Center for US-Mexican Studies, San Diego.

ERNST, C. (2008), "Recent Dynamics in Brazil's Labour Market", *Economic and Labour Market Analysis Department Working Paper* No. 10, ILO, Geneva.

EYRAUD, F. and C. SAGET (2008), "The Revival of Minimum Wage Setting Institutions", *in* J. BERG and D. KUCERA (eds.), *In Defence of Labour Market Institutions: Cultivating Justice in the Developing World,* Houndmills, Basingstoke, Hampshire and New York, Palgrave MacMillan, ILO, Geneva, pp. 100-118.

FIELDS, G. (1975), "Rural-urban Migration, Urban Unemployment and Underemployment, and Job-search Activity in LDCs", *Journal of Development Economics*, Vol. 2, No. 2, pp. 165-187.

FIELDS, G. (1990), "Labor Market Modelling and the Urban Informal Sector: Theory and Evidence", *in* D.TURNHAM, B. SALOMÉ and A. SCHWARZ (eds.), *The Informal Sector Revisited*, OECD Development Centre, Paris, pp. 49-69.

FIELDS, G. (2004), "Dualism in the Labour Market: A Perspective on the Lewis Model After Half a Century", *The Manchester School,* Vol. 72, No. 6, pp. 724-735.

85

FIELDS, G. (2005a), "A Welfare Economic Analysis of Labor Market Policies in the Harris-Todaro Model", *Journal of Development Economics,* Vol. 76, No. 1, pp.127-146.

FIELDS, G. (2005b), "A Guide to Multisector Labor Market Models", *World Bank Social Protection Discussion Paper Series* No. 0505, World Bank, Washington, D.C.

FRASER INSTITUTE (2008), http://fraserinstitute.org

FREEMAN, R. (2005), "Labour Market Institutions without Blinders: The Debate over Flexibility and Labour Market Performance", *NBER Working Paper,* No. 11286, National Bureau of Economic Research, Cambridge, MA.

FRIEDMAN, E., S. JOHNSON, D. KAUFMANN and P. ZOIDO-LOBATON (2000), "Dodging the Grabbing Hand: The Determinants of Unofficial Activity in 69 Countries", *Journal of Public Economics*, Vol. 76, No. 3, pp. 459-493.

FUGAZZA, M. and J. JACQUES (2003), "Labor Market Institutions, Taxation and the Underground Economy", *Journal of Public Economics*, Vol. 88, pp. 395-418.

GALLI, R. and D. KUCERA (2004), "Labor Standards and Informal Employment in Latin America", *World Development,* Vol. 32, No. 5, pp. 809-828.

GALLI, R. and D. KUCERA (2008), "Gender, Informality and Employment Adjustment in Latin America," *ILO Policy Integration Department Working Paper* No. 85, ILO, Geneva.

GASPARINI, L. and L. TORNAROLLI (2007), "Labor Informality in Latin America and the Caribbean: Patterns and Trends from Household Survey Microdata", *CEDLAS Working Paper* No. 0046, Centro de Estudios Distributivos, Laborales y Sociales, La Plata.

GEREFFI, G. (1994), "The Organization of Buyer-Driven Global Commodity Chains: How US Retailers Shape Overseas Production Networks," *in* G. GEREFFI and M. KORZENIEWICZ (eds), *Commodity Chains and Global Capitalism*, Praeger, Westport, pp. 95-117.

GEREFFI, G. (2005), "The New Offshoring of Jobs and Global Development," *ILO Social Policy Lectures*, ILO, Jamaica.

GLOBAL URBAN INDICATORS DATABASE (2000), http://ww2.unhabitat.org/programmes/guo/guo_indicators.asp

GUNTHER, I. and A. LAUNOV (2006), "Competitive and Segmented Informal Labor Markets", *IZA Discussion Paper* No. 2349, Institute for the Study of Labor, Bonn.

HANSON, G. (2001), "Should Nations Promote Foreign Direct Investment?" *UNCTAD (United Nations Conference on Trade and Development) and Center for International Development G-24 Discussion Paper* No. 9, UNCTAD and CID, Geneva.

HARRIS, J. and M. TODARO (1970), "Migration, Unemployment and Development: A Two-Sector Analysis", *American Economic Review,* Vol. 60, No. 1, pp. 126-142.

HART, K. (1973), "Informal Income Opportunities and Urban Employment in Ghana", *The Journal of Modern African Studies*, Vol. 11, No. 1, pp. 61-89.

HECKMAN, J. and C. PAGES (eds.) (2004), *Law and Employment: Lessons from Latin America and the Caribbean*, University of Chicago Press, Chicago.

HECKMAN, J. and C. PAGES-SERRA (2000), "The Cost of Job Security Regulation: Evidence from Latin American Labor Markets", *Economia: The Journal of Latin American and Caribbean Economic Association,* Vol. 1, No. 1, pp. 109-154.

HESTON, A., R. SUMMERS and B. ATEN (2006), *Penn World Tables Version 6.2.* Center for International Comparisons of Production, Income and Prices at the University of Pennsylvania, PA.

HUSSMANNS, R. (2005), "Measuring the Informal Economy: From Employment in the Informal Sector to Informal Employment", *ILO Policy Integration Department Working Paper* No. 53, ILO, Geneva.

ISBN: 978-92-64-05923-8 - © OECD 2009

ILO (2002), *Decent Work in the Informal Economy*, International Labour Office, Geneva.

ILO (2007), *Key Indicators of the Labour Market,* 5th Edition, ILO, Geneva.

ILO (2008), Employment Relationship, www.ilo/public/english/dialogue/ifpdial/areas/legislation/employ.htm, accessed 6 November 2008.

IPEA (2006), *Brasil: O Estado de uma naçao*, Instituto de Pesquisa Econômica Aplicada, Brasilia.

Lee, B-H and S. Lee (2007), "Minding the Gap: Non-regular Employment and Labour Market Segmentation in the Republic of Korea", *ILO Conditions of Work and Employment Series* No. 19, ILO, Geneva.

Lemos, S. (2007), "Minimum Wage Effects across the Private and Public Sectors in Brazil", *Journal of Development Studies*, Vol. 43, No. 4, pp. 700-720.

Levi, M. (1988), *Of Rule and Revenue*, University of California Press, Berkeley.

Lewis, W.A. (1954), "Economic Development with Unlimited Supplies of Labour", *The Manchester School,* Vol. 22, No. 2, pp. 139-191.

Loayza, N. and J. Rigolini (2006), "Informality Trends and Cycles", *Policy Research Working Paper Series* No. 4078, World Bank, Washington, D.C.

Maloney, W. (2004), "Informality Revisited", *World Development,* Vol. 32, No. 7, pp. 1159-1178.

Maloney, W. and J. Nuñez Mendez (2003), "Measuring the Impact of Minimum Wages: Evidence from Latin America", *NBER Working Paper* No. 9800, National Bureau of Economic Research, Cambridge, MA.

Paes de Barros, R. and C. Corseuil (2004), "The Impact of Regulations on Brazilian Labor Market Performance", *in* J. Heckman and C. Pagés (eds.), *Law and Employment: Lessons from Latin America and the Caribbean*, University of Chicago Press, Chicago, pp. 273-350.

Pieper, U. (2000), "Deindustrialisation and the Social and Economic Sustainability Nexus in Developing Countries: Cross-country Evidence on Productivity and Employment", *The Journal of Development Studies*, Vol. 26, No. 4, pp. 66-99.

Posthuma, A. (2009), "Challenges for Promoting Decent Work in Global Production Networks: Emergence of a Next Generation of Labour Regulation", *in* A. Posthuma and D. Nathan (eds.), *Labour in Global Production Networks,* Oxford University Press, New Delhi, forthcoming.

Ranis, G. and F. Stewart (1999), "V-Goods and the Role of the Urban Informal Sector in Development", *Economic Development and Cultural Change*, Vol. 47, No. 2, pp. 259-288.

Saavedra, J. and M. Torero (2004), "Labor Market Reforms and their Impact over Formal Labor Demand and Job Market Turnover: The Case of Peru", *in* J. Heckman and C. Pagés (eds.), *Law and Employment: Lessons from Latin America and the Caribbean*, University of Chicago Press, Chicago, pp. 131-182.

Saget C. (2006), "Wage Fixing in the Informal Economy: Evidence from Brazil, India, Indonesia and South Africa*", Conditions of Work and Employment Working Paper* No. 16, ILO, Geneva.

Sakthivel, S. and P. Joddar (2006), "Unorganized Sector Workforce in India: Trends, Patterns and Social Security Coverage", *Economic and Political Weekly*, Vol. 41, No. 21, pp. 2107-2114.

Schneider, F. (2000), "The Value Added of Underground Activities: Size and Measurement of Shadow Economies and Shadow Economy Labour Force All Over the World", mimeo. Presented at a Workshop of Australian NationalTax Centre, ANU, Canberra on 17 July 2002. Available at: http://dspace.anu.edu.au/bitstream/1885/42024/1/workshop.schneider.pdf.

Schneider, F. and D. Enste (1998), "Increasing Shadow Economies all over the World – Fiction or Reality: A Survey of the Global Evidence of its Size and of its Impact from 1970-1995", IMF and University of Linz, 21 August, Washington and Linz.

87

SCHNEIDER, F. and D. ENSTE (2000), "Shadow Economies: Sizes, Causes and Consequences", *Journal of Economic Literature*, No. XXXVIII, pp. 77-114.

SOTO, H. DE (1989*a*), *The Other Path: The Invisible Revolution in the Third World*, Harper & Row, New York, NY.

SOTO, H. DE (1989*b*), "The Informals Pose an Answer to Marx", *Economic Impact*, No. 67, Washington, pp. 56-66.

SOTO, H.DE (2000), *The Mystery of Capital: Why Capitalism Triumphs in the West and Fails Everywhere Else*, Basic Books, New York, NY.

WOODRUFF, C. (2001), "Review of de Soto's: The Mystery of Capital", *Journal of Economic Literature*, Vol 39, No. 4, pp 1215-1223.

WORLD BANK (2007*a*), WDI online: *World Development Indicators*, Washington, D.C. Available at: http://publications.worldbank.org/WDI/.

WORLD BANK (2007*b*), *Informality: Exit and Exclusion*, World Bank, Washington, D.C.

88

ISBN: 978-92-64-05923-8 - © OECD 2009

CHAPTER FOUR

Women in Informal Employment: What Do We Know and What Can We Do?

David Kucera and Theodora Xenogiani

ABSTRACT

Hundreds of millions of women work around the world but the types of job they do are often informal, of lower quality, worse paid and more precarious than those performed by men. They face cultural, social and legal obstacles. They are often casualties of economic structuring. But strategies exist to help by empowering women through education, the provision of childcare and microfinance. Public works and employment guarantee schemes, coupled with social protection schemes targeting the most vulnerable groups, have a role to play in empowering women through employment and good jobs. Women's organisations in informal employment are crucial for the protection of their rights.

89

ISBN: 978-92-64-05923-8 - © OECD 2009

INTRODUCTION

Work has a major role to play in helping in the empowerment of women. It means that they can become earners, and employment can boost their self-esteem and their integration into the societies in which they live. If women can have access to high quality jobs not only is their own well-being affected for the better, but household welfare can improve and there can be important consequences for the health and education of their children.

Until fairly recently gender-conscious analysis of employment outcomes concentrated on the low participation of women in the labour force and on the policy interventions to increase it, in particular in developing countries. This changed considerably, especially during the 1980s, as more women joined the labour market, participating in it actively and taking up jobs previously held by men (Standing, 1999; Beneria, 2001*a*). That trend continues today, although to a lesser degree. Indeed, women's participation in the labour force remained stable at 53 per cent between 1997 and 2007 (ILO, 2008*a*). But participation does not tell the entire story. A second dimension of labour market outcomes needs to be added: that of job quality.

This chapter shows that women in developing countries are over-represented in low quality, often informal jobs. There are important gender differences in the quality of jobs, with women not having the same access to good, secure and well-paid work as men, this being especially the case in developing and less developed countries. Being in informal employment – particularly in low-paid and hazardous jobs – makes women more dependent and more vulnerable to poverty.

Against this backdrop, this chapter aims to examine the reasons behind the gender differences in employment outcomes and discusses policy options to address the particular challenges that women face in the labour markets. Are labour market policies equally effective in improving job quality for both men and women? Are more specific policies needed to address these challenges? This chapter paints a comprehensive picture of employment outcomes across gender lines in terms of types and quality of jobs and discusses the main factors behind the over-representation of women in worse jobs as well as the impact of policy and the options for addressing these outcomes.

CHARACTERISTICS AND FEATURES OF WOMEN IN INFORMAL EMPLOYMENT

In developing countries, women are over-represented in the most vulnerable jobs in informal employment, for example being contributing family workers. Moreover, although generally both men and women have lower earnings on average when working informally, earning gaps between formal and informal workers are larger for women than for men.

Table 4.1 provides details about gender patterns related to employment status. It gives the most recently available gender-disaggregated data on employment status (employees, employers, own-account workers and contributing family workers) for a wide selection of countries. Some interesting features emerge. On a cross-sectional basis there is a wide diversity between countries in terms of the access of women and men to waged and salaried work and it is not possible to draw any firm conclusion as to whether there exists a gender disparity in terms of access to formal jobs.

Therefore, there is no clear-cut evidence that women are systematically more likely than men to be in informal employment. However, when the composition of informal employment is considered, there is evidence that women are over-represented in the lower tier of informal employment (Table 4.1 and Figure 4.2).

ISBN: 978-92-64-05923-8 - © OECD 2009

Table 4.1. Employment by Status and Gender (percentage out of total)

Country	Year	Employees Women	Employees Men	Employers Women	Employers Men	Contributing Family Workers Women	Contributing Family Workers Men	Own Account Workers Women	Own Account Workers Men	Other / Not defined Women	Other / Not defined Men
Argentina	2000	77.5	69.5	2.6	5.3	1.6	0.6	18.3	24.6	0.0	0.0
Bolivia	2000	42.4	56.7	1.4	4.0	11.3	4.4	44.8	34.0	0.1	1.0
Botswana	2001	84.6	88.2	2.9	4.7	0.7	0.3	11.8	6.7	0.0	0.0
Brazil	2001	65.2	61.1	2.4	5.3	3.6	1.8	15.0	21.9	13.9	10.0
Bulgaria	2002	93.1	88.5	1.7	4.5	1.1	0.6	3.9	6.1	0.2	0.3
Colombia	2002	52.0	49.5	2.4	6.4	8.2	3.6	37.2	40.3	0.2	0.3
Costa Rica	1999	76.2	72.6	4.1	9.0	3.4	1.2	16.3	17.3	0.0	0.0
Croatia	2001	92.8	86.8	3.2	6.7	0.4	0.3	3.5	6.2	0.1	0.1
Egypt	1998	88.4	72.8	2.3	10.6	3.5	2.8	5.8	13.8	0.0	0.0
Ethiopia	1999	19.8	46.2	0.4	1.2	23.9	8.3	54.6	42.0	1.3	2.2
Hungary	2004	90.8	84.4	2.4	4.3	0.4	0.2	6.3	11.0	0.1	0.0
Indonesia	2006	47.5	56.4	1.4	4.5	15.7	2.7	35.4	36.4	0.0	0.0
Iran, Islamic Rep. of	1996	61.6	63.1	0.7	4.0	14.4	1.0	18.2	28.4	5.2	3.5
Latvia	1999	95.9	92.9	2.1	4.3	0.1	0.1	1.8	2.5	0.0	0.2
Lithuania	1999	94.5	90.4	1.8	2.5	0.5	0.5	2.7	5.8	0.4	0.5
Madagascar	2003	43.0	62.9	6.1	5.5	15.9	8.4	33.1	21.8	1.9	1.4
Malaysia	2007	1.4	5.2	82.5	79.3	5.5	1.6	10.5	13.9	0.0	0.0
Mauritius	2004	86.6	79.0	1.0	4.0	4.1	0.7	8.2	16.1	0.1	0.2
Mexico	1999	65.8	71.4	1.9	6.0	9.9	3.3	22.3	19.2	0.0	0.0
Moldova, Republic of	2000	91.3	88.4	0.3	1.6	0.2	0.2	7.7	9.6	0.5	0.2
Morocco	2002	62.9	53.2	0.9	3.5	3.7	4.6	14.4	25.1	18.0	13.6
Nicaragua	2006	53.6	63.7	2.2	4.8	0.0	0.0	36.5	28.0	0.0	0.0
Oman	1996	98.2	95.4	0.0	1.1	0.2	0.1	1.0	3.4	0.0	0.0
Pakistan	2002	65.2	59.2	0.7	1.4	13.8	7.7	20.3	31.7	0.0	0.0
Panama	2003	79.8	68.6	1.4	3.3	1.9	0.5	16.9	27.6	0.0	0.0
Philippines	2004	60.3	72.6	1.9	2.6	6.7	2.8	31.2	21.9	0.0	0.0
Poland	2000	91.3	85.5	2.5	4.6	0.8	0.4	5.4	9.4	0.0	0.0
Romania	2000	96.2	91.3	0.8	2.5	0.4	0.3	2.0	5.7	0.0	0.0
Serbia	2006	93.4	84.5	2.5	5.9	0.5	0.5	3.6	9.1	0.0	0.0
South Africa	2007	82.1	84.1	16.4	15.0	0.6	0.3	0.6	0.3	0.3	0.3
Thailand	2003	59.5	64.6	1.6	5.9	15.4	7.1	23.2	22.3	0.2	0.1
Trinidad and Tobago	2002	84.9	77.3	2.1	5.5	1.3	0.3	10.7	15.6	1.0	1.2
Turkey	2002	86.2	70.9	2.1	9.3	6.2	3.5	5.5	16.3	0.0	0.0
West Bank and Gaza Strip	2002	85.7	64.1	0.6	4.7	4.9	4.5	8.7	26.7	0.0	0.0

Source: OECD Development Centre based on Laborsta (2008): see Chapter 2 for detailed sources and methods.
StatLink ⬛ http://dx.doi.org/10.1787/533721731247

91

ISBN: 978-92-64-05923-8 - © OECD 2009

Figure 4.1 gives more details about the types of jobs women and men are doing within employment. The four diagrams depict the share of working women and men outside agriculture by employment status. The 45-degree lines represent equality across gender lines. Women are less likely to be employers and more likely to be contributing family workers in the great majority of countries. The picture changes considerably if the distribution of own-account workers is considered: here men in most of the countries reviewed outnumber women.

Figure 4.1. **Women are Over-Represented in the Most Vulnerable Jobs**

Women and men by employment status
as percentages of employed women and men (respectively)

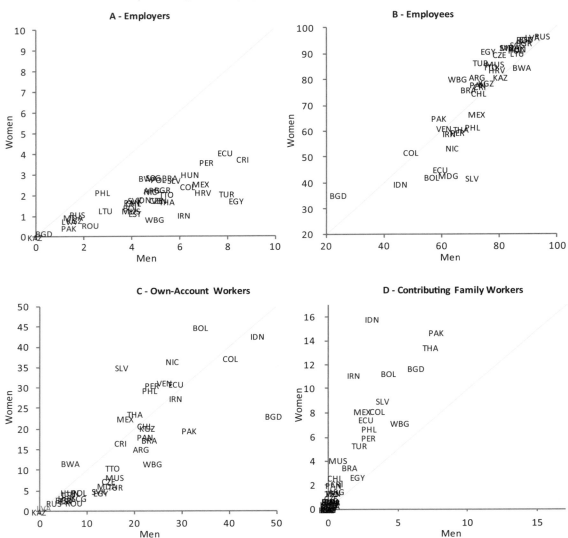

Source: See methodological notes to Chapter 2.
StatLink ⟶ http://dx.doi.org/10.1787/533436018578

This pattern is consistent with earlier evidence. Based on a review of a wide range of empirical literature, a hierarchy of job statuses in the informal economy was constructed by Chen *et al.* (2004). Ranked by average earnings, these job statuses are:

1) employers;

2) own-account operators;

3) employees of informal enterprises;

4) other informal wage workers

5) industrial outworkers/home-workers;

6) unpaid family workers.

Data on earnings and wage gaps between men and women from Chapter 2 are presented in Figure 4.2. The data presented are for different points in time depending on their availability for each country. Figure 4.2 shows that overall there are significant gender gaps in both entrepreneurs' incomes and wages. Women entrepreneurs in Brazil, Turkey and Morocco earn about half as much as their male counterparts. In Tunisia, the gender gap in entrepreneurs' incomes is much lower, at about 11 to17 per cent. In terms of wages, substantial gender gaps are found in Ethiopia, Morocco and Tunisia, where women earn about 32 to 36 per cent less than men.

Figure 4.2. Earnings and Wage Gap Between Women and Men in Selected Countries

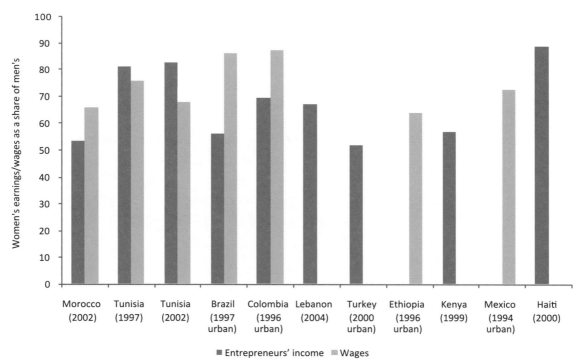

Note: Average monthly income and wages in national currency. (1) Main activity (2) Main and secondary activities (3) Own-account workers (4) Employers of micro-enterprises (fewer than ten workers)

Source: Charmes (2002), for the ILO *Women and Men in the Informal Economy*, 2002. For Western Asia and Northern Africa: Charmes (2008).

StatLink 🔗 http://dx.doi.org/10.1787/533436703025

93

There is an additional element of gender segregation emphasised by Chen *et al.* (1999) that also contributes to the aggregate gender earnings gap, and that is within these six informal job statuses. From this Chen (2006) concludes that:

> "Women tend to work in different types of activities, associated with different levels of earning, than men – with the result that they typically earn less even within specific sectors of the informal economy".

One example given is street vendors, of whom men are more likely to sell non-perishable goods from pushcarts or bicycles whereas women are more likely to sell perishable goods from baskets or the ground. Another example is domestic work, which employs a very high proportion of women. These are among the most vulnerable informal workers, typically working very long hours without social protection, even though such protection is legally mandatory for domestic workers in many countries (Lee *et al.*, 2007; Mesa-Lago, 2007).

Earnings Gaps

Surveys of the literature also show that earnings gaps between formal and informal workers are greater for women than for men and also that returns to education within informal employment are lower for women than for men (Chen *et al.*, 2004; Galli and Kucera, 2003). Funkhouser (1996) examines patterns of employment and earnings in the formal and informal[1] sectors in five countries in Central America (Costa Rica, El Salvador, Guatemala, Honduras and Nicaragua). His results suggest there is a higher gender earnings gap in the informal sector compared with the formal one. The estimated male-female differential in the informal sector is about 25 per cent and is as high as 40 per cent in Nicaragua, whereas the gender earnings gap in the formal sector is around 10 per cent. In other words, the earnings penalty of informal work tends to be greater for women than for men.

Evidence of gender earnings gaps is also found in Bangladesh, South Africa and Tanzania (Chen *et al.*, 2004). In particular in Bangladesh, "men own-account workers earn more than three times the earnings of women own-account workers, while male employers earn about four times more than female ones". Differences can be also found in terms of hours worked and other dimensions of work conditions (Chen *et al.*, 2004): underemployment, seasonality of work, occupational health hazards, multiple activities.

While the described over-representation of women in the most vulnerable sectors of informal employment jobs is widely acknowledged, the debate about the determinants and reasons behind is far less settled.

WHAT EXPLAINS GENDER DIFFERENCES IN INFORMAL EMPLOYMENT PREVALENCE AND OUTCOMES?[2]

Informal Institutions

Informal institutions, i.e. evolved practices with stable rules of behaviour that are outside the formal system (Sen, 2007), determine to a large extent the types of jobs that are available to women and the particular working conditions associated with them. They are omnipresent in human interaction, from the most private sphere of sexuality to the public forums of economic and political life. Informal institutions can exert their influence in two ways: directly, where traditions, customs and social norms can constrain women's activities – for example by not allowing them to start their own businesses, by refusing to allow them to do jobs in which they are in contact with, or are managing, men, or by simply forbidding them to leave the house alone; and indirectly, where there are restrictions on women's access to resources such as education, credit and information that are essential if they are to compete with men for formal employment. In both cases, constraints on women's movements and the activities available to them lead to an exclusion of women from entrepreneurial activities that are often the first step towards independence, self-esteem and freedom of choice.

Women from poor households can be particularly affected by informal institutions as they may have to choose between self-employment, which pays less but allows them to combine work with family care, and waged work, which may pay more but conflicts with their family responsibilities and the social restrictions placed on women's mobility (Morrisson and Jütting, 2005; Pfau-Effinger, 2003; Chen *et al.*, 2005; Beneria, 2001*b*). To give an example, a survey in Morocco in 1997-98 showed that 85 per cent of women said they needed the permission of their husband or guardian to leave the house (World Bank, 2004).

Women's work, women's lack of rights

The often hidden role of informal institutions in shaping employment outcomes for women becomes fairly visible when the type of work mainly performed by women is considered, in particular in agriculture. Helping out with farming, most often in an informal way, is still seen as a woman's obligation to the family in many developing countries. This is, according to some, the result of women's lack of control over agricultural resources (Rebouché, 2006). The patriarchal nature of most rural societies does not provide women with the same rights to land as it does men. In most Muslim countries, for example, inheritance laws and government land-grant programmes favour men (Lastarria-Cornhiel, 2006; Agarwal, 2003), and other religions, e.g. Hinduism, do not recognise women's rights to land. Even in countries and religions that recognise women's rights to possess land, significant issues remain about their ability to claim these rights. Consequently, women have access to land only through the land market, for which savings and/or credit are needed. In addition, marriage rarely helps a woman to become a joint owner of land (Chen *et al.*, 2005). Moreover, in some countries, as in Kenya, women are still denied property rights to land upon divorce or separation from their husbands or even following the death of their spouses. This is because inheritance laws (whether official or traditional) lay down that property passes to the deceased's male child rather than to his daughter or to his wife (Rebouché, 2006). Even when women do own land, male family members often take control over it. Informal institutions and practices are in some cases reinforced by formal legislation. For example, the labour laws of many countries in the Middle East and North Africa (MENA) region clearly define the types of jobs women may do as well as the hours and conditions of work (World Bank, 2004).

Box 4.1. **Measuring Informal Institutions – The GID Database**

To help governments choose effective policies that will improve women's labour market performance, the OECD Development Centre created the Gender, Institutions and Development Database (GID). Compiled from various sources, the database provides comparative data for 160 countries on the socio-economic status of women. Its true innovation is the inclusion of institutional variables that range from intra-household behaviour to social norms. Information on cultural and traditional practices is coded so as to measure the level of discrimination, making the GID a unique tool-box for a wide range of analytical queries and allowing a case-by-case adaptation to specific research or policy questions.

Aid effectiveness and the Millennium Development Goals call for coherent and inclusive strategies that address the institutional obstacles preventing social and economic development. By identifying cultural and traditional practices that discriminate against women, from forced marriages and female genital mutilation to restrictions on inheritance and ownership rights, the GID helps design effective policies for sustainable development. In order to address women's over-representation in informal employment, the underlying causes of discrimination need to be addressed. Building new classrooms, for example, will make no difference for gender equality if girls are simply not allowed to enter them. The Gender, Institutions, and Development Database is open to researchers and policy-makers alike and can be accessed free of charge at the GID's homepage at: www.oecd.org/dev/gender/GID.

Further reading:
JÜTTING, J. *et al.* (2008*a*), "Measuring Gender (In)Equality", *Journal of Human Development and Capabilities,* Vol. 9, Issue 1, pp. 65- 86.

Barriers to women's access to formal employment are likely to be transmitted from one generation to the next. As women earn less in informal work than in formal work, they are confronted with much lower bargaining power than their husbands when it comes to the household's allocation of resources, including expenses for the education of children. Several studies emphasise that women's insufficient participation in decision making in the household can lower the investment in the education of their daughters (Heintz and Pollin, 2003; Agarwal, 1997; Agarwal, 2003) giving rise to a vicious cycle which is difficult to break. Chen *et al.* (2005), point out that the transfer of informal activities between generations can also follow cultural norms and patriarchal traditions. In caste-specific occupations in India, for example, women follow in the hereditary occupation of their family or social group, which is passed on from one generation to the next.

To sum up, informal institutions can both directly and indirectly impact on the economic role of women. The following paragraphs develop further how better education, access to healthcare and productive resources have an impact on women's chances to participate in the labour market. While looking at these factors is very important, one should always be bear in mind that often informal institutions might be at the heart of the problem. Addressing the symptoms by, for instance, increasing female enrolment rates while not addressing high female drop-out rates due to traditional forms of labour sharing in households might not be good enough.

Access to Resources

Education

Literacy and numeracy are essential skills if the individual is to be able to compete in the labour market and are becoming increasingly important in today's information society (Clark, 2003). Not surprisingly, women with basic skills in literacy and numeracy have a better chance of winning access to formal employment (Jütting *et al.*, 2008*b*; Leach, 1999; Clark, 2003). Furthermore, education enables women to change their status within informal work and even to move from informal to formal activities over the course of their lives (Jütting *et al.*, 2008*b*). Women may start as informal contributing family workers, and, after having accumulated additional human capital, are then able to move on to paid work in the informal sector, to become self-employed in the informal sector or even to gain a foothold in the formal workforce (Jütting *et al.,* 2008*b*). This indicates that not only education but also experience, vocational training and life-long learning are important for women to have a choice between formal and informal work, and a choice between good and bad jobs. Leach (1999) confirms the importance of experience and further learning by emphasising that school, in many developing countries, does not provide girls with relevant marketable skills but still focuses on traditionally feminine skills that offer little opportunity for a sustainable income. Furthermore, in an empirical analysis for Kenya, Atieno and Teal (2006) point out that women with high levels of education and experience are more likely than men to have a public sector job which offers relatively high levels of social protection and pay[3]. The fact that public employment is traditionally one of the main destinations for educated women in the labour markets of many countries all over the world confirms this finding (Jütting *et al.,* 2008*b*).

Despite significant efforts during the last years in closing the education gender gap, important gender differences in educational attainment persist. Deficient investment in girls' education and basic skills fundamentally limits their access to formal employment opportunities and pushes women towards informal employment, as their only survival labour market strategy. According to the UNESCO Institute for Statistics (2002), women make up two-thirds of all illiterates in the world. It must be noted that over the course of the last decades, the educational gap between boys and girls has been closing, but in many developing countries the educational system is simply not appropriate for girls, who lack both the time and freedom to attend school (Leach, 1999). The World Bank (2001) underlines that the mere provision of schools is not enough to improve girls' access to education and that it is necessary to consider girls' needs in a larger context: toilet facilities for them, short distance from their villages, provision of transport to school, etc.

ISBN: 978-92-64-05923-8 – © OECD 2009

The link between education and poverty is often handed down from one generation to the next, with mothers playing a major role. Heyzer (2006) indicates that educational poverty is often transferred to their children by mothers. Lastarria-Cornhiel (2006) shows for Ecuador, Colombia, South Africa and Kenya that girls are often pulled out of school early to help meet basic survival needs of the family. While mothers are away at work, daughters must take over the housework and care for younger children. Their educational disadvantages keep girls from developing skills that would enable them later on to compete in the formal labour market (UN, 2005). Hence, women's lower education pushes them towards informal work, bad working conditions and low pay.

Land, credit and information networks

Access to land, credit and information networks is extremely important for women if they are to improve their chances in the labour market, whether this is waged employment, farming or self-employment. The 2008 *World Development Report* (World Bank, 2008) highlights the important differences in women's access to land compared with that of men. A sample of countries in Latin America has shown that only 11 to 27 per cent of all landowners are women. Even in countries where women account for a large share of agricultural production, such as Uganda, they often have no, or only limited, rights on the land (World Bank, 2008).

As indicated, institutions – formal and informal – shape the access to land and often grant only limited, if any, rights to land to women. Consequently, in most developing countries there is a deep contrast between female land control and ownership and their contribution to land development (Agarwal, 2003; Rebouché, 2006). Furthermore, privatisation of land rights, commercialisation of community resources (communal land, forests, water) and increasing land scarcity (for example in southern Niger) have significantly weakened women's claim to land, a factor which pushes women further into certain forms of informal activities (Lastarria-Cornhiel, 2006).

Not least because of insufficient access to land ownership, women face various constraints in their decisions to engage in formal entrepreneurial activities (Esim and Kuttab, 2002). Restricted land laws for women and their related poor resources often mean women have restricted access to capital (Lastarria-Cornhiel, 2006; Agarwal, 2003; ILO, 1998*a*; Kabeer, 2008). Furthermore, socio-cultural barriers frequently hinder women's access to credit and to entrepreneurial assistance and consultancy (Esim and Kuttab, 2002). Finally, men also have better access to productive assets and financial capital relative to women because the returns of their entrepreneurial activities are often higher than those of women, who engage mainly in survivalist activities with limited returns. Men have better tools of the trade and operate from better work spaces and consequently they produce or sell higher volumes and different ranges of goods and services. Because of their limited returns, women often rely on informal sources of finance, such as friends and family, and consequently risk having only limited control over their enterprises (ILO, 1998*a*). Evidence from Botswana (Ntseane, 1999) shows that women are occasionally successful in setting up their own businesses but often face major constraints and barriers not only in terms of access to credit but also because of the patriarchal structures.

Another important factor in determining women's selection into formal and informal activities is their degree of access to information networks. In many countries, social norms prevent women from entering networks that offer formal employment opportunities or support entrepreneurial activities. Hence, women rely on networks mediated to them through relationships to men in order to acquire professional contacts, information and support (Chen *et al.*, 2005). Furthermore, the lack of contacts in financial, marketing or client networks prevents women's access to other opportunities offered by these institutions, such as consultancy, training, education or information (ILO, 1998*a*). Because of the limited access to networks, informal work is often the only option to generate income.

At the same time, the informality of women's work also hinders their access to professional networks and institutional approaches that facilitate the access to resources. For example, women who work informally are excluded from formal sector workshops that organise collective

97

renting of expensive tools and equipment or offer technical consultancy and legal coverage (Esim and Kuttab, 2002). Moreover, their limited integration into professional networks further hinders their participation in mechanisms of collective decision making, e.g. trade unions, work councils or other formal organisations of workers (Beneria and Floro, 2004).

Gender differences in job quality and informal employment are related to a number of economic factors, including economic structure, trade liberalisation and migration. The following sections discuss them separately.

Economic Structure and Changes

Women in informal employment and the economic structure

Shifts in economic structure have a profound impact on the differing positions of women and men in the labour market. Because of structural constraints (e.g. less access to education and skill development), women can frequently adapt less easily to changing demands in the labour market. As a consequence, they tend to be crowded into agriculture in developing countries; into manufacturing in fast-growing countries; and into services in industrialised countries.

When the share of the agricultural sector started to decline in the 1970s, men increasingly left agriculture for better-paid work. At the same, time the involvement of women in agricultural activities began to rise in many countries. This "feminisation of agriculture" (World Bank, 2008) has had important consequences: in many developing countries women are now over-represented in farming activities, and work in agriculture is the most common form of female employment and the largest source of income for women (Lastarria-Cornhiel, 2006; Esim and Kuttab, 2002; Agarwal, 2003; Heyzer, 2006).

As a rule of thumb, the proportion of informal employment is greater in the agricultural sector than in the non-agricultural sectors. In fact, in developing countries almost all female activities in agriculture can be considered to be informal (Parlevliet and Xenogiani, 2008; Lastarria-Cornhiel, 2006; Esim and Kuttab, 2002; Unni and Rani, 2000). In some of the former Communist countries in Central and Eastern Europe, as for example in Romania, the introduction of the market economy in the 1990s has sharply decreased the options for women in formal employment and so they have been pushed into different forms of informal employment, such as cross-border trade, craft work, food-processing, piece-rate home-work and home-based services, and subsistence farming (Parlevliet and Xenogiani, 2008; Esim, 2001).

Different types of work within agriculture

Furthermore, differences exist in terms of the activities women perform within agriculture compared with men. Women largely work to contribute to their family's income, whereas men in informal agricultural activities tend to work as own-account farmers. In developing countries, on average 69.1 per cent of those working as contributing family workers are women against 30.9 per cent of men, whereas 71 per cent of men are self-employed in informal work in agriculture against 29 per cent of women (Jütting *et al.*, 2008*b*). Moreover, women tend to work in subsistence farming and in smallholder production, in traditional agro-export agriculture (crops grown on plantations such as coffee, sugar or cocoa) and in the labour-intensive field of non-traditional agro-export agriculture (horticulture crops such as vegetables, flowers, fruits), whereas men in agriculture tend to work in machinery-driven, large-scale production of non-traditional agricultural exports and tend to be involved in supervision and management (Lastarria-Cornhiel, 2006; Chen, 2004). Consequently, informal work in agriculture is characterised by strong gender-based differences in status and income when compared with informal work in the non-agricultural sectors. Women's informal work in agriculture is often low paid, unpaid or paid in food rather than wages (Jütting *et al.*, 2008*b*; Rebouché, 2006). Esim and Kuttab (2002) show that in the West Bank and Gaza, women in agriculture still mainly perform unpaid family labour, whereas women's informal activities in non-agriculture are mainly remunerated.

98

Additionally, in many regions in Africa, Latin America and Asia, the proportion of women in informal work is also increasing in non-agricultural sectors. In the growing regions in South Asia for example, more and more women work in manufacturing as well as in services, both sectors with a substantial prevalence of informal employment (Unni and Rani, 2000). As in agriculture, the informal activities that women usually perform are quite different from those of men. Women are more likely than men to be pushed into informal work in export-oriented light manufacturing (e.g. clothing, textiles, leather, footwear, electronics) where they perform simple manual tasks and labour-intensive operations (Chen *et al.*, 1999). The need for low-skilled and low-paid workers favours female informal employment without offering them status benefits or the chance to accumulate technical skills (Standing, 1999; Seguino, 2000 and 2005; Beneria, 2001a; Chen *et al.*, 2005). Lastarria-Cornhiel (2006) also shows that own-account women in Ahmedabad City in India tend more to be home-workers, whereas own-account men work more as street vendors and often own their own businesses.

Gender differences in informal employment are linked to a distinction between rural versus urban employment. Naturally, much of the difference between women's and men's representation in rural versus urban informal employment is determined by each group's representation in agricultural versus non-agricultural activities. However, increasingly important in rural areas are off-farm activities, many of them household-based and informal. Off-farm activities account for between 30 to 40 per cent of rural incomes in Asia, Latin America and sub-Saharan Africa (Wisana, 2006). These activities include the processing and packaging of food, beverage and tobacco products; textile and apparel production; construction and the production of construction materials; and a wide range of services (Carr, 1984).

Finally, gender differences may also be explained depending on whether employment is in the public or the private sector. Public sector employment is generally characterised as formal employment, offering relatively secure employment with social protection benefits (e.g. Hussmanns, 2005). There has been a decline in the share of public sector employment in many countries going back roughly to the late 1980s. The degree to which women are particularly affected by the decline in the share of public sector employment is not clear and depends on the relative vulnerability of men and women to job loss as well as their ability to find other formal employment. Based on data going up to 1994, one study finds a rise in the female share of public employment in a sample of developing countries (Standing,1999). Consistent with this, another study of ten Latin American countries shows that women's representation in informal employment from 1990 to 2000 was either stable or declining, even in the face of overall declines in the share of public sector employment (Galli and Kucera, 2008). The public sector has thus been an important source of formal employment for women while the decline in public sector employment does not appear to have contributed to an over-representation of women in informal employment.

99

Trade liberalisation, technological change and economic restructuring

Trade liberalisation has brought important changes to domestic labour markets in terms of reallocation of labour across countries, sectors, and across types of jobs (Freeman and Katz, 1991; Revenga, 1992; Gaston and Trefler, 1994 and 1997; Grossman, 1986 and 1987)[4]. It has not only affected women's participation in the labour market but also the types of jobs women hold and the conditions under which they work. Overall, trade liberalisation and associated changes of economic activities have created benefits for women but to a lesser degree compared with men. This being said, while job opportunities have greatly improved in the moment of an economic expansion, risks and vulnerabilities also increased in particular in a moment of economic downturn.

Trade liberalisation can impact on female employment and working conditions in various ways. On the one hand, it has expanded opportunities for women through sectoral allocation of work towards export-led industries and specific types of services, benefiting women (see Nordas, 2003; Joekes, 1999, for a review of the related literature). According to trade theory, trade liberalisation will lead to the expansion of employment in labour-intensive industries in developing countries. Since women are often over-represented in those sectors of the economy, they are expected to benefit from trade liberalisation. On the other hand, many of the new jobs created and taken by women are of low quality; most of them are informal and offer low pay and bad working conditions. In addition, it is also believed that women may be more hurt by the adverse effects of trade liberalisation and import competition, compared with men.

Joekes (1999) argues that women may also gain from trade liberalisation in terms of higher wages, if these are compared to their earnings in the sectors (e.g. agriculture, domestic services and small-scale commerce) where they were mostly found before changes induced by liberalisation. In addition he argues that export companies in the formal sector conform to minimum wage legislation and hence pay fair wages to men and women. To take the example of manufacturing, trade liberalisation at least in early years led to a large increase in the share of employment in export-led manufacturing which has benefited women. The creation of Export Processing Zones (EPZs) offered opportunities for job creation, especially for women, in labour-intensive industries such as garments, footwear, electronics, clothing and toys (ILO, 1998b; Joekes, 1999; Nordas, 2003). Women in Southeast Asia represent a very significant share of informal manufacturing, especially in garment shops, shoe factories, craft industries but also farming and building (Ghosh, 2004). An important part of the work is often subcontracted to domestic companies which further subcontract to home-workers, many of them women. Evidence from Bangladesh, based on a computable general equilibrium model (Fontana and Wood, 2000), shows labour relocation from agriculture to manufacturing, and employment and wage gains for women. Ozler (2000) shows a positive relation between exports and the share of female employment at the firm level in Turkey for the period 1983-85.

With respect to agriculture, trade liberalisation tends to favour medium and large producers. Women, mainly holders of small plots of land, lose out when their farming land is taken to produce export-oriented agricultural goods. Constraints in women's access to credit, transport and storage facilities (Baden, 1998) further limit their ability to increase their production and gain from trade. The situation is even more acute in horticulture, a form of agriculture dominated by women and on the rise since 1980 (UN, 1999: up to 90 per cent of workers are women). Large corporations dominate and hence women are often found on large-scale farms working for low wages and in bad conditions. Women working in this sector might be even more vulnerable than those in manufacturing as there are more health risks associated with the agricultural work, as well as the seasonal nature of this work. Gideon (2007) argues that increased female employment rates in low quality jobs have created new health risks for women. This problem is even more acute as many of these workers lack basic health protection coverage. In the services sector, women have benefited at least to some degree from the expansion of jobs such as those in call centres. However jobs in this sector are also of poor quality, with low wages and missing benefits, as the level of workers' unionisation is fairly low.

Finally, trade-related factors have led to a deterioration of work conditions for some women. First, changes in the nature of work and the increasing demand for skills are expected to have a negative effect on low-skilled women and those with incomplete access to information and limited mobility. Second, the relocation of foreign investment to cheaper regions and countries around the world, coupled with the crisis in the garment industry, can also explain the loss of an important number of jobs in Asia, very often held by women. Finally, globalisation has been associated with lower subsidies for domestic non-tradeable goods that are usually produced by women (Standing, 1999).

To sum up, women have benefited, at least in some way, from trade liberalisation and the changing characteristics of economic activity, but it is possible that their limited access to resources and institutional and societal factors, determined to a large extent by informal institutions, have not allowed them to benefit as much as men. Most importantly, women are not a homogenous group and some might have benefited while others are losing. Whether women benefit more or less relative to men depends on the specific country characteristics in terms of economic structure, its abundance in labour, the position of women in the labour market and society, the stage of development and the flexibility of labour markets.

Migration

Migration impacts on informal employment for women in two ways. First, through the labour market status of female migrants in the destination country and second through the impact of male migration on labour market outcomes of the women left behind.

According to the UNFPA (2006) in 2005, there were about 95 million women migrants, corresponding to 49.6 per cent of total migrants and to an increase of 3 percentage points between 1960 and 2005. The largest increase (Morrison *et al.*, 2007) is observed in Oceania, Latin America and the Caribbean, Africa and the former Soviet Union[5]. Migration status and hence the labour market status of migrants in the destination country are strongly determined by migration policies. In early periods in migration history, family reunification policies allowed women to follow their husbands who migrated for work purposes. Hence women were mainly reduced to lives as housewives because of the limited work options that were granted in the destination country. The creation of female migrants' networks, the lower cost of migration and the empowerment of women in terms of participation in economic and social life led to the sharp increase of the number of female migrants that we experience today. Now many men migrate in turn as accompanying family members, following their wives' migration.

Despite this "feminisation of migration", women's lower education in some countries, as well as the barriers some face in terms of access to land, credit and information networks, may prevent them from fully benefiting from migration. There are various ways in which female migration is linked to informal employment and the quality of jobs that women hold. First, female migrants can themselves be informally employed in the destination country. The probability of informal work is in general higher for migrants than for native residents, especially if it concerns illegal migration. This is even more the case for low-skilled workers, among whom many are women. As women are less likely than men to be able to use their own land resources and cash to cover the cost of migration, they are more constrained in their migration destination choices. As a consequence, discrimination against women may lead to higher representation of female migrants in informal employment, both relative to male migrants and natives. Supporting evidence from internal migration in Colombia (Florez, 2003) shows that migrant women from rural areas are more likely to be in informal employment and in particular in the subsistence part of the informal sector than local women and men (whether migrants or locals).

Migration also impacts on women's labour market options if it is not the women migrating, but their husbands. Male migration to urban labour markets increases women's responsibilities in the rural labour market and in particular in farming activities (World Bank, 2008). Moreover, business start-ups by returning migrants and their families (Mesnard and Ravallion, 2001; Leichtman, 2002; Wahba, 2004) create opportunities for work for household members, in particular for women who manage small businesses in the case of absence of male family members and/or become contributing family workers. In addition, remittances sent home by male migrants have an effect on women's labour supply (OECD, 2007), and they can alter labour allocation and decisions within the households, in the form of reduced work hours or change in the type of work. Finally, male out-migration can have an empowering effect on women through their physical and financial independence (International Organisation for Migration (IOM), 2004) as well as their self esteem as contributors to the community. Zachariah *et al.* (2002) show that the so-called "Gulf wives", that is the wives of male migrants in the Gulf region, gain independence, autonomy, status, management skills and experience in dealing with the world outside their homes following their husbands' departure.

101

HOW TO ACHIEVE BETTER JOBS FOR WOMEN?

Building Capacity and Promoting Productivity at Work

Several studies emphasise that education is an important factor in determining the selection of women into formal and informal activities (Jütting *et al.*, 2008*b*; UN, 2005; Chen, 2004; Leach,

1999). However, important gender differences exist worldwide not only in basic education but also in take-up rates of vocational training and apprenticeship schemes. Gender differences also exist in the impact of these programmes on employment prospects and earnings, with women often benefiting less than men. This evidence is not confined to developing countries, but is also supported by data in developed countries. For example apprenticeships have a smaller impact on women than men in many countries around the world (for a review of the literature see Ryan, 2001). Technical and vocational education (TVE) "appears to have a limited impact on changing gender patterns of employment" (Adams, 2007).

For developing countries, Kabeer (2008) argues that women are less likely to receive vocational training compared with men. In addition, even in cases where women were as likely as men to receive training, there were significant differences in terms of the amount of training they received. Kabeer (2008) provides a detailed review of the literature and shows that this is indeed the case in Nigeria as well as Côte d'Ivoire, Uganda and Guinea[6]. Adams (2007) gives a detailed description of how cultural factors determine women's participation in TVE programmes in male-dominated sectors and hence their subsequent employment in these sectors.

The described shortcomings and limitations can be overcome with careful design and implementation. Encouraging evidence in this sense comes from evaluations in Peru and Colombia; and Bulgaria, Poland and Slovakia. The ProJoven[7] programme in Peru is a labour training programme for poor young people in urban areas, first introduced in 1996. A careful evaluation by Ñopo *et al.* (2007) shows that the programme has been extremely successful in terms of the subsequent labour market outcomes of women participating in it. ProJoven not only promotes equal participation among men and women but also offers special subsidies to young women with children. Ñopo *et al.* show that the programme increases employment rates of women more than those of men, and the overall effect (taking into account employment rates, occupational field, hours of work and wages) is found to be "substantially higher for females than for males" (Ñopo *et al.,* 2007). Another training that targets disadvantaged young people in Colombia is the Jóvenes en Acción scheme, introduced between 2002 and 2005[8] and offering standard training and on-the-job training as well as additional stipends for women with children. The evaluation of the scheme by Attanasio *et al.* (2008) shows that the benefits were higher for women, both in terms of employment and of wages. Katz (2008) argues that part of the success of the Jóvenes en Acción programme is that it was operated by non-governmental organisations (NGOs) located in the young person's neighbourhood. Both Jóvenes en Acción and ProJoven were very well targeted and provided links with private sector labour demand, which according to Katz (2008) accounts for part of their success. In addition, they were better adapted to women's needs and focused on providing the skills required for the types of tasks women usually undertake. Programmes that offer post-training guidance, career counselling and job placement can be also extremely useful, especially for women with no prior labour market experience[9].

Childcare policies

A major obstacle to better jobs for women is the scarcity of childcare provision. This relationship is substantiated by studies of informal women workers in Angola, Bangladesh, Costa Rica, Guatemala, the Philippines and Zambia (surveyed in Cassirer and Addati, 2007). The challenge of balancing family responsibilities with paid work has arguably become increasingly difficult as a result of the breakdown of traditional family support (resulting in part from internal and international migration) and the increased number of female-headed households. Moreover, the scarcity of childcare provision can contribute to the growth of informal employment in that it creates demand for informal domestic workers as childcare providers (*ibid.*).

An in-depth study of existing childcare programmes in 13 developing countries was undertaken by Cassirer and Addati (2007). Each of these programmes was established to address the needs of a wide range of informal women workers, including domestic workers, vendors, workers in agriculture and fishing, and home-based workers. The programmes vary considerably in their design and implementation mechanisms, such as the extent to which they rely on parents' contributions and co-operate with partner institutions including national and local governments,

ISBN: 978-92-64-05923-8 - © OECD 2009

employers, trade unions and NGOs. A key challenge for these programmes is their financial sustainability, particularly given the generally low earnings of informal workers. Cassirer and Addati argue that, in a number of cases, the sustainability of these programmes rested on their being supported by multiple partner institutions.

Some of the schemes reviewed by Cassirer and Addati (2007) were successful as women reported that "childcare enabled them to work more productively, with fewer interruptions to attend to children's needs and fewer concerns about children's safety". In addition in some schemes, women reported higher earnings associated with the childcare facilities (Nairobi and Chile). The location of the childcare facilities was identified as important in determining outcomes.

Microfinance

The origins of microfinance are commonly associated with the Grameen Bank in Bangladesh, established in the 1980s. The Grameen Bank provides loans without collateral requirements to small groups of poor workers, the majority of them women. The basic model has subsequently become very influential, with microfinance programmes now operating in many developing countries. There are several microfinance paradigms, differing in their criteria for success and modes of operation. These have been referred to as the "financial self-sustainability", the "poverty alleviation" and the "feminist empowerment" paradigms, though different programmes may combine several elements of them (Mayoux, 2000). Microfinance involves not only microcredit, but insurance and savings facilities, and the last of these may be particularly important for the poorest women (Burjorjee *et al.,* 2002).

The *financial self-sustainability paradigm* is argued to be "dominant within most donor agencies" (Mayoux, 2000). In one sense, this paradigm could be argued to work in women's favour in receiving loans, given that women tend to have higher repayment rates. However, one concern with this paradigm is that it may tend to overlook the needs of the poorest women, for whom returns to investments may be lower (Burjorjee *et al.*, 2002). A particular concern here is the opportunity cost of time for poor women to join local groups that form the basis of most MFIs (microfinance institutions). Weinberger and Jütting (2001) have shown that poor women in particular simply do not have the time to spend to participate actively as their opportunity costs are too high.

The *poverty alleviation paradigm* sees microfinance as an alternative or complement to traditional poverty alleviation programmes rather than an investment in the narrow sense of the term, as in the financial self-sustainability paradigm. For example, this paradigm may focus on smoothing families' income and consumption patterns in the face of cyclical or seasonal fluctuations.

In the *feminist empowerment paradigm*, microfinance is seen as part of a broader package of improving women's economic, social and political status, and is associated with the development of participatory women's organisations. In assessing these approaches Mayoux (2000) writes that: "Unless poverty reduction and empowerment goals are explicitly integrated throughout programme design and implementation, microfinance may have little positive impact".

In evaluating best practice in microfinance programmes, a report by the United Nations Capital Development Fund (UNCDF) states:

> "Experience has shown that increasing women's access to microfinance has wide-ranging benefits, not only for women's well-being but also for the welfare of the family and the health of the larger economy" (Burjorjee *et al.*, 2002).

Yet the report also cautions that larger loans made by microfinance institutions are disproportionately taken out by men rather than women. Moreover, there is a positive correlation between the benefits from microfinance and clients' initial assets, which can perpetuate gender inequality given that those of women are generally smaller. The report also argues that microfinance institutions need to account for the greater constraints on women's time and mobility in providing services. Again, as with the other policies presented, the specific design is crucial for the success of a specific programme.

103

Providing Better Protection

Workers' organisations play a fundamental role in improving their welfare. They contribute to enhancing the capacity of women as well as providing them with means for improving social protection. The relevance of such organisations for informal workers is potentially wide-ranging, as suggested by studies of organisations of informal workers in South Africa (Goldman, 2003; Devenish and Skinner, 2004). These organisations represent the interests of members to local governments, manage the number of members operating in an area, resolve conflicts among members, co-ordinate orders and bulk buying, facilitate access to benefits and credit and savings facilities, and organise education and training, in addition to engaging in negotiations and collective bargaining.

Perhaps the best known organisation of informal women workers is the Self-Employed Women's Association (SEWA) in India, with nearly a million members in 2006. As with workers' organisations in South Africa, SEWA is engaged in a wide range of activities, including the provision of childcare and healthcare (Gallin and Horn, 2005). The fact that SEWA is not tied to a recognised employer created difficulties in its being formally recognised as a union, both nationally and internationally (SEWA, 2008). Yet SEWA addressed this concern and received legal recognition as a union by the Indian government in 1972 and joined the International Confederation of Trade Unions (ICFTU) in 2006. SEWA has served as the model for SEWA Turkey, SEWA Yemen and the Self-Employed Women's Union (SEWU) in South Africa (ILO, 2007). SEWA also played a role in the adoption of the ILO Home Work Convention (C177) of 1996 (Gallin, 2007).

Domestic workers are among the most difficult to organise, yet unions of domestic workers – some claiming membership extending to the thousands – have been established in East Asia, South Asia, sub-Saharan Africa, and Latin America and the Caribbean. As an example of the potential effectiveness of these unions, the National Federation of Domestic Workers in Peru was instrumental in the passage in 2003 of legislation providing domestic workers with social security and healthcare coverage, vacation time and an eight-hour working day. Also established was a confederation of national unions of domestic workers in Latin America and the Caribbean (Gallin and Horn, 2005).

Street vendors would also seem difficult to organise, but here, too, there have been success stories. The National Association of Street Vendors in India (NASVI) claimed to represent 168 000 street vendors from 20 states of India in 2003 (ILO, 2007). A confederation of eight national unions of street vendors in Latin America and the Caribbean was established in 2005 (Gallin and Horn, 2005). StreetNet, established in Durban, South Africa in 2002, is an international alliance of membership-based organisations of street vendors, including unions, co-operatives and associations (StreetNet, 2008). The number of membership-based organisations representing street vendors compiled by StreetNet is noteworthy: 120 in Africa, 40 in Asia and 113 in Latin America.

Finally, the Women in Informal Employment: Globalizing and Organizing (WIEGO) is a global research-policy network that seeks to improve the status of the working poor, especially women, in the informal economy. WIEGO has gained some considerable influence in bringing informal employment to the debate of researchers, policy makers and donors.

These examples suggest that the legal and logistical obstacles to organising informal women workers are surmountable, providing a potentially important path to better jobs for women.

Employment guarantee schemes and public works

A wide variety of employment guarantee schemes exist throughout the world (see Antonopoulos, 2007, for an overview). The largest of these is India's National Rural Employment Guarantee Scheme (NREGS), which provides up to ten days of employment benefits to rural households upon request at the national minimum wage. Passed in 2005, NREGS started to be implemented on a nationwide basis in 2008 (*The Economist,* 2008). An important precursor to NREGS was the Employment Guarantee Scheme of the State of Maharashtra, beginning in the early 1970s, in which earnings were paid as piece rates.

ISBN: 978-92-64-05923-8 - © OECD 2009

Insofar as women are disproportionately represented among the poor, one indicator of the effectiveness of these programmes is that women are well represented within them. In the state of Rajasthan under NREGS, 70 per cent of participants are reported to be women (*The Economist,* 2008). Similarly, the *Jefes* Programme (Programme for Unemployed Male and Female Heads of Households), implemented in Argentina following the economic crisis of 2001-02, was also effective in this respect, with about 75 per cent of participants being women as of 2005 (Tcherneva and Wray, 2007). Summarising the effects of *Jefes* on women in Argentina, Tcherneva and Wray write: "Some of the benefits women report are: working in mother-friendly jobs, getting needed training and education, helping the community, and finding dignity and empowerment through work". These examples suggest that employment guarantee schemes can indeed be of benefit to women provided that they are adequately designed and implemented.

Overall, there are major problems in reaching out to women, and in particular women in more disadvantaged groups, for at least two main reasons. Women's limited access to information and/or misunderstanding of the eligibility and conditions of the scheme are often suggested as explanations of the limited success of these programmes. In addition, public work schemes often require physical work and hence may be less appealing to women. Furthermore, women can be less represented in public work programmes that require long journeys to work, given the social constraints imposed on them by social and cultural norms and their family responsibilities.

Public works and employment guarantee schemes offer several lessons learnt and examples of good practice. If the main constraints on women's participation are cultural norms and customs, then projects that target solely women (or even women-only components of projects) can help. If the issue is more about family constraints and the non-availability of childcare facilities, then the distance of the programme from women's houses matters most. In addition on-site provision of childcare facilities can also help overcome these constraints. Finally broad access to information and clear presentation of the requirements and conditions of participation are crucial for women (Kabeer, 2008). Successful programmes in attracting/targeting women such as the rural maintenance programme in Bangladesh use for instance loudspeakers to inform people about the programme and women were offered access of women-only projects, hence addressing issues related to cultural norms and restrictions. Reaching out to women is at least as important as the effectiveness of the programme.

Social protection schemes

A large number of social protection schemes around the world either target or extend to informal workers. They comprise a large range of activities, from health and life insurance to pensions and childcare or also education and health-related conditional cash transfers. Lund and Srinivas (2000) review many of these schemes in Bangladesh, Bolivia, Colombia, India, Japan, the Philippines, South Africa and Zimbabwe, whereas Perry *et al.* (2007) provide rich information on such schemes in Latin America[10]. Information on various types of social protection schemes is also provided by Kabeer (2008). Overall, the quality of targeting and the progressivity of these schemes vary significantly.

According to Kabeer (2008), women may benefit more than men from social pension schemes and cash transfers. This will be the case if women live longer and/or because female-headed households depend more on social pensions compared with male-headed ones. A large set of interesting examples of schemes targeting women directly or indirectly are reviewed in Kabeer (2008). For example, the Previdência Social in Brazil, which expanded in 1988 to provide universal entitlement to a basic pension to the elderly and those in informal rural employment, was successful in extending its coverage, especially among women workers in the informal economy and female-headed households. Universal social pensions in Namibia seem to be more important for women than men as more female-headed households depend on the pensions as their main income source than male-headed households. Zambia's social cash transfer for the ultra-poor is another example of a well targeted scheme that covers a large number of women. Finally, Bangladesh recently introduced a social assistance programme for widows and destitute women. Conversely, India's state social assistance programme, which was introduced

105

in 1995 and includes family benefits, a maternity scheme and an old age pension scheme, has not successfully managed to extend coverage to women, who only constitute 37 per cent of the total.

The financial sources of these schemes and their management vary widely. The role of the state is most often very important, but recently initiatives have emerged that engage the private sector, and trade unions and civil organisations. The interventions can come from the state and the formal sector of the economy, but can also be based on the informal community (Lund and Srinivas, 2000). Indeed, involving community-based organisations in social protection is another approach that has recently appeared. According to Kabeer (2008), concluding these partnerships between the state and the private sector can be very beneficial and may therefore be desirable. The state can not only channel development funds to social protection but also create incentives for the private sector to participate in the markets for social protection. Other emerging actors in this arena are the trade unions and occupation-based cooperatives, as well as micro-finance institutions that move from the sole provision of credit to more diversified loans and financial products. Finally, formal unions have made their first steps in extending their services to the informal sector. Overall, the provision of social protection involves various ministries and hence co-ordination among them is needed (Shepherd *et al.*, 2004, cited in Kabeer, 2008).

CONCLUSION

This chapter has shown that women are over-represented in the most disadvantaged positions within the informal sector. This has important implications for their earnings and their access to social protection and other work-related benefits. Overall, important differences between men and women are found in terms of their endowments, the types of jobs open to them and the constraints they face. It appears that the same factors that are responsible for the limited participation of women in the labour force are often also those responsible for their over-representation in low quality and informal jobs.

First, informal institutions and discrimination shaped by cultural and social norms introduce important constraints on the types of jobs women can do and the conditions of work. In addition, informal institutions also limit women's access to resources, such as education, land, credit and information networks, which further limit the opportunities women have in the labour market. These factors impose constraints on the way and the extent to which women adapt to, and benefit from, a labour market change induced by globalisation. Secondly, the access to resources (credit, land, communication, etc.) matters a great deal for female labour force outcomes. Finally the economic structure and continuing changes in the context of globalisation determine how many women participate and in which types of jobs.

Policies addressing gender disparities with respect to labour force outcomes should expand the work options women have in the formal sector, improve mobility towards better jobs, enhance productivity and improve the conditions of work for those in informal jobs with limited options elsewhere, through, among other things, the provision of social protection. The policy discussion in the previous section has shown that interventions in different moments of a woman's life are necessary. Early interventions aiming to increase access to education and training on the one hand, and change stereotypical views of the gender roles of the young generations on the other, can increase a woman's chances of getting a good job. Later interventions in the form of employment-specific schemes, microfinance and childcare policies can further increase the options open to women. Finally, for those women who have no other choice but jobs in the informal sector, schemes to expand social protection to them, as well as workers' organisations, can improve their conditions of work.

From the discussion in the previous section, it becomes clear that the design of specific schemes is an important factor in determining the participation of women and subsequently the success

ISBN: 978-92-64-05923-8 - © OECD 2009

of the programme. A few conclusions can be drawn from existing schemes around the world. First, and very importantly, reaching out to women – and particularly to the most disadvantaged among them – is not straightforward. Hence special provisions should be made for women, given their limited access to information and networks. Innovative and more women-friendly methods, such as those used in the Indian Employment Guarantee scheme (use of loudspeakers with the objective of reaching out to a larger number of people), can be successful in attracting women. Second, special provisions should be made to satisfy the constraints women face with respect to their family responsibilities and limited geographic mobility, offering them options of work close to their house and childcare facilities. Finally co-ordination is necessary, not only among policy actors but also between them and social partners such as women's organisations that know better the needs of women and the constraints they face.

ISBN: 978-92-64-05923-8 - © OECD 2009

NOTES

1. Informal sector is defined to include the "self-employed, domestics, family workers, wage and salary workers in firms of four or fewer persons except professional and technical occupations" (Funkhouser, 1996: p. 1739).

2. This section has largely benefited from inputs by Angela Luci, consultant to the OECD Development Centre.

3. Study based on the Kenyan Labour Force Survey (late 1990s), multinomial logit regression analysis for occupational outcomes: utility of labour market outcome (non-participation, participation formal sector, participation informal sector) as a function of education, gender and experience.

4. The debate continues on whether trade liberalisation has significant effects on inter-sectoral allocation of labour. When sectors are broadly defined, there is consensus that trade liberalisation has brought important structural changes within sub-sectors in manufacturing and services (Wacziarg and Wallack, 2004).

5. This is to some extent due to the break-up of the Soviet Union.

6. Impact of education on probability of getting a public sector job and a lower wage effect for women, compared to men.

7. It provided training to 42 000 16-24 year olds between 1996 and 2003.

8. "It provided three months of in-classroom training and three months of on-the-job training to 80 000 young people between the ages of 18 and 25 in the two lowest socio-economic strata of the population" (Katz, 2008, p. 18).

9. Katz (2008) discusses two such programmes in rural India: the Baatchit Project and the Bharatiya Yuva Shakti Trust.

10. Examples of such schemes include: mutual health insurance schemes in West Africa, universal health insurance or pension schemes (national pension system in Japan), extension of existing statutory schemes, the Mexican Seguro popular, the Asociacion Mutual "Los Andes" (AMUANDES) in Colombia, Cooperative-life mutual services association (CLIMBS) in the Philippines, Grameen Kalyan in Bangladesh, the Seguro universal de salud del instituto politecnico Tomas Katari (IPTK) in Bolivia, the SEWA integrated social security scheme in India, the social health insurance/networking and empowerment in the Philippines and the South African old age pension (SA-OAP) among others.

ISBN: 978-92-64-05923-8 - © OECD 2009

REFERENCES

ABOWD, J. and R. FREEMAN (eds.), *Immigration, Trade and the Labor Market*, University of Chicago Press, Chicago.

ADAMS, A.V. (2007), "The Role of Youth Skills Development in the Transition to Work: A Global Review", *HDNCY Working Paper Series No. 5, Children and Youth Discussion Papers,* World Bank, Washington, D.C.

AGARWAL, B. (1997), "Bargaining and Gender Relations: Within and Beyond the Household", *Feminist Economics*, Vol. 3, No. 1, pp. 1-57.

AGARWAL, B. (2003), "Gender and Land Rights Revisited: Exploring New Prospects via the State, Family and Market", *Journal of Agrarian Change* Vol. 3, Nos. 1 and 2, pp. 184-224.

ANTONOPOULOS, R. (2007), "Employment Guarantee Policies and Related Gender Dimensions", Paper prepared for the 8th International GEM-ING Conference Engendering Macroeconomics and International Economics, Istanbul, 20-22 July.

ATIENO, R. and F. TEAL (2006), "Gender, Education and Occupational Outcomes: Kenya's Informal Sector in the 1990s", *Global Poverty Research Group*, Economic and Social Research Council, University of Oxford, Oxford.

ATTANASIO, O., A. KUGLER and C. MEGHIR (2008), "Training Disadvantaged Youth in Latin America: Evidence from a Randomized Trial", *NBER Working Paper* No. 13931, National Bureau of Economic Research, Cambridge, Mass.

BADEN, S. (1998), "Gender Issues in Agricultural Liberalisation", Topic paper prepared for Directorate General for Development (DGVIII) of the European Commission, *Bridge* (*Development-Gender*) Report, No. 41. Brighton: Institute of Development Studies (IDS). Available online at: www.ids.ac.uk/bridge/Reports/re41c.pdf.

BENERIA, L. (2001a), "Changing Employment Patterns and the Informalisation of Jobs: General Trends and Gender Dimensions", ILO, Geneva.

BENERIA, L. (2001b), "Shifting the Risk: New Employment Patterns, Informalisation and Women's Work", *International Journal of Politics, Culture, and Society,* Vol. 15, No. 1.

BENERIA, L. and S. FLORO (2004), "Labour Market Informalisation and Social Policy: Distributional Links and the Case of Homebased Workers", *Vassar College Economics Working Paper* No. 60, Poughkeepsie, NY.

BURJORJEE, D., R. DESHPANDE and J. WEIDEMANN (2002), *Supporting Women`s Livelihoods: Microfinance that Works for the Majority,* United Nations Capital Development Fund, Special Unit for Microfinance, New York, NY.

CARR, M. (1984), *Blacksmith, Baker, Roofing-sheet Maker…Employment for Rural Women in Developing Countries,* IT Publications, London.

CARR, M. and M.A. CHEN (2001), "Globalization and the Informal Economy: How Global Trade and Investment Impact on the Working Poor", *Women in Informal Employment: Globalizing and Organizing (WIEGO) Working Paper*, Cambridge, MA.

CASSIRER, N. and L. ADDATI (2007), "Expanding Women's Employment Opportunities: Informal Economy Workers and the Need for Childcare", mimeo, ILO, Geneva.

CHARMES, J. (2002), "Self-employment, Informal Employment, Informal Sector Employment: Trends and Characteristics. A Tentative Assessment of their Statistical Knowledge", contribution to the ILO/WIEGO report on informal employment for the International Labour Conference 2002 and to *Women and Men in the Informal Economy: a Statistical Picture*.

CHARMES, J. (2008), "Statistics on Informal Employment in the Arab Region", Chapter 3 of *Gender Equality and Workers' Rights in the Informal Economies of Arab States*, ILO Regional Office for the Arab States and CAWTAR (Center of Arab Women for Training and Research, Beirut and Tunis pp.54-72.

CHEN, M. (2004), "Women in the Informal Sector: a Global Picture, the Global Movement", WIEGO, Cambridge, MA.

CHEN, M. (2006), "Rethinking the Informal Economy: Linkages with the Formal Economy and Formal Regulatory Environment", in B. GUHA-KHASNOBIS, R. KANBUR and E. OSTROM (eds.), *Linking the Formal and the Informal Economy: Concepts and Policies,* Oxford University Press, Oxford.

CHEN, M., J. SEBSTAD and L. O'CONNELL (1999), "Counting the Invisible Workforce: The Case of Homebased Workers", *World Development* Vol. 27, No. 3, pp. 603-610.

CHEN, M., J. VANEK and M. CARR (2004), *Mainstreaming Informal Employment and Gender in Poverty Reduction: A Handbook for Policy Makers and Other Stakeholders*, Commonwealth Secretariat/IDRC, London.

CHEN, M.A., J. VANEK, F. LUND, J. HEINTZ, with R. JHABVALA and C. BONNER (2005), *Progress of the World's Women 2005: Women, Work & Poverty,* United Nations Development Fund for Women, New York, NY.

CLARK, R. (2003), "Female Literacy Rates, Information Technology and Democracy", *Working Paper,* Canadian Political Science Association Annual Conference, Vancouver.

DEVENISH, A. and C. SKINNER (2004), "Organising Workers in the Informal Economy: The Experience of the Self Employed Women's Union, 1994-2004", School of Development Studies, University of KwaZulu-Natal, Durban.

ECONOMIST, THE (2008), "Shovelling for Their Supper", 24 April.

ESIM, S. (2001), "Women's Informal Employment in Central and Eastern Europe", Department of Economic and Social Affairs, Division for the Advancement of Women, United Nations, New York, NY.

ESIM, S. and E. KUTTAB (2002), "Women's Informal Employment in Palestine: Securing a Livelihood Against All Odds", Economic Research Forum. Background Paper for the 9th Forum of ERF, Cairo.

FLOREZ, C.E. (2003), "Migration and the Urban Informal Sector in Colombia", Paper prepared for the Conference on African Migration in Comparative Perspective, Johannesburg, 4-7 June.

FONTANA, M. and A. WOOD (2000), "Modelling the Effects of Trade on Women, at Work and at Home", *World Development*, Vol. 28, pp. 1173-1190.

FREEMAN, R. and L. KATZ (1991), "Industrial Wage and Employment Determination in an Open Economy", in J. ABOWD and R. FREEMAN (eds.), *Immigration, Trade and the Labor Market*, University of Chicago Press, Chicago.

FUNKHOUSER, E. (1996), "The Urban Informal Sector in Central America: Household Survey Evidence", *World Development,* Vol. 24, No. 11, pp. 1737-1751.

GALLI, R. and D. KUCERA (2003), "Informal Employment in Latin America: Movements Over Business Cycles and the Effects of Worker Rights", *International Institute of Labour Studies (IILS) Working Paper* No. 145 ILO, Geneva.

GALLI, R. and D. KUCERA (2008), "Gender, Informality and Employment Adjustment in Latin America", *Policy Integration and Statistics Department Working Paper* No. 85, ILO, Geneva.

GALLIN, D. (2007), "The ILO Home Work Convention: Ten Years Later", paper presented at Women Work and Poverty: SEW/UNIFEM Policy Conference on Home Based Workers of South Asia, New Delhi, 18-20 January.

GALLIN, D. and P. HORN (2005), "Organizing Informal Women Workers", paper prepared for UNRISD Gender Policy Report. Available at: http://streetnet.org.za/english/GallinHornpaper.htm (accessed 15 October 2008).

GASTON, N. and D. TREFLER (1994), "The Role of International Trade and Trade Policy in the Labor Markets of Canada and the United States", *World Economy*, Vol. 17, No. 1, pp. 45-62.

ISBN: 978-92-64-05923-8 - © OECD 2009

GASTON, N. and D. TREFLER (1997), "The Labor Market Consequences of the Canada-US Free Trade Agreement", *Canadian Journal of Economics*, Vol. 30, No. 1, pp. 18-41.

GHOSH, J. (2004), "Informalisation and Women's Workforce Participation: A Consideration of Recent Trends in Asia", paper prepared for the UNRISD report *Gender Equality: Striving for Justice in an Unequal World*.

GIDEON, J. (2007), "A Gendered Analysis of Labour Market Informalisation and Access to Health in Chile", *Global Social Policy,* Vol. 7, No. 1, pp. 75-94.

GOLDMAN, T. (2003), "Organizing in South Africa's Informal Economy: An Overview of four Sectoral Case Studies", Series on Representation and Organization Building, *SEED Working Paper* No. 60, ILO, Geneva.

GROSSMAN, G. (1986), "Imports as a Cause of Injury: The Case of the United States Steel Industry", *Journal of International Economics,* Vol. 20, pp. 201-233.

GROSSMAN, G. (1987), "The Employment and Wage Effects on Import Competition in the United States", *Journal of International Economic Integration*, Vol. 2, pp. 1-23.

HEINTZ, J. and R. POLLIN (2003), "Informalization, Economic Growth and the Challenge of Creating Viable Labor Standards in Developing Countries", *PERI Working Paper* No. 60, Political Economy Research Institute, Amherst.

HEYZER, N. (2006), "Poverty and Women's Work in the Informal Economy", United Nations Development Fund for Women, World Bank, Washington, D.C.

HUSSMANNS, R. (2005), "Measuring the Informal Economy: from Employment in the Informal Sector to Informal Employment", *ILO Policy Integration Department Working Paper* No. 53, ILO, Geneva.

ILO (1998*a*), "Women in the Informal Sector and their Access to Microfinance", paper prepared for the Inter-Parliamentary Union (IPU) Annual Conference, Windhoek, 2-11 April.

ILO (1998*b*), "Labour and Social Issues Relating to Export Processing Zones", ILO, Geneva.

ILO (2007), "Fourth Item on the Agenda: The Informal Economy", Governing Body, 298th Session, Geneva, March.

ILO (2008*a*), *Global Employment Trends for Women*, ILO, Geneva, March.

ILO (2008*b*), *LABORSTA Database*. Geneva. Bureau of *Statistics,* ILO, Geneva. *http://laborsta. ilo.org*, Accessed July. 2008

INTERNATIONAL ORGANISATION FOR MIGRATION (2004), *Essentials of Migration Management: A Guide for Policy Makers and Practitioners,* Vol. 2, IOM, Geneva.

JOEKES, S. (1999), "A Gender-Analytical Perspective on Trade and Sustainable Development", *in* UNCTAD, *Trade, Sustainable Development and Gender* (Papers prepared in support of the themes discussed at the pre-UNCTAD X expert workshop on Trade, Sustainable Development and Gender in Geneva, 12-13 July.

JÜTTING, J., C. MORRISSON, J. DAYTON-JOHNSON and D. DRECHSLER (2008*a*), "Measuring Gender (In)Equality", *Journal of Human Development and Capabilities,* Vol. 9, Issue 1, pp. 65- 86.

JÜTTING, J., J. PARLEVLIET and T. XENOGIANI (2008*b*), "Informal Employment Re-loaded", *Working Paper* No. 266. OECD Development Centre, Paris.

KABEER, N. (2008), *Mainstreaming Gender in Social Protection for the Informal Economy,* Commonwealth Secretariat, London.

KATZ, E. (2008), "Programs Promoting Young Women's Employment: What Works?", Background paper for Adolescent Girls Initiative, World Bank, Washington, D.C.

LASTARRIA-CORNHIEL, S. (2006), "Feminization of Agriculture: Trends and Driving Forces", paper prepared for the *World Development Report* 2008, World Bank, Washington, D.C.

111

LEACH, F. (1999), "Women in the Informal Sector: The Contribution of Education and Training", in Oxfam, *Development with Women,* Oxfam Publishing, Oxford, pp. 46-62.

LEE, S., D. McCANN and J. MESSINGER (2007), *Working Time Around the World: Trends in Working Hours, Laws and Policies in a Global Comparative Perspective*, Routledge, New York, NY.

LEICHTMAN, M.A. (2002), "Transforming Brain Drain into Capital Gain: Morocco's Changing Relationship with Migration and Remittances", *Journal of North African Studies*, Vol. 7, No. 1.

LUND, F. and S. SRINIVAS (2000), *Learning from Experience: A Gendered Approach to Social Protection for Workers in the Informal Economy,* ILO, Geneva.

MAYOUX, L. (2000), "Micro-finance and the Empowerment of Women: A Review of Key Issues", *SFP Working Paper* No. 23, ILO, Geneva.

MESA-LAGO, C. (2007), "The Extension of Healthcare Coverage and Protection in Relation to the Labour Market: Problems and Policies in Latin America", *International Social Security Journal*, Vol. 60, No. 1, pp. 3-31.

MESNARD, A. and M. RAVALLION (2001), "Is Inequality Bad for Business? A Nonlinear Micro Model of Wealth Effects on Self-employment", *World Bank Research Paper* No. 2527, World Bank, Washington, D.C.

MORRISON, A.R., M. SCHIFF and M. SJÖBLOM (2007), *The International Migration of Women*, for the World Bank, Palgrave Macmillan, Basingstoke.

MORRISSON, C. and J. JÜTTING (2005), "Women's Discrimination in Developing Countries: A New Data Set for Better Policies", *World Development,* Vol. 33, No. 7, pp. 1065-1081.

ÑOPO, H., J. SAAVEDRA-CHANDUVI and M. ROBLES (2007), "Occupational Training to Reduce Gender Segregation: The Impacts of ProJoven", *RES Working Papers* No. 1068, Research Department, Inter-American Development Bank, Washington, D.C.

NORDAS, H. (2003), "Is Trade Liberalization a Window of Opportunity for Women?" *Staff Working Paper ERSD*, World Trade Organization, Geneva.

NTSEANE, G. (1999), "A Botswana Rural Women's Transition to Urban Small Business Success: Collective Struggles, Collective Learning", unpublished doctoral dissertation, The University of Georgia, Athens, Georgia, US.

OECD (2007), *Policy Coherence for Development: Migration and Developing Countries,* OECD Development Centre, Paris.

OZLER, S. (2000), "Export Orientation and Female Share of Employment: Evidence from Turkey", *World Development,* Vol. 28, pp. 1239-1248.

PARLEVLIET, J. and T. XENOGIANI (2008), "Report on Informal Employment in Romania", *Working Paper* No. 271, OECD Development Centre, Paris.

PERRY, G., W. MALONEY, O. ARIAS, P. FAJNZYLBER, A. MASON and J. SAAVEDRA-CHANDUVI (2007), *Informality: Exit and Exclusion,* World Bank, Washington, D.C.

PFAU-EFFINGER, B. (2003), "Development of Informal Work in Europe; Causal Factors, Problems, Approaches to Solutions", Keynote Speech at EU Workshop: Informal/Undeclared Work: Research on its Changing Nature and Policy Strategies in an Enlarged Europe, held in Brussels, 23 May.

REBOUCHÉ, R. (2006), "Labor, Land and Women's Rights in Africa: Challenges for the New Protocol on the Rights of Women", *Harvard Human Rights Journal*, Vol. 19, Spring.

REVENGA, A. (1992), "Exporting Jobs? The Impact of Import Competition on Employment and Wages in US Manufacturing", *Quarterly Journal of Economics*, Vol. 107, No. 1, pp. 255-284.

RYAN, P. (2001), "The School-to-Work Transition: A Cross-National Perspective", *Journal of Economic Literature,* American Economic Association, Vol. 39(1), pp. 34-92, March.

ISBN: 978-92-64-05923-8 - © OECD 2009

Seguino, S. (2000), "Gender Inequality and Economic Growth: A Cross Country Analysis", *World Development* No. 28: pp. 1211-1230.

Seguino, S. (2005), *Gender Inequality in a Globalizing World*, UNRISD Conference, New York, 7 March.

Self Employed Women's Association (SEWA) (2008), *SEWA's structure.* Available at: www.sewa.org/aboutus/index.asp, accessed 14 May 2008.

Sen, G. (2007), "Informal Institutions and Gender Equality", *in* J. Jütting, D. Dreschler, S. Bartsch and I. De Soysa (eds.), *Informal Institutions – How Social Norms Help or Hinder Development*, Development Centre Studies, OECD, Paris.

Shepherd, A., R. Marcus and A. Barrientos (2004), *"General Review of Current Social Protection Policies and Programmes"*, paper prepared for the UK Department for International Development, Overseas Development Institute, London.

Standing, G. (1999), "Global Feminization Through Flexible Labour: a Theme Revisited", *World Development*, Vol. 27, No. 3, pp. 583-602.

Streetnet International (2008), Background, Database of Organisations. Available at: http://streetnet.org.za, accessed 14 May 2008.

Tcherneva, P. and L. Wray (2007), "Public Employment and Women: The Impact of Argentina`s Jefes Program On Female Heads of Poor Households", Working Paper No. 519, The Levi Economics Institute, Annadale-on-Hudson.

UN (1999), *World Survey on the Role of Women in Development: Globalization, Gender and Work,* Department of Economic and Social Affairs, Division for the Advancement of Women, United Nations, New York, NY.

UN (2005), "A Spotlight on Inequality", *in The Inequality Predicament, the Informal Economy,* Chapter II, UN Report on the World Social Situation 2005.

UNCDF (2002), *Supporting Women`s Livelihoods: Microfinance that Works for the Majority,* United Nations Capital Development Fund, Special Unit for Microfinance, New York, NY.

Unesco Institute for Statistics (2002), "Literacy Statistics", UNESCO, Paris.

UNFPA (2006), *State of World Population. A Passage to Hope: Women and International Migration*, United Nations, New York, NY.

Unni, J. and U. Rani (2000), "Women in Informal Employment in India", presented at the International Association for Feminist Economics Conference, Bogazici University, Istanbul.

Wacziarg, R. and J.S. Wallack (2004), "Trade Liberalization and Intersectoral Labor Movements", *Journal of International Economics*, Vol. 64, No. 2, pp. 411-439.

Wahba, J. (2004), "Does International Migration Matter? A Study of Egyptian Return Migrants", *in Arab Migration in a Globalised World*, International Organization for Migration, Geneva.

Weinberger, K. and J. Jütting (2001), "Women's Participation in Local Organizations: Conditions and Constraints", *World Development*, Vol. 29, No. 8, pp. 1391-1404.

Wisana, D.G.K.I. (2006), "Determinants of Off-farm Work Participation in Rural Indonesia", Master Thesis, Norwegian University of Life Sciences, Ås.

World Bank (2001), "Engendering Development", World Bank, Washington, D.C.

World Bank (2004), Gender and Development in the Middle East and North Africa: Women in the Public Sphere, World Bank, Washington, D.C.

World Bank (2008), *World Development Report: Agriculture for Development*, World Bank, Washington, D.C.

Zachariah, K., E. Mathew and S. Irudaya Rajan (2002), "Social, Economic and Demographic Consequences of Migration on Kerala", International Migration, Vol. 39, No. 2, pp. 43-71.

113

Moving Out of Bad Jobs – More Mobility, More Opportunity

Jason Gagnon

ABSTRACT

One way for the poor to improve their living standards is to move from bad jobs to better ones. That can involve switching within sectors, between them, or from one place to another. This mobility is not an option for everyone and many barriers exist: nor is it necessarily the case that leaving one job for another will automatically bring extra earnings. But there is more mobility in informal employment than might be expected and overall in many cases mobility for the poor does increase their earnings. Integrated policy frameworks spanning employment, social policies and migration are needed in order to ease the transition to better jobs.

ISBN: 978-92-64-05923-8 - © OECD 2009

INTRODUCTION

This chapter looks at the ways that the poor can improve their earnings and standard of living if they are ready to move: between jobs in the informal sector; between the formal and informal sectors in both directions; and by physically changing from one place to another.

Three broad questions emerge.

— Can labour mobility help poor people get out of bad informal jobs and, if so, what are the conditions under which mobility leads to an increase in earnings and so has an impact on poverty?

— What conditions need to exist for mobility to lead to a better standard of living?

— What can policies do to influence the environment in which labour mobility takes place to ease voluntary mobility?

The mobility of individuals between various states or categories of employment in the labour market may take several forms, notably from one job to another or from one place to another. To determine what happens when people change jobs and whether they earn more or less, researchers typically observe individuals over a period of time to see whether their incomes rise or fall, and whether these changes take place inside or outside the widely identified division of the labour market into formal and informal sectors.

This chapter is specifically concerned with ways to increase individual earnings through the mobility of the poor in developing countries. It discusses policies that make it possible for workers to move out of *bad* jobs and into *better* ones. The framework used in this chapter considers moves by individuals between four different states in the labour market: *i)* inactivity; *ii)* informal work in a bad job; *iii)* informal work in a good job; and *iv)* formal work. It looks at the contribution to changes in income following shifts between these states. The aim is to determine who has more economic mobility and who has less.

Many of the studies find surprisingly high mobility between sectors in developing countries, but they do not necessarily find similar results in terms of pay. Some find that moves from formal jobs to informal jobs mean a drop in income while movement in the opposite direction brings financial gain. Other studies show that to earn more there is not necessarily any need to leave informal employment. Informal jobs are therefore not necessarily bad jobs, although there is much overlap. Moves both *within* the informal sector, as well as moves *between* different labour market segments, may lead to increases in well-being.

The questions of whether mobility can increase earnings and of the forms of mobility under which this takes place have important implications for policy. If moving from informal to formal is critical in increasing earnings, then the focus should be on creating formal jobs and accompanying the transition to formality. But if people can earn more irrespective of the formal-informal division of the labour market, which is an important finding in this chapter, and if government policies seek to increase earnings and the job opportunities of individuals in their countries, they should aim to do so in both the formal and the informal sectors.

This chapter contains three major elements. First, using evidence pointing to increases in earnings mobility in developing countries, it is shown how mobility, informality and poverty are linked and how they affect the incomes of the poor. Second, it shows that job mobility and spatial (or geographical) mobility are prevalent in developing countries. It also offers an overview of factors which may determine the individual's ability to move and also the factors which may inhibit their movement to better paying jobs. Finally, policies in the labour market, in the education sector, in social security provision and on migration are reviewed to see how they may affect the mobility of individuals, with the aim of helping people move into better jobs and get paid more, with the end result that poverty is reduced.

ISBN: 978-92-64-05923-8 - © OECD 2009

MOBILITY, INFORMALITY AND POVERTY

Different Sorts of Mobility

Labour mobility, by which is meant the ease with which workers move between employment activities, is regarded as an indicator of a high degree of overall labour market flexibility within a given country (Nickell, 1997). Greater mobility can be seen as a means for better matching between workers and jobs. If it can lead to increased returns for the poor, it therefore also constitutes a key element of a poverty reduction strategy. This observation builds on the notions and evidence of labour markets presented in Chapter 3 and formulates a framework within which individuals may shift between labour market states and where mobility does not necessarily have to mean crossing the boundary between formal and informal labour markets. Labour mobility can be defined as individual changes in labour market activity. Such changes can come about in many ways and take many forms. Two broad categories are job mobility and spatial mobility.

Job Mobility concerns moves between jobs. They can take place within a firm or enterprise through either moves sideways or upward promotions. The category also includes moves between firms, which can similarly be sideways or upward. Job mobility can be further split between industrial mobility and occupational mobility. The first refers to changes between industries (e.g. agricultural to manufacturing industries) and the second to changes in work occupation (e.g. building worker to brick-layer) (for example in Moscarini and Thomsson, [2008] on mobility in the US). This category also embraces movements in and out of active employment, including moves into and out of the labour force (not actively searching, discouraged searchers, not-of-age or retired) and unemployment (actively searching but not employed).

Spatial Mobility is about geographical movement. Such transitions can cover very short distances and micro-level adjustments, such as moves from urban peripheries to city centres. But they can also cover longer distances, within a country (internal migration) or between countries (international migration).

An analysis of labour mobility in developing countries should not ignore moves between informal jobs. A key feature of labour mobility in developing countries is the possibility of moves not only across defined labour market segments, such as that between formal and informal jobs, but also within informal employment. Mobility is important in improving the efficiency of labour markets but also has distributional consequences. In particular, and when poverty reduction is a major policy objective, moves from *bad* jobs to *good* jobs[1] and the policies that can foster them are of particular interest.

A New Look at Informality, Poverty and Mobility

As was argued in Chapter 3, a division may exist not only between formal and informal employment in the labour market, but also one between an upper and a lower-tier informal sector (Fields, 1990). This chapter follows that view of the labour market, in arguing that the good job/bad job division cuts across formality. Indeed, earnings distributions for formal and informal jobs largely overlap, as shown for Mexico by Maloney (1998) and Laiglesia et al. (2008), though the lowest earners are typically found in the informal sector[2].

This has two implications. First, it is necessary to analyse labour dynamics *within* informal employment rather than treating it as a residual sector. Second, informal employment contains both bad and good jobs, so that transitions involving informal employment should be distinguished according to job quality within informal employment[3].

117

Diagram 5.1. **Labour Market Transitions**

TRANSITION DIAGRAM

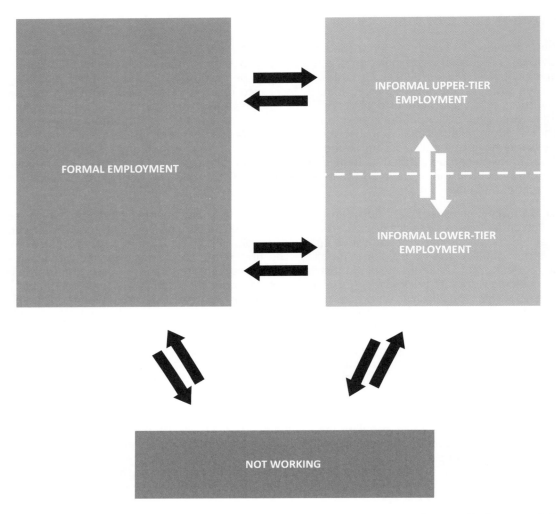

Source: author's own compilation.

Earnings Mobility and Poverty: Can Mobility Lead to Increased Earnings?

What are the effects of job mobility and spatial mobility on the earnings mobility of individuals? Put another way, this section considers who moves and why they move, and whether their incomes rise or fall, and to what degree, when they leave their existing jobs. For this purpose, earnings mobility refers to changes in individual earnings. Increases in earnings originate from three possible sources: *i)* increases in hours worked; *ii)* increases in productivity and; *iii)* changes in returns for a given level of productivity (Paci and Serneels, 2007). Earnings mobility may also be negative, especially when it concerns moves from either informal or formal employment to unemployment, or even ambiguous when they concern individual earnings which do not normally appear in tangible form (i.e. housework).

ISBN: 978-92-64-05923-8 - © OECD 2009

An important feature of earnings mobility in developing countries is the evidence linked to the phenomenon of "unconditional convergence": a situation in which individuals with the reported lowest initial incomes, earnings or consumption are those ones who gain and experience the most positive mobility over time[4]. Beyond the evidence on convergence, a study of South Africa shows that it is not necessary to acquire a formal sector job in order to achieve earnings gains; a majority of earnings gains due to mobility were achieved within the informal sector (Cichello *et al.*, 2005).

The finding that earnings distributions from both formal and informal employment largely overlap is consistent with the view of an upper and lower-tier segment within informal employment. The evidence presented on earnings premiums for at least part of the informal sector reflects the experience of some subgroups of individuals entering the informal sector voluntarily and *choosing* to be mobile between formal and informal sectors.

This competitive upper-tier segment is commonly associated with informal self-employment, such as that shown in Mexico (Maloney, 1999). Self-employed micro-enterprise owners may yield better outcomes and voluntarily work in the informal sector, while those with waged informal work may yield lower earnings. A study on Argentina (Arias and Khamis, 2008) demonstrates that there are no wage differences between formal workers and informal self-employed workers in Argentina, but that informal salaried employment comes with a significant wage penalty. Premiums may therefore exist for some types of moves and not others, and associated notably with moves into self-employment[5].

Mobility patterns are consistent with the existence of two different segments in informal employment. Accordingly, Pagés and Stampini (2007) find high mobility from informal salaried to formal salaried employment, and little mobility between self-employment and formal salaried in three Latin American countries and three economic transition countries, suggesting strong matching based on preference for the latter two employment states. Lehmann and Pignatti (2008) also point to evidence of earnings premiums associated with voluntary moves into the informal labour market in Ukraine, but that the voluntary segment itself is considerably small compared with the overall informal sector. Finally, Packard (2007) also shows that the informal self-employed segment is fairly competitive in Chile, with new entrants regularly pushing out marginally productive workers[6].

It is important to note that mobility is not necessarily associated with increasing earnings *per se*. On the contrary, moves to informal wage employment often lead to a drop in earnings. In Argentina, Mexico and Venezuela, workers who moved from formal wage employment to informal wage employment experienced a decline in monthly earnings on average, while the reverse move produced the opposite effect (Duryea *et al.*, 2006). Other empirical studies have also pointed to earnings mobility within and across segmentation but with major differences across countries. Marcouiller *et al.* (1997), for instance, show that while characteristics of informal workers are relatively similar across Mexico, El Salvador and Peru, results from wage regressions differed. Mexican data revealed a wage premium associated with informal work, while data from the other two countries did not. Why such differences may exist between countries is important for policy making and will be covered in the next section of the chapter.

A mobility pattern where individuals move from the lower tier of informal employment to salaried formal employment and then to the upper tier of informal employment, often as entrepreneurs or as self-employed, is consistent with the evidence presented above. But there is also evidence of certain segments of informal work being segmented and acting as poverty traps. Extended duration in the informal sector has been shown to yield lower returns for moves into the formal sector (Saha and Sarkar, 1999). It may be, in this case, that after long droughts in the informal labour market, moves within the informal sector are more advantageous. This is linked to what Szerman and Ulyssea (2006) find in Brazil and dub the "informality trap". As the probability of transiting out of informal employment declines rapidly over time, an individual not leaving the informal labour market soon enough risks remaining there for an extended amount of time[7].

119

ISBN: 978-92-64-05923-8 – © OECD 2009

Box 5.1. The Case of Mexico

An OECD Development Centre case study on Mexico reveals interesting trends on earnings mobility there. Using the Mexican Family Life Survey (MxFLS) panel dataset for the years 2002 and 2005, the study confirms that bad jobs, in terms of lower earnings and higher poverty, are found in the informal sector, despite longer working hours for individuals. Informal waged workers yielded the lowest earnings with MXN 1 379 (Mexican pesos) on average with income for the self-employed (MXN 2 016) and the formal waged workers markedly higher (MXN 3 083). One positive finding for informal waged workers was that, on average, they had a shorter journey to work than formally waged workers. As might be expected, self-employed workers had the shortest commute.

Earnings changes between two states of employment (formal-informal) between 2002 and 2005 show that those moving from formal jobs to other formal jobs experienced the biggest gains followed by those moving from informal to formal jobs, those remaining in informal jobs and finally those moving from formal jobs to informal jobs. Similar results were found for women as for men, except that moves to informal jobs in general yielded losses. Moreover, moves by women from informal to formal yielded the largest gains and even larger than those for men. The study also found similar results when considering non-economic variables such as those pertaining to mental health. Mental health symptoms were most severe for those entering or remaining in the informal sector.

Finally, the study demonstrated that levels of informality may change considerably depending on definitions applied for informal employment. Informal employment in the MxFLS is estimated at 48 per cent when using the registration/contract definition, 61 per cent when considering social security coverage and 53 per cent when considering the size of the company.

Source: Laiglesia *et al.* (2008).

The analysis above has limited itself to mobility and increases in earnings, to explain general increases in welfare. Undoubtedly, other forms of welfare-enhancing factors may be linked with mobility, such as educational and health outcomes, career development and recognition. Elements such as job stability, occupational hazard and access to social security are also sure to be of major importance.

While it may be true that mobility may not automatically lead to an increase in earnings, evidence generally points to high earnings mobility within and between sectors in developing countries for the poor. It also highlights a dualistic feature within the informal sector. The upper-tier segment of the informal sector is associated with positive earnings movement and voluntary entry. It is small and competitive. In the lower-tier, free-entry informal labour market, individuals are highly vulnerable to negative shocks and face a rationing problem in quitting informal employment. The next section reviews determinants and economic conditions which may influence whether individuals benefit from being mobile.

MOBILITY OF INDIVIDUALS: STRATEGIES, EFFECTS AND BARRIERS

Why and How People Move

Individuals in developing countries may gain financially by changing jobs and these job changes do not necessarily have to cross the formal/informal divide of the labour market to be positive. This section reviews evidence of labour mobility in developing countries. It gives an overview of aggregate and individual determinants of mobility as well as of how institutions, economic shocks and economic shifts may affect labour mobility. It then turns to individuals who do not, or cannot, move and the barriers some of them face in improving their employment options.

Setting industrialised economies as a benchmark, it can be seen that job mobility forms part of the standard set of efficient labour market principles in these countries (Nickell, 1997), as expected. Yet evidence also points to notable differences even between many of these countries (Ours, 1990).

Table 5.1 also shows that this is the case for developing countries. Intensity levels of mobility[8] for three South American countries are presented, backing the notion that job mobility is also prevalent in developing countries and that rates differ from country to country, even between seemingly similar countries (Bosch and Maloney, 2005). Gong and van Soest (2002) show that in Mexico, mobility between the formal and informal sectors is actually very large compared with other OECD countries, and in some countries such as Ethiopia, mobility rates between these sectors is growing (Bigsten *et al.*, 2007). Moreover, a study on Brazil has shown that job mobility between informal and formal labour markets exhibits similar characteristics as in job-to-job mobility in the US, indicating that in particular cases, segmentation may not be an impediment (Bosch *et al.*, 2007). Conclusively, it can be seen that individuals in developing countries do indeed move fairly frequently, especially when their economic situation is not optimal.

Table 5.1. Geweke, Marshall and Zarkin (1986) Mobility Indexes

	Argentina		Brazil		Mexico	
	Male	Female	Male	Female	Male	Female
Mobility of workers	0.5724	0.6515	0.6973	0.7742	0.7724	0.8224
(Standard Errors)	(0.0111)	(0.0132)	(0.0057)	(0.0068)	(0.0037)	(0.0042)

Note: Reproduced from Table 4 in Bosch and Maloney (2005).

Source: Computations are based on 10 000 Monte Carlo draws.
StatLink ⬛ http://dx.doi.org/10.1787/533735112538

One method used to observe the intensity of mobility between sectors is to produce transition matrices derived from panel data. In this way we can observe the labour market profile of the same individual over time. Sandefur *et al.* (2007) have examined mobility for Ethiopia, Ghana and Tanzania, through the construction of transition matrices, showing the proportion of individuals remaining in the same job or changing sector. They find relatively little mobility. Their study is, however, marred by short time windows for the panel; in two of the three cases, panel surveys were conducted twice within a year. This shows that not all studies using transition matrices find high mobility, but also highlights the need for better and longer panel data as job mobility may be part of a longer term strategy and not necessarily noticeable using short-term data.

ISBN: 978-92-64-05923-8 - © OECD 2009

Box 5.2. The Mexican Case – Transition Between Sectors

For a good example of job mobility intensity rates across segmented labour markets, we return to the Mexican case study conducted by the OECD Development Centre, where the percentage of informal employment has decreased between 1995 and 2007, but where the absolute number of informal workers is still increasing.

Using the Mexican Family Life Survey waves in 2002 and 2005 and following the same individuals in both years, transition matrices between three labour market states (formal, informal, without a job) were constructed.

There is a striking level of transition between formal and informal sector jobs, as defined here by contract status. Only 66 per cent of formal workers in 2002 were still holding formal sector jobs in 2005, with about 18 per cent moving to an informal job and the remainder not working at all. Informal workers too exhibited high mobility, with nearly 20 per cent of them moving to a formal sector job. Notably we observe a relatively higher labour market exit rate for informal workers, with nearly 40 per cent exiting the labour force by 2005. Using different definitions of informality yields similar trends.

Transitions in and out of the formal sector:
(among individuals aged 20 to 60 years old)

Status in 2002	Individuals with or without labour contract			
	2005			
	Formal	Informal	Without job	Total
	(percentages)			
Formal	65.5	18.2	16.3	100
Informal	19.7	42.1	38.2	100
Without job	7.1	7.1	85.8	100
Total	23.9	18.8	57.3	100

Note: Weighted data.

Source: Mexican Family Life Survey. First and second waves (2002, 2005).
StatLink http://dx.doi.org/10.1787/533743345417

Source: Laiglesia *et al.* (2008).

Many industrialised country studies point to the importance of institutions in influencing labour mobility (i.e. Ours [1990]). The context is similar for developing economies. Haltiwanger *et al.* (2008) analyse a sample of 16 industrialised and emerging economies at the firm level and find, when controlling for industry and firm size, that greater hiring and firing costs reduce job turnover. Zenou (2008) also finds that reducing entry costs for firms in developing countries promotes formal employment. He also finds that policies which subsidise the hiring process *decrease* informal employment while policies which subsidise wages *increase* it. Individuals may also be attracted by prospective job satisfaction associated with successful transition into entrepreneurship. Furthermore, the perceived relative benefits of unregistered activity may simply outweigh the risks associated with detection (Arabsheibani *et al.*, 2006). In fact, when a control for taxes on entrepreneurial earnings in South Africa is applied, the wage penalty associated with working in the informal labour market disappears (El Badaoui *et al.*, 2008). For these reasons, individuals may opt out of the formal sector and transit into informal employment.

Economic transition, economic shocks and sectoral shifts play a large role in determining mobility between sectors. In downturns, the formal sector may shrink and force many individuals to transit either into unemployment or informal employment. Informal employment then acts as a buffer to the shock. A comprehensive review by Horton *et al.* (1991) for instance showed that in 12 country case studies, aggregate shifts of labour from formal to self-employment evolved as a form of labour market adjustment during difficult economic periods. This fact is again evidenced in Khamis (2008) for Argentina during the 1999-2002 crisis; unemployed workers were more likely to find employment in the low-skilled, labour-intensive informal sector in Argentina. Between 1993 and 2001 in Argentina, 3.5 per cent of the population between the ages of 15 and 64 transited from unemployment to employment or from employment to unemployment.

ISBN: 9789264044692 © OECD 2008

Moreover, within the subset of the employed, approximately 12 per cent transited between formal sector jobs and informal sector jobs in a six-month time frame (Inter-American Development Bank, 2004). However, in times of rapid expansion the reverse does not necessarily hold. The Bosch and Maloney (2005) study on Mexico showed that the growth period following the Mexican peso crisis accompanied transition into informal self-employment.

Job mobility can, moreover, result from sectoral economic shifts, such as that resulting from the intense transition period experienced in Eastern Europe during the 1990s (Jovanovic and Moffit, 1990; Munich *et al.*, 2005). Evidence from seven Eastern European countries points to the fact that, in the advanced stages of transition, moves into entrepreneurship are prevalent, although mainly undertaken by middle-aged and educated males (Dutz *et al.,* 2001). In the early stages of transition the informal sector serves as a buffer in times of recession, and formal employment is often strictly preferred to informal employment when it is salaried informal employment and not informal self-employment (Pagés and Stampini, 2007; Bernabè and Stampini, 2008). For instance, in the early stages of transition the formal sector may not be large and dynamic enough to accommodate all individuals preferring to work in the formal sector. In the Dutz *et al.* (2001) study the evidence did not show preference for entry into self-employment for CIS countries, where transition efforts are still lagging compared with Eastern European countries; demographic profiles changed little with the rate of entrepreneurship in the CIS countries. Moreover, evidence from Ukraine shows that the number of the involuntarily informally employed is overwhelmingly greater than the voluntarily informally self-employed (Lehmann and Pignatti, 2008). Box 5.3 presents evidence found in an OECD Development Centre case study on the economic transition of Romania.

Box 5.3. **Economic Transition and Mobility in Romania**

The OECD Development Centre report on Romania gives three primary reasons for the persistence of informal employment rates in Romania and the mobility of workers between informal and formal sectors in the country.

First, the economic transition of Romania, through economic restructuring and privatisation, has led to a general move of individuals into informal work. Combined with transition, poor economic growth as well as general increases in poverty and inequality contributed to dimming the prospects of job creation. Romanian emigration may also contribute to levels of informal employment, as many engage in circular movements between origin and receiving country and work informally for short periods of time when back in Romania.

Second, institutional factors in Romania have forced or led many to opt for informal work. Regulations on the labour market, the tax and social security system structure, general bureaucratic nuances combined with corruption are thought to have contributed to this.

Third, social institutions and norms in Romanian society have also played a part in maintaining or leading individuals to the informal labour market. Aspects in this category include the general culture of non-compliance, the lack of trust in public institutions, the negative perception of the state and a general misunderstanding of the social security system.

The combination of these three determinants has led many Romanians to enter voluntarily the informal sector to work.

Source: Parlevliet and Xenogiani (2008).

What Factors Help People Move?

Looking at the characteristics of mobility is important as it provides an identifiable profile of who is likely to move and who is less likely to move, key notions when prescribing policy affecting mobility and poverty. There are several ways to look at the issue, generally by observing individual or aggregate and institutional characteristics. This section will summarise the evidence of individual characteristics which appear to enable and facilitate workers to move in the labour market.

The characteristics of the mobile worker in developing countries are not dissimilar to those found in developed economies. Education and characteristics raising potential human capital drive positively the prevalence of mobility. In general, educated males tend to be more mobile when they are of prime working age. Developing country evidence also points to an important networking component of mobility. Individuals in certain social classes, ethnic groups or with certain education levels seem to be better connected and thus able to move within the upper ranks of the labour market. Additionally, Kumlai (2008) shows that in Thailand, low-paid workers are more susceptible to movement, possibly because they see opportunity to climb the earnings scale.

A very important determinant of individual mobility is investment in human capital, which has been useful in explaining why and how individuals transit between various labour market states both within and across firms (Bartel and Borjas, 1981; Jovanovic and Mincer, 1981; Farber, 1994; Neal, 1999; Topel, 1986 and 1991). Several interpretations have been advanced, the most common being that transit is facilitated by formal education, general or firm-specific training, employer sponsorship and investment in job search (Creedy and Whitfield, 1988). According to classical human capital theory, workers choose their desired level and type of training and this in turn determines individual wages as well as their future prospects for mobility.

The mobility induced by the investment in human capital can itself take shape in various forms: either within a firm (i.e. a promotion or a change of occupation), a change of employer or a change of employment sector. Workers who have undertaken firm-specific training and those with longer tenures in their jobs are most likely to experience upward mobility in their jobs, with an associated increase in their earnings, and are hence less likely to change firms. For this reason, job-to-job mobility is much lower among older workers compared with younger ones. Those who invest more in general training and education are more mobile as their accumulated human capital can be appreciated and compensated outside their firm. Individuals choose an optimal career path depending on their own preferences, expressed by the utility they derive from every possible outcome and their individual characteristics, including education and human capital investment. If the expected benefits in the current job are lower than those in alternative job options, workers may decide to move.

Evidence from Slovenia, for instance, shows that education plays a major role in voluntary labour mobility as well as exits from unemployment during transition periods (Orazem and Vodopivec, 1997). Sorm and Terrell (2000) also examine labour mobility and labour market dynamics in the Czech Republic during this period and find that economic restructuring improved efficiency in the local labour market. Their findings suggest that young individuals and single men were most likely to be involuntarily mobile (change jobs or become unemployed), whereas the relatively more educated were less likely to change jobs and more likely to exit unemployment or job inactivity. In Georgia as well, queuing for a formal job while remaining unemployed is largely a device for educated individuals (Bernabè and Stampini, 2008)[9].

In many developing countries, the lack of transition into formal sector jobs may be due to the short supply of highly skilled individuals. It is often believed that the existence of the informal sector implies a reserve army of workers easily at the disposal of the formal sector. Andersen and Christensen (2006) show this is not necessarily the case in Bolivia where the public sector and the formal private sector compete for a limited number of individuals with the required necessary skills. Their findings suggest that skilled workers may quit their jobs voluntarily while job separations for unskilled workers may be involuntary. Benhassine et al. (2006) have also shown using matched employer-employee data for 11 African countries that the education-wage gap is due more to occupational selection than firm selection (sorting across occupations is more important in explaining the gap than sorting across firms). The study also confirms that returns to experience in Africa are large. Skilled and experienced workers are hence a scarce commodity in developing countries, and in high demand.

ISBN: 978-92-64-05923-8 - © OECD 2009

Box 5.4. Mexico Revisited – Transition Conditional on Human Capital

The Mexican case study portrays the important case of transition between informal and formal sectors conditional on education levels. It is known from employment data in Mexico that more educated individuals tend to be in the formal sector

The two tables below furthermore display transition matrices between various labour market states, for two classes of education levels: individuals with six years or less of formal education and individuals with more than six years of formal education. There are two figures which are striking. The first is that tenure in the best jobs, identified here by salaried jobs with contract, is highest for the educated group: 62.5 per cent of educated individuals were in this category in 2002 and remained in it in 2005, while this figure was 45.7 per cent for the less educated group. The second figure shows that while mobility is high for both groups, what could be termed as bad mobility is more prevalent for the less educated, while the opposite holds for the educated group. Of less educated individuals 26 per cent transited from salaried jobs with contracts to salaried jobs without contracts, nearly twice as many as made the opposite transition (14 per cent). For the educated group only 14.9 per cent transited into salaried jobs without contracts while 23.4 per cent moved to more secure salaried jobs with contracts. In general, less educated individuals also transited more into inactive employment status.

Transitions in and out of formal employment: percentage of individuals with or without labour contracts
(among individuals **with six years or less of education**)

Status in 2002	2005				
	With labour contract and salaried	Without labour contract and salaried	Without labour contract and self-employed	Not working	Total
	(percentages)				
With labour contract and salaried	45.7	26.0	8.7	19.7	100
Without labour contract and salaried	14.0	43.8	15.6	26.6	100
Without labour contract and self-employed	2.8	14.7	53.2	29.3	100
Not working	1.2	5.8	8.5	84.5	100
Total	7.2	14.7	17.1	61.0	100

Transitions in and out of formal employment: percentage of individuals with or without labour contracts
(among individuals **with more than six years of education**)

Status in 2002	2005				
	With labour contract and salaried	Without labour contract and salaried	Without labour contract and self-employed	Not working	Total
	(percentages)				
With labour contract and salaried	62.5	14.9	8.6	14.0	100
Without labour contract and salaried	23.4	41.1	14.9	20.7	100
Without labour contract and self-employed	9.3	14.5	54.4	21.8	100
Not working	13.1	7.5	8.7	70.3	100
Total	30.1	16.0	16.5	37.4	100

Note: Weighted data, based on Mexican Family Life Survey. First and second waves (2002, 2005).

Source: Laiglesia *et al.* (2008)
StatLink 🔗 http://dx.doi.org/10.1787/533768565575

125

ISBN: 978-92-64-05923-8 - © OECD 2009

Migration and Informal Employment

The arguments so far have centred on labour mobility without considering movements over space or distance. *Spatial* mobility, in the form of migration, accounts for an important part of the observed movement in developing countries and is an important employment strategy for poor individuals and households. Therefore another characteristic of the informal labour market includes recently arrived, transitory and circular migrants. Several empirical papers provide evidence of informally employed rural-to-urban migrants such as Meng (2001) for China and Florez (2003) for Colombia.

According to classical economic theory, movement into the informal sector is relatively more common for migrants than non-migrants[10]. Dualistic models of informal labour markets set out to explain the apparent paradox of high rates of migration and relatively poor outcomes for migrants. The Harris and Todaro (1970)[11] model tells us that migration can become a two-step process, with migrants not fortunate enough to find a formal sector job queuing while making a living in the informal sector. The migration of individuals to cities often accompanies economic development, as proximity produces better synergies between economic agents. In such dualistic models (Lewis, 1954; Harris and Todaro, 1970), the informal sector feeds subsistence living and eventually disappears with the advent of industrialisation. This turns out to be a rather one-dimensional approach to explaining migrant informality in urban areas. Among the assumptions of the model, individual productivity in informal work is zero and primarily for subsistence. Traditional dualistic approaches to the labour market fail to account for the competitive, upper-tier informal labour market and the possibility of voluntary entry.

Recent research provides evidence that in some countries, migrant-induced informal labour markets are dynamic and productive. Cornwell and Inder (2004) point to South African evidence that migrants are remarkably adept at finding employment; given the risks and sacrifices they have made to migrate, they are likely to be highly motivated to find work. Meng (2001) also shows that internal migrants in China are not necessarily temporarily entering the informal sector as they wait to transit into the formal sector. Rather, he shows that regardless of whether migrants are self-employed or receive informal wages, both are often better off than in the formal sector. Evidence also points to higher mobility between employers and sectors for migrants than non-migrants; in China it is almost six times that of urban workers (Knight and Yueh, 2004).

While typically rural-to-urban migration may be thought of as forming part of the development process, evidence points to the prevalence of other forms of internal migration. Thus, while internal migration may have once taken the form of one-way schemes, the evidence shows that today migration is increasingly temporary. In both developed and developing countries, a sizeable number of migrants engage in either circular behaviour, returning to rural areas or moving from rural to other rural regions, perhaps for seasonal reasons. As the duration of these episodes is often short, many migrants remain in the informal sector before returning or moving on.

This could be a response, based on preference, to easier travel and increasing information, making it simpler for migrants to cease economic opportunity. De Brauw (2007) finds that in Viet Nam, seasonal migration contributed to household moves out of labour-intensive crops to more profitable capital-intensive crops. It could, on the other hand, also be a consequence of migration policy or land rights policy, as in China (Rupelle *et al.*, 2008). Additionally, while counter-urbanisation[12] has been documented in developed economies, the developing world has also begun to experience urban-to-rural migration. Beauchemin *et al.* (2004) document such trends in Côte d'Ivoire and Burkina Faso as do Andrzejeweski *et al.* (2006) in Ghana. These cases suggest that internal migrants may remain informal, operating temporarily between both urban and rural regions. Policy has also played a role in inciting individuals to engage in urban-to-rural migration; Ciupagea *et al.* (2004) argue that urban-to-rural migration in Romania followed important land reforms; the incentive to reinvest in land encouraged urban dwellers to leave the cities.

ISBN: 978-92-64-05923-8 - © OECD 2009

Zohry (2005) gives an account of entry into informal labour markets from internal migration in Egypt. Many internal migrants in Egypt engage in circular migration (or labour circulation) behaviour, keeping one foot in both regions (or more) while remaining informal. One reason for this is that temporary migrants typically do not change their legal place of residence. This makes it difficult to infer rates of internal migration, or rates of entry into informal labour markets, and thus put in place effective policy measures. He finds that temporary migrants are very poor and often young males, in contrast with Andrzejeweski et al. (2006) who show that circular migrants in Ghana are educated and display no differences along gender lines.

These cases show that internal migration is prevalent yet contains major differences between groups. For instance, while migrants may display higher mobility in urban labour markets than their resident counterparts, this mobility may stem from either voluntary or consequential motives. The mobility of migrants in China, as in the Knight and Yueh (2004) paper cited above, may be high because migrants are simply not able to obtain tenure in *any* job, and therefore must continuously change jobs. Moreover, migrants in China may also not be necessarily looking for a formal job because the chances of obtaining one are slim, and thus investment in job search is more profitable in the informal sector.

These cases also show that, while earnings mobility from internal migration may be positive (for example de Brauw [2007] on Viet Nam), it should be remembered that many migrants are forced into the informal sector, where they are not protected by the state, earn less than urban dwellers and must deal with the tremendous social and psychological costs associated with being away from their home in an uncertain environment. Looking solely at migrant individuals who experienced a change in employment situation a year after an initial survey took place in Australia, Hugo et al. (2006) find that those who changed employers declared themselves as being less satisfied with their employment than those who had changed occupation but remained with the same employer. Moreover, as migration implies a household strategy, the impact this has on household members left behind, who must now deal with the loss of a productive household member, should not be forgotten.

International migration is also a way to improve livelihoods. International migration may have a sizeable impact on informality in developing countries within South-South regional unions. De Vreyer et al. (2007) show that international migration within the West African Economic Monetary Union (WAEMU) zone often leads to informal sector work (at least more likely than for non-migrants), with the majority of migrants being less educated than non-migrants. In contrast, for migrants going to richer countries, education is often an important determinant for labour mobility (see Larson and Mundlak, 1997). Zohry (2005) also adds that increases in border constraints are a major factor in determining the type of migrant and the sector into which he or she self-selects. He makes the case for Egypt by pointing to differing migration policy in Libya and Jordan; in Libya, the relative ease at the border enables Egyptian migrants to engage in circular behaviour – and thus in informal sectors – while in Jordan, a costly work visa is required, forcing a certain level of formalisation.

Irregular migration has been particularly significant in filling labour market shortages in relatively low-paid service sectors in international cities, much of which is informal (Baláz et al., 2004). In Berggren et al. (2007), it is shown that the increasingly stringent migratory system has led to an increase in irregular migration in European OECD countries, with most of these migrants remaining in the informal sector. Munck (2007) adds that this change has led to an increase in trafficking for forced labour, further jeopardising the welfare of these migrants. Irregular migration to the informal sector is also particularly high in the USA where, according to Passel (2005), the numbers exceeded 11 million individuals in 2004, without including regular migrants choosing to work informally.

Another channel by which international migration may positively impact earnings mobility within the informal sector in the sending region is through return migration. Many recent studies (Arif and Irfan, 1997, and Ilahi, 1999, on Pakistan; McCormick and Wahba, 2001, on Egypt; Carletto et al., 2007, and Piracha and Vadean, 2008, on Albania) have provided evidence of individuals leaving informal sector jobs, migrating internationally, and then returning to their home country to set up a business. These types of occupational changes into self-employment often lead to higher earnings.

Job and spatial mobility can therefore provide opportunities for individuals in developing countries to seize better opportunities of employment; evidence shows both forms of mobility accompanying positive earnings mobility, given the right mix of incentives and policy. However, for certain individuals, being mobile is not a possibility and the informal sector remains their only outlet for employment. The next section will look at existing barriers to mobility which may make good jobs inaccessible for certain individuals.

Barriers to Mobility

The analysis so far has focused on individuals with the ability to be mobile, and has dealt with how and why mobility may lead to positive earnings mobility. The other side of the story deals with individuals who are not able, or less able, to be mobile and therefore barred access to better jobs. In general, individuals facing such barriers form the lower tier of the informal sector. The biggest barrier to mobility is the lack of good and productive jobs. The rationing of these jobs means that many individuals will never have the option of obtaining them. Good jobs are not necessarily only those in the formal sector; the better paid, competitive upper-tier informal jobs are also subject to entry barriers, in particular in the form of skills and capital accumulation.

A second reason is the high cost of job search, especially in the absence of unemployment insurance. If good jobs are rationed, then searching for one comes with high opportunity cost as finding a match may take months. Most individuals in developing countries cannot afford to do so and prefer to work, at least from a financial perspective, doing any menial task. They may search for an upgrade part-time rather than devoting full time attention to this task. Rama (2003) and Bernabè and Stampini (2008) show this to be the case in Sri Lanka and Georgia respectively, with wealthier individuals able to queue for good jobs. Evidence of this is consistent with labour market segmentation. For the poorest this may send them into a poverty trap and reinforce their employment situation or lack of it; Bosch and Maloney (2005), moreover, point to evidence that spells of individual duration in unemployment or lower-tier jobs can be a determinant of long-term immobility.

Finally, the level of immobility may simply be a result of self-selection resulting from available capital. The amount of human, but also financial, capital required to enter better paid segments of the labour market makes it difficult for many to access these jobs. Initial conditions (and changes in these), such as the employment status of the household head (Cichello et al., 2003b) or the value of household assets (Barrett and Carter, 2007) can make individuals particularly vulnerable to poverty and immobility. Other factors have been associated with lower mobility rates, such as large initial household size, poor initial education, poor initial asset endowment, poor initial employment access (Klasen and Woolard, 2005, on South Africa), gender and race (Michaud and Vencatachellum, 2003, on South Africa). In support of this view, Chankrajang et al. (2008) provide evidence that entrepreneurs in the formal sector in Ecuador are not necessarily those with the highest levels of wealth, and in fact show that the case may indeed be the reverse: that those who are voluntarily in the informal sector have relatively high wealth. Similarly, those who may transit into informal sector jobs may be those with the means to do so. Therefore the factors that predetermine a higher likelihood of being in bad informal work also affect the likelihood of moving out of bad informal jobs.

In the absence of these three barriers, are there policies or norms which may lead to a disadvantaged system or discrimination for certain individuals? Some individuals face a plethora of barriers in moving to better jobs. Generally, barriers to mobility in this sense can come from a country's social institutions and cultural norms, its legal and institutional climate, geographic barriers or migration policies and/or the lack of infrastructure.

128

ISBN: 978-92-64-05923-8 - © OECD 2009

First, discrimination in the labour market can result either from social institutions (or norms) or from policy (or lack of it). Chapter 4 brought an important component of the informal employment-poverty nexus to the fore: that of gender. Men in general can be more mobile than women. In household migration decisions, for instance, the human capital of men is perceived to be higher than that of women (and thus also their ability to generate income for the household) and therefore it is men who are sent to migrate for work. Many other studies also show that men generally are financially advantaged, more educated and thus display greater rates of labour mobility to better jobs (for instance, Bosch and Maloney, 2005). Bernabè and Stampini (2008) demonstrate that in Georgia women are more likely than men to move to less desirable jobs or exit the labour force altogether.

Funkhouser (1997) finds that pre-labour market characteristics are even more important for women than for men in determining mobility. Women become especially immobile after marriage; in many developing countries, marriage comes with the extra household task of childcare and general household management. Wives are often tied to their husband's location and job status, which may not always be the best fit for her skill set (e.g. Ofek and Merrill, 1997, on the US). Arntz and Assaad (2005) have linked this argument to female job immobility and thus lower earnings in the case of Egypt[13].

Given their socially imposed care workload, women may prefer to opt for employment which is more compatible with their everyday lives. Andersen and Muriel (2007) find that in Bolivia women have a strong preference for the informal self-employment sector, with nearly half of employed women in their sample with this characteristic[14]. What is more surprising, however, is that women make on average 40 per cent less than men in this sector, mostly because they operate on a smaller scale and have less access to capital. While there appear to be strong barriers to overcome to gain greater access to capital (unrealistic terms, few opportunities), the authors also find that women have little incentive to grow their business as they face rapidly decreasing returns to capital.

Other forms of discrimination can also emerge in the labour market. Old age can be a source of immobility; the elderly have typically shown lower rates of job mobility in developed countries (Groot and Verberne, 1997; Huffman and Feridhanusetyawan, 2007; Jorgensen and Taylor, 2008) than their younger counterparts, but also lower levels of pay (Arunatilake and Vodopivec, 2008). As individuals grow older, financial incentives to move shrink and the costs of moving increase. In developing countries, this immobility may play a detrimental role for non-migrating household members left behind in rural regions. For instance, the mass migration of rural Chinese to the coast has left many elderly folk behind to deal with agricultural duties and other household management chores, while remaining in the lower tiers of informal employment. Finally, discrimination on the labour market may also come in the form of race, ethnicity and physical disability.

The legal and institutional climate of a country might also lead to the inability of certain individuals to be mobile in labour markets. Mobility may rest with institutional restrictions on movement. This is the case in China, for instance, where the *Hukou* system of registration makes it difficult for rural individuals to obtain good jobs in urban areas (Box 5.5). Combined with the restriction of movement, the lack of a portable social security system diminishes the incentive of many individuals to move, as social security access features importantly in individual welfare. Other legislated distorting practices may also affect the opportunity to seize job opportunities, such as rigid property rights or housing market legislation. Complicating the issue is the fact that these formal institutions interact closely with informal institutions and norms, previously covered.

129

Box 5.5. Migration Policy and Discrimination in China

An OECD Development Centre case study on two rural counties in China[15] revealed the degree and impact of migration from rural to urban regions of China. Both counties have seen continued growth of migration rates to economic centres, with currently more than 40 per cent of the population classified as migrants in each county.

Most migrants are men with junior middle school education and most find work in low-skilled jobs such as construction. The returns to migrating are high compared with opportunities back home and a large percentage of their savings is remitted back home. Although migrant employment is increasingly stable compared with previous years, and also compared with opportunities back home, most migrants have little intention of staying in the cities in the long term and plan to return and invest their savings and put to use their accumulated human capital. Many engage in temporary and circular migration movements.

Migration policy in China is highly influenced by the country's *Hukou* registration system. The system essentially classifies individuals as being rural or urban, which then determines where they have access to public services and consequently their level. This has had major ramifications in solidifying segmentation in the Chinese labour market; individuals with urban *Hukou* registrations have been able to access better formal jobs, which provide better pay, occupational safety, better conditions and social security. Migrants, on the other hand, self-select into the informal labour market and engage in circular migrant behaviour, so as to keep their rights to political participation in their region of origin and over their land in the community from which they originally came. This decision clearly compromises their welfare while they are in urban areas, as trying to obtain a good job in an urban region of China with a rural *Hukou* status can undoubtedly lead to disadvantages (Gagnon *et al.*, 2008).

Source: OECD and Development Research Centre of the State Council, China (2009) for country case study on China.

THE ROLE OF POLICIES AND INSTITUTIONS IN EXPANDING MOBILITY AND OPPORTUNITY

Governments have a number of tools with which to help people into better jobs and out of poverty. One of these is a set of measures to create both demand and supply, provide job assistance and help small businesses. There is some dispute as to how effective these programmes have been. Education and training are also fields where governments are active. Social policies to help those must vulnerable have a role to play, not least in helping migrants. Initiatives to lessen the rural-urban divide and to make life easier for migrants should be fostered.

Labour Market Policies

Active labour market policies (ALMPs), common in OECD countries, can have an important influence on the upward mobility of individuals. In general these policies seek to increase the quality of the labour supply (e.g. training), increasing and creating new demands for labour (e.g. employment subsidies) and improving general matching mechanisms or job-assistance schemes (e.g. public employment services). They also target more general benefits associated with labour market participation, such as the benefits associated with inclusion in working society. While ALMPs generally target the formal sector, the general purpose is to improve the probability of individuals finding a *good* job while increasing overall productivity and individual earnings. As developing country contexts undoubtedly pose a different set of labour market dynamics, some ALMP frameworks may be difficult to apply in these countries (Betcherman *et al.*, 2000). In light of this, Albrecht *et al.* (2006) observe that even if ALMPs are targeted towards the formal sector, they can have important spillover effects on the informal sector.

ALMPs aim to maintain or increase employment rates through job creation (demand) by supporting public works, self-employment, wage subsidies and training (supply), yet a primary role for improving labour mobility lies in public employment services (PES). Mobility incentives and other employment services can reduce structural labour market imbalances between jobs

130

and unemployed job-seekers by improving matching and sorting mechanisms between workers and employers; they serve as a sort of brokerage function between the two. These mechanisms are relatively inexpensive and offer high rewards; by providing job seekers with information on work opportunities (even informal), they can shorten unemployment spells. In developing country contexts, community organisations are often in a position to play this mediating role in the informal sector.

ALMP programmes which can affect mobility include micro-enterprise development programmes such as loans, fiscal advantages and labour-hiring facilitation. This type of intervention affects relatively older and better educated individuals, although surveys demonstrate that participation rates are low among the unemployed (Abrahart et al., 2000 on Middle Eastern and North African (MENA) countries). Nevertheless, in the developing country context, governmental institutions and non governmental organisations (NGOs) alike could help mediate the links between individual desire to create a start-up and informational and capital needs. Labour market policies, particularly micro-enterprise support programmes, need to take into account preferences compatible with individual lifestyles. The Andersen and Muriel (2007) study on Bolivia showed that households preferred to operate several identical micro-enterprises in order to spread economic risks but also market influence, while remaining under a certain taxation threshold[16].

The overall consensus on ALMPs is mixed. Public employment services and job assistance schemes have been shown to have negative effects on employment since they make being unemployed less unattractive in a study of 15 industrialised countries (Estevao, 2003). On the other hand, a number of such policies targeting job assistance schemes have been successfully implemented. In the case of Romania, they have helped reduce unemployment drastically since 1991 (Ecobici and Paliu-Popa, 2007).

Minimum wage legislation may also affect job mobility, especially in developing countries. Ghana's minimum wage policies during the 1970s and 1980s, for instance, reduced formal sector employment opportunities and sent workers into the informal sector (Jones, 1998). Khamis (2008), on the other hand, has shown that employers react differently to different levels of legislation. In Argentina, a change in the legislated minimum wage had a stronger impact on wages in the informal sector than in the formal sector. It would appear in this context that employers may want to comply with some labour legislation but ignore other elements, such as social security. The reason for this, however, is not fully understood as it is unclear whether this is a sign that there is in fact no segmentation in the labour market and that informal labour market employers have to pay the going wage rate.

Educational, Skill-Building and Training Policies

An area of policy intervention which enjoys public support and great returns is that of education, skill-building and training. Active labour market policies tend to apply training programmes in order to stimulate employment and create job mobility. One reason for their popularity is due to the evidence linking low levels of education and bad informal work (Loayza, 2007). As Radwan (2006) puts it, the skills of the labour force do not always match the requirements of the labour market. In migration also, education programmes seem to find support for policy intervention. In reviewing possible pro-poor paths for Ghana, Al-Hassan and Diao (2007) describe the low levels of education and skills of migrants from the north of the country migrating to the south. With such low levels of skills brought to the labour market, the returns, including remittances, are also inherently low.

131

As educated individuals are less likely to be working informally, ALMPs aim at providing training support, either through direct provision or through informational sources, such as licensing (Betcherman et al., 2000). Different training support is needed depending on whether the individual has been unemployed in the long or short term, is young or is a displaced worker. Efficient implementation requires co-ordination between the public and private sectors as well as a thorough analysis of demand and supply of the current labour market, including the informal sector.

A relevant example of a concerted effort in this field is the Technical and Vocational Skills Development (TSVD) initiative in Africa (OECD, 2008), present mostly in the informal sector. It is hoped that such programmes will lead not only to moves out of informal work, but mostly to moves out of *bad* jobs. The initiatives touch upon several key elements of labour mobility previously mentioned, such as programmes for skills development outside urban areas, where low levels of education and high levels of informality are found (especially true in the context of rural-urban migration). In terms of matching and co-ordination schemes, they facilitate moves from informal to formal sectors by creating recognition standards for skills that are useful and learned outside the formal sector, as well as support for entrepreneurship initiatives. Further analysis on TSVD in Africa is elaborated in the following chapter (see Box 6.1 in Chapter 6).

In addition to the TSVD initiatives for the informal sector, the World Bank also advocates Grassroots Management Training (GMT) programmes, which specifically target vulnerable groups (Monnet, 2002). GMT programmes, often aimed at women, are used to train individuals to create marketable products to be sold and used as a basis for informal self-employment. The work provides them not only with extra revenue, but also with technical and managerial training, access to markets and capital, and it leads to diversification, improved credit-worthiness, an improvement in literacy and varying levels of economic and social empowerment. It is often an important first step towards entry into a competitive labour market.

Social Policies

Anti-discrimination policies should be integrated into labour market policies, preventing harmful and potentially divisive practices against elderly individuals, women and certain ethnic groups. Specific policies should also be devised to take into account specific aspects of each group. For instance, the difficulty experienced by the elderly in being mobile and adopting new ways of societal living, or female family-related aspects such as child-bearing, must be considered when drafting policies affecting mobility. Policies should also create the incentive to create diverse and multi-ethnic workplaces to enhance a better understanding of society and minimise stereotypes.

A second important social issue relating to the spatial mobility of individuals is the level of portability of basic state-sponsored social services. For instance, rural-urban migration in China bars migrants in urban regions who wish to retain their rural rights from obtaining the same rights they enjoyed in their rural hometowns. Migration is used by households as a tool for risk diversification, helping them escape exposure to financial risk which keeps them in danger of poverty traps. It may in this sense be seen as a form of social protection, although it fails to protect them in other fundamental ways. Migrants arriving in urban areas, other regions or states or in irregular situations in other countries lack access to vital services such as sickness and unemployment insurance. As such, internal social security policies should include portability across the country, so as to ensure that the individual move from bad jobs to good jobs also includes access to health, education and housing, allowing the individual the same basic amenities that other similar workers enjoy. The immediate benefits to the individual will spill over into productivity and inclusion into normal working society. In fact, in some developed economies, social security schemes are devised to accelerate job mobility (Usuki, 1999). Such portability of social services can also be envisaged for moves between formal and informal work.

132

The implications resulting from helping individuals to be mobile will certainly bring to light a host of social issues regarding vulnerable groups who may not be able to participate in the advantages it provides. As such, policies must consider that certain non-mobile groups may need to be targeted for subsidies, and other forms of protection and policy schemes must be devised so as not to worsen the plight of vulnerable groups.

Migration Policies

A main policy element in this area is to increase the circulation of information and improve communication facilities. As a result, information on employment opportunities, living conditions and daily urban costs will not grow to mythological proportions in rural regions. This is only one side of the coin, however, as push factors also need to be dealt with. Rural region investments, taxation benefits, employment creation and adequate infrastructure in health, education and transport in rural areas can help diminish the pressures for people in the countryside to leave home. In summary, what is needed is the reduction in geographical inequality in living conditions. In developed economies, and even some developing economies, balanced rural-urban growth projects have incited individuals to return to or stay in rural regions.

A certain level of internal labour readjustment is necessary, however, to achieve economic growth and development. Policies can help mitigate this migratory pressure and its prevalence to drive individuals towards low living conditions in the informal labour market. Internal migration can be exploited as an agent for development while remaining compatible with existing social protection schemes. Several solutions have been proposed and different initiatives have been put in place; overall they aim to improve the plight of migrants, by improving infrastructure to accommodate their needs and by facilitating mobility and circular migration.

The growing mobility of individuals in China and India, where circular migration appears to be emerging as the dominant form of spatial mobility (Deshingkar, 2006), provides a good starting point to evaluate potential policies. Several projects have been launched in these countries (for instance, the UK Department for International Development (DFID) funded the Andhra Pradesh Urban Services Project), mostly with the aim of improving the lives of migrants, identifying vulnerable groups and generating local development.

In general, policies promoting internal migration and development target the removal of barriers to movement, the provision of social protection (and security) for migrants, the improvement of remittance-sending infrastructure, the creation of migrant-friendly services, the building of relevant labour market skills for migrants and the implementation of systematic migration surveys. Migrant community organisations, for instance, can play an important role – similar to that of hometown associations (HTAs) in the international context – in providing vital information on job opportunities, housing, migrant rights and support groups. Moreover, some regions of the world, such as East Africa, have displayed greater regional mobility following regional integration (Ammassari *et al.*, 2004). Mobility in this specific case was facilitated by the combined creation of regional passports and regional migration arrangements. Similar observations are found in West Africa, where as many as 8 million Sahelians can be found in other parts of West Africa (Black *et al*, 2004). Such mobility-facilitating policies, however, must take into account the rapid change of labour resources, including the important loss of rural labour and the degradation of land resources because of its conversion to cropland.

CONCLUSION

The chapter addressed three questions. In seeking to answer them, it has analysed important issues relating to mobility, informal employment and poverty: the role of mobility in bringing people out of bad informal employment; the conditions that need to be in place for people to move and which lead to positive earnings increases; and policy lessons. The overall finding is that in many cases, mobility for the poor yields increases in their earnings, even when mobility does not transcend the division between formal and informal labour markets. In other words, there is much more mobility within informal employment than one would expect. This is the good news. The rather bad news, and this relates to the second point, is that mobility bringing about an increase in earnings depends on individual characteristics (education, networks, etc.) as well as a healthy economic, institutional and social environment. Many barriers can prevent people from moving out of bad jobs, such as discrimination and formal and social institutions.

ISBN: 978-92-64-05923-8 - © OECD 2009

The impact of these barriers on individuals can have devastating effects on welfare and poverty, violating individuals' rights to occupational and social protection as well as their right to decent work and equal treatment.

On the other hand, there are also cases in which mobility is not the voluntary choice of an individual but rather imposed by force or unfortunate circumstances. Economic shifts and shocks force people to change jobs. Those most likely to gain from these changes are those with high human capital profiles. For spatial mobility, policy plays an important role in determining who gains and who loses. Internal migrants may find it difficult to integrate and fully gain by a move, while international return migrants may find it difficult to reintegrate into their home country.

As a consequence of the above, policy makers need to recognise that informal labour markets are fundamentally linked to the welfare of many poor individuals, who rely on them for a living and who do not necessarily possess the option of opting out of them. Policies which shape labour markets, educational opportunities, social cohesion, social security and migration must therefore take into account poverty implications in both the formal and informal sectors. They must also recognise that labour mobility and development are intrinsically linked, and that this link is growing in no small because of the large windfalls associated with the current wave of globalisation.

ISBN: 978-92-64-05923-8 - © OECD 2009

NOTES

1. A *bad* job is one that does not allow a worker holding that job to exit poverty and eliminate the risk of falling into poverty. So defined, *good* jobs are typically formal jobs with social protection but may also include better paid informal jobs, to the extent that better pay can compensate for the additional risk borne by the worker.

2. Earnings differentials by themselves are insufficient to prove or disprove segmentation along the formal-informal division because of unobservable characteristics of both workers and jobs (see Maloney, 1998).

3. In practice, distinguishing according to job characteristics is best approximated by discriminating according to more readily available information on employment status.

4. Cichello *et al.* (2003*a*) show this to be the case for Indonesia, South Africa (for the province of KwaZulu-Natal) and Venezuela with respect to income: the poor enjoyed the largest absolute gains. Khor and Pencavel (2006) also find unconditional convergence but moreover show that income mobility across quintiles or clusters in China in the 1990s was greater than that in the United States. A similar finding in China was shown in Deng *et al.* (2006) for the period 1991-95, and in Indonesia and Peru by Grimm (2005).

5. Other papers have followed and have confirmed this view. Günther and Launov (2007) for Côte d'Ivoire and Bernabè and Stampini (2008) for Georgia confirm the existence of a dualistic informal sector characterised by a free-entry segment, where earnings are low relative to a competitively entered upper-tier segment.

6. This fact corresponds to a similar finding in the state of Georgia in the US. Hotchkiss and Quispe-Agnoli (2008) show that an increase in the supply of labour in the informal sector is associated with decreases in low-skill wages, mostly for other informal workers.

7. In fact, Yamada (1996) finds evidence of competitive earnings and voluntary choice into the informal self-employment sector in Peru, but only those who did well stayed in the sector. Others left for more suitable employment.

8. These are summary measures derived from transition matrices.

9. Pagés and Stampini (2007) however, find that wage differences and mobility patterns between informal and formal sectors were not different across skill levels in three transition countries (Albania, Georgia and Ukraine) and three emerging market countries in Latin America (Argentina, Mexico and Venezuela). The study suggests that segmentation in these countries is not solely caused by policies affecting low-skilled job sectors.

10. Although contingent on skill composition and human capital characteristics, urban residents nevertheless have better knowledge of local labour conditions, not to mention social networks, which enable them to obtain formal jobs.

11. The Harris and Todaro model supposes that during this process, armies of informal workers gather within the confines of urban sprawl waiting to obtain a job in the formal sector. The framework centres on potential migrants who compare the expected utility of migrating with the expected utility of remaining in the rural economy. This "urban reserve army" acts as a buffer and an adjustment mechanism between rural and urban wages, which in turn leads to migratory pressure. The size of the informal labour market is then a function of the urban wage; if the wage is set high, the amount of formal workers is small and the informal labour market larger.

12. Also commonly referred to as *population deconcentration*.

ISBN: 978-92-64-05923-8 – © OECD 2009

13. When economic hardship hits the household, women may even increase their labour supply and enter the lower segment of the informal labour market in addition to covering other tasks. This may also lead to positive social effects; an increase in earnings, such as this, may accompany increases in household bargaining power (Khan and Qureshi, 1996).

14. A similar conclusion is made in Laiglesia *et al.* (2008).

15. The two counties were Yi county in Hebei province and Zizhong in Sichuan province

16. Similarly, the Pagés and Stampini (2007) study on transition in Latin American countries showed that there was little movement between self-employment and formal salaried jobs, even when conditioning on education levels. Benefits, amenities but also compatibility with individual lifestyle surely account for this observation.

ISBN: 978-92-64-05923-8 - © OECD 2009

REFERENCES

ABRAHART, A., I.KAUR and Z. TZANNATOS (2000), "Government Employment and Active Labor Market Policies in MENA in a Comparative International Context", Paper presented at MDF3 in Cairo.

ALBRECHT, J., L. NAVARRO and S. VROMAN (2006), "The Effects of Labor Market Policies in an Economy with an Informal Sector", *IZA Discussion Papers* No. 2141, Institute for the Study of Labor (IZA), Bonn. Available at: http://ideas.repec.org/p/iza/izadps/dp2141.html.

AL-HASSAN, R. and X. DIAO (2007), "Regional Disparities in Ghana: Policy Options and Public Investment Implications", *IFPRI Discussion Paper* No. 693, IFPRI, Washington, D.C.

AMMASSARI, S., R. BLACK, S. MOUILLESSEAUX and R. RAJKOTIA (2004), "Migration and Pro-Poor Policy in West Africa", *DRC Working Paper C8*, Sussex Centre for Migration Research, University of Sussex, Brighton.

ANDERSEN, L. and B.J. CHRISTENSEN (2006), "Labor Mobility in Bolivia: On-the-job Search Behavior of Private and Public Sector Employees", *Development Research Working Paper Series 01/2006,* Institute for Advanced Development Studies, La Paz. Available at: http://ideas.repec.org/s/adv/wpaper.html.

ANDERSEN, L. and B. MURIEL (2007), "Informality and Productivity in Bolivia: A Gender Differentiated Empirical Analysis", *Development Research Working Paper Series 07/2007,* Institute for Advanced Development Studies, La Paz. Available at: http://ideas.repec.org/p/adv/wpaper/200707.html.

ANDRZEJEWSKI, C., H. REED and M. WHITE (2006), "An Event-History Analysis of Internal Migration in Ghana: Determinants of Interregional Mobility among Residents of Coastal Central Region", mimeo, Population Studies and Training Center, Brown University, Providence, RI.

ARABSHEIBANI, G., F. CARNEIRO and A. HENLEY (2006), "On Defining and Measuring the Informal Sector", *IZA Discussion Papers* No. 2473, Institute for the Study of Labor (IZA), Bonn.

ARIAS, O. and M. KHAMIS (2008), "Comparative Advantage, Segmentation and Informal Earnings: A Marginal Treatment Effects Approach", *IZA Discussion Papers* No.3916, Institute for the Study of Labor (IZA), Bonn.

ARIF, G.M. and M. IRFAN (1997), "Return Migration and Occupational Change: The Case of Pakistani Migrants Returned from the Middle East", *The Pakistan Development Review*, Vol. 36(1), pp.1-37, Pakistan Institute of Development Economics, Islamabad. Available at: http://ideas.repec.org/s/pid/journl.html.

ARNTZ, M. and R. ASSAAD (2005), "Constrained Geographical Mobility and Gendered Labor Market Outcomes Under Structural Adjustment: Evidence from Egypt", *World Development,* Vol. 33, No. 3, pp. 431-454.

ARUNATILAKE, N. and M. VODOPIVEC (2008), "Population Aging and the Labor Market: The Case of Sri Lanka", *World Bank SP Working Paper* No. 0821, World Bank, Washington, D.C.

AVIRGAN, T., J. BIVENS and S. GAMMAGE (eds.) (2005), *Good Jobs, Bad Jobs, No Jobs,* Economic Policy Institute, Washington, D.C.

BALÁŽ, V., C. WALLACE and A.WILLIAMS (2004), "International Labour Mobility and Uneven Regional Development in Europe: Human Capital, Knowledge and Entrepreneurship", *European Urban and Regional Studies*, Vol. 11(1): 27-46.

BARRETT, C. and M. CARTER (2007), "Asset Thresholds and Social Protection: a 'Think-Piece'", *IDS Bulletin*, Vol. 38, No. 3, pp. 34-38(5). Available at: www.ingentaconnect.com/content/ids/idsb;jsessionid=1uavghevadza4.alexandra.

BARTEL, A. and G. BORJAS (1981), "Wage Growth and Job Turnover: an Empirical Analysis," *in* S. ROSEN (ed.) *Studies in Labor Markets,* pp. 65-90, University of Chicago Press, Chicago.

137

BEAUCHEMIN, C., S. HENRY and B. SCHOUMAKER (2004), "Rural-Urban Migration in West Africa: Toward a Reversal? Migration Trends and Economic Conjuncture in Burkina Faso and Côte d'Ivoire", Paper submitted for the 2004 PAA Annual Meeting in Boston.

BENHASSINE, N., M. FAFCHAMPS and M. SÖDERBOM (2006), "Job Sorting in African Labor Markets", Centre for the Study of African Economies, WPS/2006-02, University of Oxford, Oxford.

BERGGREN, E.L., B. LIKIC-BRBRIC, G. TOKSÖZ and N. TRIMIKLINIOTIS (eds.) (2007), "Irregular Migration, Informal Labour and Community: A Challenge for Europe", Shaker Publishing, Maastricht.

BERNABÈ, S. and M. STAMPINI (2008), "Labour Mobility during Transition: Evidence from Georgia", *LICOS Discussion Papers* No. 20608, LICOS - Centre for Institutions and Economic Performance, K.U.Leuven. Available at: http://ideas.repec.org/s/lic/licosd.html.

BETCHERMAN, G., A. DAR, A. LUINSTRA and M. OGAWA (2000), "Active Labor Market Programs: Policy Issues for East Asia", *SP Discussion Paper* No.0005, World Bank, Washington, D.C.

BIGSTEN, A., T. MENGISTAE and A. SHIMELES (2007), "Mobility and Earnings in Ethiopia's Urban Labor Markets: 1994-2004", *World Bank Working Paper* No. 4168, World Bank, Washington, D.C.

BLACK, R., L. MCLEAN HILKER and C. POOLEY (2004), "Migration and Pro-Poor Policy in East Africa", *University of Sussex DRC Working Paper C7,* Sussex Centre for Migration Research, University of Sussex, Brighton.

BOSCH, M., E. GONI and W. MALONEY (2007), "The Determinants of Rising Informality in Brazil: Evidence from Gross Worker Flows", *IZA Discussion Papers* No. 2970, Institute for the Study of Labor (IZA), Bonn. Available at: http://ideas.repec.org/p/iza/izadps/dp2970.html.

BOSCH, M. and W. MALONEY (2005), "Labor Market Dynamics in Developing Countries: Comparative Analysis Using Continuous Time Markov Processes", *Policy Research Working Paper Series 3583,* World Bank, Washington, D.C.

BRAUW, A. DE (2007), "Seasonal Migration and Agriculture in Vietnam", *Working Paper* No. 07-04, Agricultural and Development Economics Division, Food and Agriculture Organization of the United Nations (FAO-ESA), Rome. Available at: http://ideas.repec.org/p/fao/wpaper/0704.html.

CARLETTO, C., B. DAVIS, T. KILIC and A. ZEZZA (2007), "Investing Back Home: Return Migration and Business Ownership in Albania", *Policy Research Working Paper Series* No. 4366, World Bank, Washington, D.C.

CHANKRAJANG T, K.P. HUYNH and D. JACHO-CHAVEZ (2008), "Entrepreneurship and Informality in Ecuador: Choice or Necessity?", mimeo.

CHEN, M. and J. VANEK (2005), "Informal Employment: Rethinking Workforce Development", *in* AVIRGAN, T., J. BIVENS and S. GAMMAGE (eds.), *Good Jobs, Bad Jobs, No Jobs,* Economic Policy Institute, Washington, D.C.

CICHELLO, P., G. FIELDS, S. FREIJE, M. MENENDEZ and D. NEWHOUSE (2003a), "For Richer or For Poorer? Evidence from Indonesia, South Africa, Spain and Venezuela", *Journal of Economic Inequality,* Vol. 1(1), pp.67-99.

CICHELLO, P., G. FIELDS, S. FREIJE, M. MENENDEZ and D. NEWHOUSE (2003b), "Household Income Dynamics: A Four Country Story", *Journal of Development Studies* 40(2), pp. 30-54.

CICHELLO, P., G. FIELDS and M. LEIBBRANDT (2005), "Earnings and Employment Dynamics for Africans in Post-Apartheid South Africa: A Panel Study of KwaZulu-Natal", *Journal of African Economies,* 14(2): pp.143-190.

CIUPAGEA, C., S. ILIE and R. NEEF (2004), "Economic and Social Developments in Romania since 1990", *in* NEEF, R. and R. ADAIR (eds.), *Informal Economies and Social Transformation in Romania*, Lit Verlag, Münster.

CORNWELL, K. and B. INDER (2004), "Migration and Unemployment in South Africa: When Motivation Surpasses the Theory", Monash University Working Paper 02/04, Monash University, Victoria.

ISBN: 978-92-64-05923-8 - © OECD 2009

CREEDY, J. and K. WHITFIELD (1988), "Job Mobility and Earnings: An Internal Labour Market Analysis", *Journal of Industrial Relations*, Vol. 30, No. 1, pp.100-117.

DENG, Q., S. LI and H. YING (2006), "Income Mobility in Urban China", *Economic Research Journal* (in Chinese), 10: pp.30-43.

DESHINGKAR, P. (2006), "Internal Migration, Poverty and Development in Asia", Paper presented for the Asia 2015 Conference in London.

DURYEA, S., G. MARQUEZ, C. PAGÉS and S. SCARPETTA (2006), "For Better or for Worse? Job and Earnings Mobility in Nine Middle and Low-Income Countries", *Brookings Trade Forum, Global Labour Markets*, pp. 187-203.

DUTZ, M., C. KAUFFMANN, S. NAJARIAN, P. SANFEY and R. YEMTSOV (2001), "Labour Market States, Mobility and Entrepreneurship in Transition Economies", *EBRD Working Paper* No. 65, EBRD, London.

ECOBICI, N. and L. PALIU-POPA (2007), "Active Measures for Stimulating the Employment of Labour Force and its Impact in the Gorj County", *MPRA Paper* No. 8043, p.19, Munich Personal RePEc Archive, Munich.

EL BADAOUI, E., E. STROBL and F. WALSH (2008), "Is There an Informal Employment Wage Penalty? Evidence from South Africa", *Economic Development and Cultural Change*, Vol. 56, pp.683-710.

ESTEVAO, M. (2003), "Do Active Labor Market Policies Increase Employment?", *IMF Working Paper* No. 03/234, International Monetary Fund, Washington, D.C.

FARBER, H.S. (1994), "The Analysis of Interfirm Worker Mobility", *Journal of Labor Economics,* Vol.12 (4), pp. 554-593.

FIELDS, G. (1990), "Labour Market Modelling and the Urban Informal Sector: Theory and Evidence", *in* TURNHAM, D., *The Informal Sector revisited*, OECD, Paris.

FLOREZ, C. (2003), "Migration and the Urban Informal Sector in Colombia", Paper prepared for the Conference on African Migration in Comparative Perspective in Johannesburg, 4-7 June.

FUNKHOUSER, E. (1997), "Mobility and Labor Market Segmentation: The Urban Labor Market in El Salvador", *Economic Development and Cultural Change*, Vol. 46, No. 1, pp. 123-153.

GAGNON, J., T. XENOGIANI and C. XING (2008), "Are All Migrants Really Worse off in Urban Labour Markets? New Empirical Evidence from China", mimeo, OECD Development Centre, Paris.

GEWEKE, J., R.C. MARSHALL and G. ZARKIN (1986), "Mobility Indices in Continuous Time Markov Chains", *Econometrica*, Econometric Society, Vol. 54(6), pp. 1407-23.

GONG, X. and A. VAN SOEST (2002), "Wage Differentials and Mobility in the Urban Labour Market: A Panel Data Analysis for Mexico", *Labour Economics*, Vol. 9(4), pp.513-529. Available at: http://ideas.repec.org/a/eee/labeco/v9y2002i4p513-529.html.

GRIMM, M. (2005), "Removing the Anonymity Axiom in Assessing Pro-Poor Growth", *Discussion paper* No. 113, Ibero-America Institute for Economic Research, Georg-August-Universität Götingen.

GROOT, W. and M.VERBERNE (1997), "Aging, Job Mobility and Compensation", Oxford Economic Papers, New Series, Vol.49(3), 380-403.

GÜNTHER, I. and A. LAUNOV (2007), "Competitive and Segmented Informal Labor Markets", *Ibero America Institute for Economic Research (IAI) Discussion Paper* No. 153, Ibero-America Institute for Economic Research. Available at: http://ideas.repec.org/p/got/iaidps/153.html.

HALTIWANGER, J., S. SCARPETTA and H. SCHWEIGER (2008), "Assessing Job Flows Across Countries: The Role of Industry, Firm Size and Regulations", *NBER Working Paper* No. 13920, National Bureau of Economic Research, Cambridge, MA.

HARRIS, J.R. and M. TODARO (1970), "Migration, Unemployment and Development: A Two-sector Analysis", *American Economic Review*, No. 60.

139

HORTON, S., R. KANBUR and D. MAZUMDAR (1991), "Labour Markets in an Era of Adjustments: An Overview", *World Bank Working Paper* No. 694, World Bank, Washington, D.C.

HOTCHKISS, J. and M. QUISPE-AGNOLI (2008), "The Labor Market Experience and Impact of Undocumented Workers", *Federal Reserve Bank of Atlanta Working Paper* No. 2008-7c, Atlanta, GA.

HUFFMAN, W. and T. FERIDHANUSETYAWAN (2007), "Migration, Fixed Costs, and Location-Specific Amenities: A Hazard Analysis for a Panel of Males", *American Journal of Agricultural Economics*, Vol. 89, No. 2, pp. 368-382.

HUGO, G., S. KHOO and P. MCDONALD (2006), "Temporary Skilled Migrants' Employment and Residence Outcomes: Findings from the follow-up survey of 457 visa holders", Third Report on the Australian Research Council Linkage Project "Temporary Overseas Migration to Australia", Prepared for the Australian Department of Immigration and Multicultural and Indigenous Affairs, Canberra.

ILAHI, N. (1999), "Return Migration and Occupational Change", *Review of Development Economics,* Vol. 3, No. 2, pp. 170-86.

INTER-AMERICAN DEVELOPMENT BANK (2004), *Good Jobs Wanted*, Inter-American Development Bank, Washington, D.C.

JONES, P. (1998), "The Impact of Minimum Wage Legislation in Developing Countries where Coverage is Incomplete", *Centre for the Study of African Economies Working Paper* No. 98-2, Oxford University, Oxford.

JORGENSEN, B. and P. TAYLOR (2008), "Older Workers, Government and Business: Implications for Ageing Populations of a Globalising Economy", *Economic Affairs*, Vol. 28, No. 1.

JOVANOVIC, B. and J. MINCER (1981), "Labor Mobility and Wages", *in* S. ROSEN (ed.) *Studies in Labor Market,* University of Chicago Press, Chicago.

JOVANOVIC, B. and R. MOFFITT (1990), "An Estimate of a Sectoral Model of Labor Mobility", *Journal of Political Economy*, University of Chicago Press, Vol. 98(4), pp. 827-52, August.

KHAMIS, M. (2008), "Does the Minimum Wage have a Higher Impact on the Informal than on the Formal Labor Market? Evidence from Quasi-experiments", *IZA Discussion Paper* No.3911, Institute for the Study of Labor (IZA), Bonn.

KHAN, A. and A.F. QURESHI (1996), "Women in the Informal Labor Market in a Developing Metropolis: Agents for Change", *Takemi Fellows Working Paper* RP 112, Harvard School of Public Health, Boston, MA.

KHOR, N. and J. PENCAVEL (2006), "Income Mobility of Individuals in China and the United States", *Economics of Transition*, 14 (3), pp. 417-458.

KLASEN, S. and I. WOOLARD (2005), "Determinants of Income Mobility and Household Poverty Dynamics in South Africa", *The Journal of Development Studies*, Vol.41, No.5, pp. 865-897.

KNIGHT, J. and L.YUEH (2004), "Job Mobility of Residents and Migrants in Urban China", *Journal of Comparative Economics*, No.32, 637-660.

KUMLAI, J. (2008), "Job Mobility and Low Wage Change in Thailand's Labor Market: Analysis Using a Multinomial Endogenous Switching Model", conference on RC28 Spring Meeting 2008, organised by the European University Institute, Florence, Italy, pp.15-18. Available at: http://kumlai.free.fr/RESEARCH/ARTICLE/lowwage.pdf.

LAIGLESIA J. DE, R. BAZILLIER, R. S. PARKER, U. QUIJANO, A. SARACHO, A. and V. SCORZA (2008), "Work and Well-being in Mexico: Integrating the Employment and Social Development Agendas", Draft report prepared for the Mexican Ministry of Social Development, OECD Development Centre, Paris.

LARSON, D. and Y.MUNDLAK (1997), "On the Intersectoral Migration of Agricultural Labor", *Economic Development and Cultural Change*, Vol. 45, No. 2, pp. 295-319.

ISBN: 978-92-64-05923-8 - © OECD 2009

LEHMANN, H. and N.PIGNATTI (2008), "Informal Employment Relationships and Labor Market Segmentation in Transition Economies: Evidence from Ukraine", *ESCIRRU Working Paper* No. 03, German Institute for Economic Research, Berlin.

LEWIS, W. A. (1954), "Economic Development with Unlimited Supplies of Labour", *The Manchester School*, Vol. 22, pp. 139-191.

LOAYZA, N. (2007), "The Causes and Consequences of Informality in Peru", *Working Paper Series* No. 2007-018, Banco Central de Reserva del Peru.

MALONEY, W. (1998), "Are LDC Labor Markets Dualistic?", *World Bank Policy Research Working Paper* No. 1941, World Bank, Washington, D.C.

MALONEY, W. (1999), "Does Informality Imply Segmentation in Urban Labor Markets? Evidence from Sectoral Transitions in Mexico", *The World Bank Economic Review*, Vol. 13, No.2, pp.275-302.

MARCOUILLER, D., V. RUIZ DE CASTILOLA and C. WOODRUFF (1997), "Formal Measures of the Informal-Sector Wage Gap in Mexico, El Salvador and Peru", *Economic Development and Cultural Change*, Vol. 45, No. 2, pp. 367-392.

MCCORMICK, B. and J. WAHBA (2001), "Overseas Work Experience, Savings and Entrepreneurship amongst Return Migrants to LDCs", *Scottish Journal of Political Economy*, Vol. 48 No. 2, pp. 164-78.

MENG, X. (2001), "The Informal Sector and Rural-Urban Migration - A Chinese Case Study", *Asian Economic Journal,* Vol. 15, No. 1, pp. 71-89(19). Available at: www.ingentaconnect.com/content/bpl/asej;jsessionid=73smghcd2t4j8.alexandra.

MICHAUD, P-C. and D. VENCATACHELLUM (2003), "Human Capital Externalities in South Africa", *Economic Development and Cultural Change,* Vol. 51(3), pp. 603-628.

MONNET, M. (2002), "Key Labor Market Issues", World Bank Institute, Presentation made for the Social Protection Learning Program, January-March, Washington, D.C.

MOSCARINI, G. and K.THOMSSON (2008), "Occupational and Job Mobility in the U.S.", *Scandinavian Journal of Economics*, Vol. 109, Issue 4, pp. 807-836.

MUNCK, R. (2007), "Irregular Migration and the Informal Labour Market: the 'Underside' of Globalisation or the New Norm?" *in Irregular Migration, Informal Labour and Community: A Challenge for Europe*, Shaker Publishing, Maastricht.

MUNICH, D., J. SVEJNAR and K. TERRELL (2005), "Returns to Human Capital under the Communist Wage Grid and During the Transition to a Market Economy", *Review of Economics and Statistics,* 2005, Vol. 87, No.1, pp.100-123.

NEAL, D. (1999), "The Complexity of Job Mobility among Young Men", *Journal of Labor Economics*, Vol. 17(2), pp. 237-61.

NEEF, R. and R.ADAIR (eds.) (2004), *Informal Economies and Social Transformation in Romania*, Lit Verlag, Münster.

NICKELL, S. (1997), "Unemployment and Market Rigidities: Europe versus North America", *Journal of Economic Perspectives,* 11(3):5-74.

OECD (2008), *African Economic Outlook*, OECD Development Centre, Paris.

OECD and DEVELOPMENT RESEARCH CENTRE OF THE STATE COUNCIL, CHINA (2009), "Migration and Poverty Alleviation in China", joint report between the OECD Development Centre, Paris, and the Development Research Centre of the State Council, China, Beijing, forthcoming.

OFEK, H. and Y. MERRILL (1997), "Labor Immobility and the Formation of Gender Wage Gaps in Local Markets", *Economic Inquiry*, Vol. 35, pp. 28-47.

ORAZEM, P.F. and M. VODOPIVEC (1997), "Value of Human Capital in Transition to Market: Evidence from Slovenia", *European Economic Review*, Vol. 41, No. 3-5, pp. 893-903.

141

Ours, J. van (1990), "An International Comparative Study on Job Mobility", *Labour*, No. 4 (3), pp. 33-55.

Paci, P. and P.Serneels (eds.) (2007), *Employment and Shared Growth: Rethinking the Role of Labor Mobility for Development,* World Bank Publications, Washington, D.C.

Packard, T. (2007), "Do Workers in Chile Choose Informal Employment? A Dynamic Analysisof Sector Choice", *World Bank Policy Research Working Paper* No. 4232, World Bank, Washington, D.C.

Pagés, C. and M. Stampini (2007), "No Education, No Good Jobs? Evidence on the Relationship between Education and Labor Market Segmentation", *IZA Discussion Paper 3187,* Institute for the Study of Labor (IZA), Bonn.

Parlevliet, J. and T. Xenogiani (2008), "Report on Informal Employment in Romania", *Working Paper* No. 271, OECD Development Centre, Paris.

Passel, J. (2005), *Estimates of the Size and Characteristics of the Undocumented Population,* Pew Hispanic Centre, Washington, D.C.

Piracha, M. and F. Vadean (2008), "Return Migration in Albania", OECD Development Centre Case Study, mimeo.

Radwan, S. (2006), "Good Jobs, Bad Jobs and Economic Performance with Reference to the MENA Region", Presentation made at the World Bank, 19 June.

Rama, M. (2003), "The Sri Lankan Unemployment Problem Revisited", *Review of Development Economics*, Vol. 7(3), pp. 510-525.

Rosen, S. (1981), (ed,) *Studies in Labor Markets,* pp. 65-90, University of Chicago Press, Chicago.

Rupelle, M. de la, Q. Deng, S. Li and T. Vendryes (2008), "Land Rights and Rural-Urban Migration", *China Perspectives*, No. 2. Available at: www.cefc.com.hk/perspectives.php?cat=1

Saha, B. and S. Sarkar (1999), "Schooling, Informal Experience and Formal Sector Earnings: A Study of Indian Workers", *Review of Development Economics*, Vol. 3, No. 2, pp. 187-199.

Sandefur, J., P. Serneels and F.Teal (2007), "Poverty and Earnings Mobility in Three African Countries", *in Employment and Shared Growth*, World Bank, Washington, D.C.

Sorm, V. and K. Terrell, (2000), "Sectoral Restructuring and Labour Mobility: A Comparative Look at the Czech Republic", *IZA Discussion Paper* No. 111, Institute for the Study of Labor (IZA), Bonn.

Szerman, D. and G.Ulyssea (2006), "Job Duration and the Informal Sector in Brazil", Instituto de Pesquisa Economica Aplicada da Brazil, mimeo, Brasilia.

Topel, R.-H. (1986), "Job Mobility, Search and Earnings Growth: A Reinterpretation of Human Capital Earnings Functions", *Research in Labor Economics*, 8(A), pp.199-233.

Topel, R.-H. (1991), "Specific Capital, Mobility and Wages: Wages Rise with Job Seniority", *Journal of Political Economy*, University of Chicago Press, Vol. 99(1), pp. 145-76.

Usuki, M. (1999), "Will Defined Contribution Pension Plans Really Encourage Labor Mobility?", NLI Research Institute, No. 135, Tokyo.

Vreyer, P. De, F. Gubert and F. Roubaud (2007), "Migration, Self-Selection and Returns to Education in the WAEMU", DIAL *Working Paper DT/2007/10*, Paris.

Yamada, G. (1996), "Urban Informal Employment and Self-Employment in Developing Countries: Theory and Evidence", *Economic Development and Cultural Change*, Vol. 44, No. 2, pp. 289-314.

Zenou, Y. (2008), "Job Search and Mobility in Developing Countries: Theory and Policy Implications", *Journal of Development Economics*, Vol. 86(2), pp. 336-355.

Zohry, A. (2005), "Interrelationships between Internal and International Migration in Egypt: A Pilot Study", *Research Reports Series,* Development Research Centre on Migration, Globalisation and Poverty, University of Sussex, Brighton.

ISBN: 978-92-64-05923-8 - © OECD 2009

Dealing With Informal Employment: Towards a Three-Pronged Strategy

Johannes Jütting and Juan R. de Laiglesia

ABSTRACT

Informal employment presents a challenge for low and middle-income countries as they strive to fight poverty and make possible fairer societies. Dealing with informal employment requires moving away from piecemeal approaches and moving beyond current mainstream thinking. An integrated policy framework is needed that follows three core axes: *i)* the creation of more formal jobs; *ii)* the provision of incentives for formalisation for those who voluntarily opt out of the formal system to become integrated into the modern economy; and *iii)* the protection and promotion of those workers who are stuck in bad jobs. Giving informal workers more rights, access to services and a voice, while reminding them of their duties as citizens, will not only contribute to development and the reduction of poverty but will also bring societies closer together.

ISBN: 978-92-64-05923-8 - © OECD 2009

INTRODUCTION

The previous chapters have shown that informal employment is normal, in the sense that it is pervasive and a common feature of labour markets in developing countries. Roughly speaking the proportion of people who work in informal employment varies between one-third and more than two-thirds, with the phenomenon most common in sub-Saharan Africa, followed by Asia and Latin America. Contrary to common belief, economic growth alone will not eliminate it. On the contrary, in some parts of the world informal employment has even increased, in spite of growing economic growth[1]. Indeed, informal employment, rather than disappearing with development, has transformed itself in both developed and developing countries. New forms have emerged, such as the increasing representation of women in informal bad jobs and the informalisation of formal work. This trend manifests itself in various forms, for example in "false self-employment" and the practice of "envelope" payments[2] (Parlevliet and Xenogiani, for Romania, 2008; OECD, 2008a).

This concluding chapter seeks to develop a strategy to deal with the practice of informal employment. It takes into account the lessons learnt from the previous chapters but also draws on conclusions from various policy experiences in different countries. The main lesson from past policy experience is that neither the "bulldozer approach" – crushing informal activities by force, the economic policy equivalent of Operation *Murambatsvina* by which Harare's slums and shanty towns were massively demolished in 2005 – nor the "laissez faire/do nothing approach" are good enough. Both are most likely to lead to adverse effects and increased poverty. An integrated policy framework is needed, built around three core policy objectives: *i)* increasing the number of good formal jobs; *ii)* providing incentives for formalising informal jobs; and *iii)* affording those excluded from the formal labour market with the necessary means to become more productive and improve their risk management. To put this framework into practice a three-pronged strategy is needed: *i)* to offer incentives to become formal to those who are in the upper tier of informal employment; *ii)* to make available the necessary means (legal, financial, social) to those who are excluded from the formal labour market (lower tier) to enable them to become more productive, while in parallel helping them improve their risk management through offering basic social services and fostering institutions for social security; and *iii)* to promote the creation of formal jobs for all workers.

For all countries the creation of more formal jobs is an important challenge, but also a huge and long-term one. While the long-term policy objective should indeed be to move the economy and labour relations towards formality[3], it is equally important to recognise that the transition to formal employment will take a very long time and that for most people in the world "informal is normal" will remain the reality for decades to come. Whether there should be a greater focus on the "upper" part of informal employment or the "lower tier" depends on country-specific conditions, and gathering enough statistical evidence is critical to an appropriate diagnostic of informal labour in a given country. The truth is that conventional policy prescriptions fall short of understanding the complexity and heterogeneity of informal employment and thereby risk neither promoting productivity nor reducing poverty.

Far from there being a clear divide, many shades of grey are to be found between formality and informality. No generally applicable policy framework can account for the diversity of situations. Indeed, an important policy prescription is to unbundle the different elements that characterise informal work and address each of them with appropriate policies. These can then be regrouped by the tier of informality they are most critical in addressing. In that sense, the framework presented in this chapter is not a recipe for policy. Rather, it is the collection of essential ingredients, organised to highlight the most important distinctions within informal employment.

The rest of this chapter presents a simple policy framework mapping out the three-pronged strategy towards informal employment with policies focusing on all informal workers, the upper tier and the lower tier. Using this framework, the main part of the chapter is then devoted to presenting the different policies in greater detail as well as the lessons learnt from country

ISBN: 978-92-64-05923-8 - © OECD 2009

experience worldwide. The chapter concludes with a few general lessons related to the need to improve policy coherence, its linkage to institutional reforms and the necessity of embedding reforms in a wider debate about the relationship between the citizens and the state.

A SIMPLIFIED POLICY FRAMEWORK

The aim of the policy framework in Figure 6.1 is to give a structured overview of the various policy arenas related to informal employment and how these policies target the different forms of workers in an economy. The proposed three-pronged strategy differentiates between policies geared towards all workers, the lower tier and the upper tier of those informally employed. With this it moves from very general non-targeted policies to very specific policy interventions.

Figure 6.1. Three-Pronged Strategy Dealing With Informal Employment

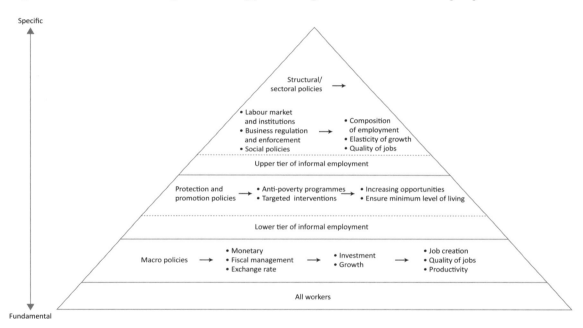

Source: Authors' own illustration.

Most important, this policy framework underlines the need for internal policy coherence. First, informal employment generates social and economic problems that call upon much more than labour or social policies alone. Macroeconomic policies, fiscal policies and generally the structural composition of value added and wealth creation are critical in steering the economy towards more and better jobs. Second, numerous interactions are to be found between actions in different policy domains. The most notable is probably the interplay between labour and social security policies on the one hand and social assistance policies on the other. Informal employment presents a challenge in extending the reach of the state to sections of the population that are often very large.

ISBN: 978-92-64-05923-8 - © OECD 2009

Macroeconomic Factors for Increasing Formal Jobs

To start with, the creation of more formal jobs demands close attention to monetary, exchange rate and fiscal management policies as they affect employment composition and productivity through their ability to stimulate (or dampen incentives for) investment and growth. Aggregate demand and investment have an important effect on the availability of good jobs in an economy. Whereas there is an emerging consensus on the role that employment has to play for effective poverty reduction and on the fact that it should be better reflected in the design of the Poverty Reduction Strategy Papers, a debate has emerged around the issue of whether there is a need to revisit the prevailing orthodoxy in macroeconomic policy to better account for the reality of labour markets in developing countries[4]. McKinley (2008) for instance argues that a macroeconomic framework that focuses only on stability can be at odds with the objective of employment creation if public investment is reduced or hampered, in particular in strategic sectors, and if not enough attention is paid to expanding productive capacity and mobilising domestic resources. Fiscal policy is also of critical importance in any strategy to deal with informal employment. While the importance of informal employment for the revenue side of fiscal policy has been stressed for a long time, less attention has been paid to the expenditure side – an issue that will be discussed in greater depth in the following section.

Beyond policies that have wide-ranging impacts on the economy and that, as such, will affect both the rate of total employment creation and the composition of employment in the economy, the proposed framework rests on the hypothesis that appropriate policies need to be designed to respond to the situation of each of the two tiers of informal employment. As such, individual policy measures addressing each of the two tiers might have many common points from one country to the next. On the other hand, the policy mix will differ markedly across countries as a function of local institutions and labour market outcomes.

In respect of policies to address the poverty and mobility of people working in the lower tier of informal employment, policies to enhance equity are of crucial importance. They are made up of two different sets of policies and instruments: poverty reduction programmes and targeted interventions such as providing social assistance. They have a direct impact on poverty and social protection through either direct employment creation in public works schemes or the provision of benefits (in kind or cash) to those outside formal social security schemes. In recent years programmes have emerged that combine both elements – the provision of assistance in a moment of crisis and an investment in human capital to break the intergenerational transfer of poverty. Conditional cash transfer programmes are examples of the latter and are getting more and more prominence. They are characterised by their twin objectives of providing for the immediate needs of the poor and of breaking the transmission of poverty from one generation to another by investing in the human capital of the children of the beneficiary families. To achieve these, they combine a cash transfer mechanism, a targeting system and a set of conditions, normally related to school attendance and compliance with healthcare programmes.

The main objective of policies targeted at the upper tier of informal employment is to generate a set of incentives that make formal employment more attractive from an individual perspective. Such incentives can come from both carrots and sticks, and will have to comprise in most cases both elements: lowering the cost of formality and providing better benefits on the one hand while at the same time strengthening the enforcement of existing rules to ensure improved compliance. Policies that affect business regulation and enforcement, as well as the design of labour market institutions, are of primary importance.

While this framework can be applied to all countries regardless of their current development status, the importance of the different policy packages varies according to the degree of informal employment in a country. Taking the example of a poor country with more than 80 per cent of informally employed, creating more and better good jobs and tailor-made policies for the lower tier should have greater weight in the policy mix. The situation is quite different in a middle-income developing country with fewer than 50 per cent informally employed where most workers move between formal and informal jobs.

ISBN: 978-92-64-05923-8 - © OECD 2009

ELEMENTS OF THE THREE-PRONGED STRATEGY

Macroeconomic Policies: A Key Driver for the Creation of Better Jobs

Macroeconomic policy has an economy-wide impact and is therefore relevant for all workers. Through their ability to stimulate or dampen investment and growth, macroeconomic policies have a crucial impact on job creation, employment composition and productivity. Whereas there is an emerging consensus that macro-polices are indeed of crucial importance for employment creation, the specific impact on the composition of employment is an unresolved question (Cook *et al.*, 2008).

What could be referred to as orthodox macroeconomic policy fixes a number of objectives and instruments to attain these objectives, including institutional arrangements. In this view, macroeconomic stability features as a key objective, and price stability as one of the critical targets to be met, along with sustainable debt management and financial discipline. This means that the objective of creating more and better jobs often comes second. Among the six key determinants for pro-poor growth identified by the World Bank macroeconomic stability features prominently alongside well-defined property rights, trade openness, a good investment climate, well-functioning labour markets and broad access to infrastructure and education (Cord, 2007).

Faster growth to cut poverty

There is agreement that faster growth that is more pro-poor is needed to halve extreme poverty and achieve the first Millennium Development Goal. However, the role of the macroeconomic policy framework and its implications in terms of labour market outcomes are the subject of controversy. Two related issues stand out in this debate: whether low inflation targets are over-emphasised, and the role of public expenditure, especially of public investment.

Critics of the orthodox approach claim that inflation targets that are too low and too rigid are inappropriate in countries that have narrow economic bases and lack price indexation mechanisms because they will respond more to external shocks even when these can be managed without recourse to monetary tightening. In this view, not only are tight inflation-targeting frameworks unnecessary but they are also counterproductive, as they can lead to deflation with the risk of initiating a downward spiral of prices, profits and incomes. They argue for a macroeconomic framework that grants more attention to employment creation, possibly accepting moderate levels of inflation[5] (McKinley, 2008; Gottschalk, 2008).

Public spending and its composition have a key role to play in directing spending towards areas that will make growth more pro-poor (basic infrastructure and other public goods are important components, as are basic economic and judicial infrastructure and institutions). On the one hand, tight control of the public purse as proposed by orthodoxy might limit investment. On the other hand, Toye (2008) argues that the Keynesian justification for expansionary fiscal policy (through its multiplier effect on consumption) hardly applies to a developing countries context with very different forms of employment, with many self-employed and limited mobility between sectors. He argues against relaxing inflation control as this would make public service delivery and spending more difficult to plan.

The Growth Report of the Commission on Growth and Development (2008) also highlights macroeconomic stability as an important ingredient for growth. While the report acknowledges that macroeconomic instability might cut off private investment, it also underlines that there is disagreement on what it means exactly and how to achieve it. The report refers to policy trade-offs mentioned above, i.e. public spending, debt and inflation control.

ISBN: 978-92-64-05923-8 - © OECD 2009

Fiscal policies

Within the overall macroeconomic framework, fiscal policies play a particularly important role for employment outcomes. Public spending has a critical role to play in ensuring that public goods are provided in adequate quantity and quality. On the revenue side, taxes affect the degree of informal employment in a number of ways. First, high payroll taxes and social security contributions increase formal labour costs and incentives to hire or work (fully or partly) undeclared. These are particularly worrying from a poverty standpoint when they are regressive, because the lowest-earning workers will have greater incentives to opt out of formality, thereby increasing their risk of falling into poverty. Regressive social security regimes can emerge not only by design, but also *de facto* when certain bundled services are not accessible to groups of workers (e.g. because of deficient health infrastructure in rural areas or when childcare costs are mutualised via social security). Second, the tax structure, in particular differences in the taxation of self-employed income or business profits compared with labour income, provides incentives to under-declare wages by the employer or for workers to declare themselves as self-employed even when in a dependent employment relationship, thereby forgoing the protections afforded to formal employees. Third, a complex tax system increases compliance costs and incentives to evade taxes. Other things being equal, higher labour taxes are associated with more informal employment, although the extent to which tax rates are enforced and the quality of governance also play a crucial role (see OECD [2008*b*] for a full discussion).

Structural and Sector Policies: Creating More Formal Jobs and Providing the Right Incentives

Towards employment-intensive growth

Policies focusing on infrastructure, labour markets, business regulations, rural development or on specific sectors have an influence on the employment elasticity of growth and on the incentives for formalising informal jobs. The multiple segmentation of labour markets in developing countries has three main implications for the relationship between growth, informal employment and poverty reduction (Hull, 2008):

1) Growth alone is not sufficient to address informal employment in economies with segmented labour markets and limited mobility as it might occur only in those sectors where the good jobs are already to be found[6]. In other words, to have an impact on informality, growth must occur in those sectors in which the informally employed are located or to which they have access.

2) Growth in those sectors with less productive jobs might simply lead to an increase of informal employment and not to a reduction. There is some evidence that the evolution of informal employment is in many cases indeed pro-cyclical. This behaviour can result from demand shocks that affect mainly non-tradeable sectors where informal employment is more prevalent (Fiess *et al.*, 2006).

3) Easing mobility from bad jobs to good jobs through structural policies is crucial. As discussed in Chapter 5, barriers to more mobility could lie, among other factors, in social institutions, as well as limitations caused by insufficient infrastructure and geography. A potential solution to this could be managed migration better to match supply and demand for good jobs.

In respect of which sector could best lead people into better jobs, the evidence is inconclusive. Using a sample of countries, Gutierrez *et al.* (2007) find some heterogeneity within manufacturing and agriculture with respect to offering "more productive" and "less productive" jobs. While overall they find that manufacturing seems to be associated with more productive jobs, in Latin America employment-intensive growth in manufacturing is not robustly correlated with poverty reduction.

Hull (2008) develops a hands-on framework that aims at helping policy analysts in identifying sectoral patterns of growth that are mostly correlated with poverty reduction in a given country

ISBN: 978-92-64-05923-8 - © OECD 2009

setting. The empirical evidence suggests, however, that while increasing job opportunities in the most productive sectors has some merits, especially if policies to facilitate mobility are implemented at the same time, structural policies should also address bottlenecks in less productive sectors. This could include improved services to small and medium enterprises, the strengthening of off-farm activities and the development of rural-urban linkages.

Structural policy that contributes to strengthening the linkages between rural and urban development will most likely affect the creation of more and better jobs. Globalisation forces have contributed to an increased linkage between the rural hinterland and urban centres around the world. Increased trading opportunities, lower transaction costs facilitating market exchange, and decentralised government structures revolutionise the structure, depth and quality of linkages. The dramatic increase in urbanisation, with accelerating urban poverty and exploding urban labour markets, poses a huge challenge to create more jobs for the inflow of young workers (Betchermann, 2002).

A more balanced development path would reduce the pull factors encouraging rural to urban migration. In order to improve rural-urban linkages von Braun (2007) suggests: *i)* fostering and promoting innovations in agriculture and related on-and off farm activities; *ii)* improving the infrastructure (transport, communication) to lower transaction costs; *iii)* developing market institutions that enable the poor to participate; and *iv)* tackling the political economy of reform in decentralised policy making by giving more influence and better services to the poor. A recent report by the OECD (2006) on "Promoting Pro-Poor Growth: Agriculture" highlights the need to "promote investments in higher productivity activities and links to new market opportunities in urban centres and in regional and global markets".

Unlike the propositions above, such a "balance" does not solely reside on the sectoral composition of growth but on the geographical balance. Balanced growth in that sense does require increased agricultural productivity but also the creation of more and better non-agricultural jobs also in rural areas.

A better business climate, stronger rules enforcement, more inclusive labour market institutions

The main aim of policies targeting the upper tier of informal employment is to put incentives in place that make formalisation more attractive from an individual perspective. Informal employment is voluntary for these workers, in the sense that they are not rationed out of the formal economy. This is not to say that upper-tier informal workers are rich (or even that they are not poor). As discussed in Chapter 3, the choice of informality at the individual level is made under a number of constraints, including the quality of accessible formal sector jobs.

This should ideally be done with the classical carrot and stick approach: lowering the cost of formalisation and providing better benefits on the one hand while at the same time strengthening the enforcement of existing rules to ensure improved compliance. But focusing on the individual cost-benefit assessment of formality is not sufficient: policy also needs to address the shortcomings of the institutional setup.

There is a strong link between the regulatory costs that businesses face and the extent of informality. In particular, the higher the cost of establishing a formal firm, the greater the share of output or employment in informal sector firms (Auriol and Warlters, 2005; Djankov *et al.,* 2002). Where the costs of establishing a formal firm are high, many entrepreneurs will fail to register their firms formally, either with the government's business registry or for tax, social security or labour regulation purposes. Reducing the cost of establishing a formal firm can increase the level of formality among firms and increase the likelihood that employees are subsequently registered for taxes and social security purposes.

How this can be done is shown by the recent experience of Czech Republic, Hungary, Korea, Mexico, Poland, Slovakia and Turkey, all of which have made significant progress in simplifying business start-up regulations over the past five years, reducing both the average number of

149

days required to register a business and the cost of doing so (OECD, 2008a). For example, in 2005 the Czech Republic simplified the registration process by introducing standard application forms for business regulation and a "silence is consent" rule whereby applications not approved after five days are automatically approved. Slovakia cut business start-up costs over the course of a few years by transferring the responsibility for approving business registrations from judges to court clerks, introducing standard documents, clarifying the grounds for rejecting registration applications and simplifying tax registration procedures. In Turkey, a number of steps in the business registration process were combined into one and delegated to chambers of commerce. Application forms were also standardised and shortened and registry officers given better training (Bruhn, 2008; Kaplan et al., 2007). Single-window services that bundle a number of procedures can also help limit the cost of registering a new business, as in the case of Mexico's SARE (Sistema de Apertura Rápida de Empresas).

There is a range of benefits to firms operating in the formal sector. To the extent that formal sector institutions (such as banks and the legal system) operate effectively, they can provide incentives for the formalisation of small informal firms, overcoming some of the costs of operating in the formal sector and promoting business growth in the longer term. Informal firms often have limited access to credit, hindering future growth potential. For example, banks may require evidence of formal registration in order to approve a loan, while inaccurate or non-existent book-keeping may make it difficult for informal businesses to convince potential creditors about the financial viability of the enterprise or the existence of assets to use as collateral for loans. Therefore the strength of formal sector institutions, and especially financial markets, is critical in providing incentives to formalise[7].

Effective enforcement of tax, social security and labour regulation must be a fundamental component of any policy package aimed at reducing informal employment in all countries. Enforcement effectiveness can be improved in a number of ways. First, well-designed regulation and transparent administration makes it easier for firms and individuals to comply with legal requirements and should increase voluntary compliance. Second, sufficient resources, including well-trained inspectors or auditors and resources to support their work, should be allocated to enforcement activities. Third, risk-assessment methods should be used to identify firms or individuals most likely to be informal and allow limited resources to be used most efficiently (OECD, 2008a).

Labour inspection services also play a vital role in combating informal employment because, in many countries, they are the only government bodies with the authority to investigate breaches of labour regulations in workplaces. Labour inspectors can also play an important educative role by working with firms and workers to encourage compliance. International studies of best practice highlight a number of characteristics of high-quality, well-functioning labour inspection services. These include adequate resources (both staff and infrastructure); recruitment and training policies designed to attract and retain high-quality inspectors; central administration to improve consistency and reduce duplication; preventative targeting of firms based on risk; integration of different types of inspections to reduce the inspection burden on business; and a focus on prevention and education as well as enforcement (Schrank and Piore, 2007; ILO, 2006; Treichel, 2004).

While easing business registration and improving the enforcement of existing, established rules are broadly accepted as means to address informal employment, the role of labour regulations and labour market institutions and their link to informal employment are the subject of great controversy. Several studies seem to suggest that more rigorous labour regulations lead to an increase in informal employment (Heckman and Pagés, 2004)[8], but others call these findings into question (Berg and Kucera, 2008). The advocates of the former view argue that cross-country evidence suggests that stringent labour regulations and their enforcement are positively related to the size of the informal sector of countries (e.g. Loayza et al., 2005; Almeida and Carneiro, 2006). High minimum wages contribute to the cost of formal employment and are associated with lower formal-sector employment, at least in countries where the minimum wage is binding in the formal sector (e.g. Carneiro [2004] and Lemos [2004] for Brazil; Infante et al. [2003], for Chile; Jaramillo [2005] for Peru; Hamidi and Terrell [2001] for Costa Rica;

ISBN: 978-92-64-05923-8 - © OECD 2009

Bell [1997] for Colombia; Jones [1998] for Ghana). In most cases, the fall in formal-sector employment caused by higher minimum wages is accompanied by an increase in informal-sector employment, so that overall, higher minimum wages are associated with a higher share of informal employment. However, in countries where minimum wages are less binding in the formal sector, there appears to be little evidence of an impact on formal employment (Bell, 1997; Hamidi and Terrell, 2001).

There is evidence to suggest that informal workers benefit *de facto* from the protection of minimum wages, at least in some countries (Saget, 2006). Even in informal employment, typically a sizeable proportion of workers earn the minimum wage. In other cases, the relationship between wages of formal and informal employees is looser, with earnings of informal workers being at different levels but increasing with increases in the minimum wage. Such developments have been observed for Brazil for workers without a signed labour card (a usual indicator of informality), for informal workers in Argentina, for farm workers and domestic workers in South Africa and to a lesser extent in some Indian states[9].

The impact of labour market institutions (minimum wage, hiring and firing procedures, collective bargaining) on the size of informal employment is inconclusive. As referred to in Chapter 3, Freeman (2007) in his review concludes that it is not yet possible to establish a causal relation between labour market institutions and employment outcomes and pinpoints many methodological problems.

Improving the benefits of formalisation, fighting corruption and improving governance

Improving governance standards and combating corruption can play an important role in reducing informality by increasing the perceived and actual benefits to taxpayers of paying taxes. Frey and Torgler (2007) find that people are less likely to evade taxes if they think that others are paying their fair share, suggesting that publicising good tax behaviour could play a role in a strategy to improve compliance. Perceptions about the quality of government services can also influence tax and social security compliance (Slemrod, 2007). Taxpayers feel less guilt about evading taxes if they think that tax revenues are being misused, either through corruption or incompetence. A number of empirical studies find a positive link between trust in government or governance quality and tax compliance or formality (e.g. Friedman *et al.*, 2000; Frey and Torgler, 2007; Hanousek and Palda, 2002).

Beyond narrow taxation issues, the benefits of formality are mainly associated with market opportunities and productivity-enhancing public goods on the one hand, including law and order, contract enforcement, and services such as health, education or housing provision on the other. Improving the quality of these services and aligning the services provided with their perceived cost can also help establish new links between citizens and the state.

If workers have some say in whether or not they are employed formally, the perception that they receive less in benefits (from social protection schemes or public services financed out of general taxation) than they pay in contributions or taxes may be a factor in encouraging informality or under-declaration. For countries with social insurance schemes where contributions are linked to formal employment, access to social protection can be considered as a benefit of working formally. For those workers who are financially able to contribute and are provided with the choice of working formally or not incentives for formalisation may be improved by increasing the link between contributions and benefits.

The perception of a link between contributions and benefits may be particularly relevant in the case of pensions and, to a lesser extent, unemployment insurance, which can be considered deferred wages. The benefits to workers of contributing to pension and unemployment insurance will depend both on the ease of access to benefits (i.e. the eligibility conditions) and on the value of benefits (i.e. the replacement rates). Different groups of workers may have different perceptions of the benefits of contributing to social protection depending on the quality of the service provided and on their discount rate. For example, young workers may prefer current

151

consumption to making contributions to a pension scheme that will have little pay-off until many years into the future: hence the importance not only of returns, but also of the transparent management and prudential rules of pension funds. This highlights an important role for governments in increasing awareness of the benefits of social protection and public services.

What is true for citizens and workers holds also for firms: Safavian and Wimpey (2007) find that firms are more likely to use informal credit when they are exposed to corruption or where they find the regulatory environment onerous. Batra *et al.*, (2003), cited in Straub (2005), find that perceptions of poor protection of property rights and more corruption lead to greater informality among firms. Although hardly automatic, incentives for firms to establish their business formally are conducive to their registering their workers.

Protecting and Promoting Those in the Lower Tier

An increase in the quantity and quality of jobs created, and incentives for those jobs to be created or become formal, can, in the long run, lead to labour relations becoming more formalised. But informal labour markets are themselves segmented. To alleviate and durably reduce poverty in the lower tier of informal employment, it is necessary to implement policies specifically designed to provide workers with better opportunities and with better tools to manage risk.

Education and training policies

Improving skills, especially of those who are working in the lower tier of informal employment, is essential. The combination of globalisation and technological progress has led to increased demand for skilled workers and increased returns to skills. As a consequence, income differentials between skilled and unskilled workers have increased dramatically, leading to larger inequality in those countries where skills themselves are unequally distributed (World Bank, 2001). Many low income countries in sub-Saharan Africa (SSA) face a vicious circle of low education and skills, low productivity and poverty. Only one fifth of boys and girls of secondary school age in these least-developed SSA countries attend school. The better jobs, i.e. the more productive ones offering decent pay, security and social protection, are often those that require a certain level of skills. The Commission on Growth and Development (2008) argues strongly in favour of investing in education on efficiency and equity grounds. The controversial issue today, though, is how best to allocate resources within the educational sector and how to increase the quality of teaching and improve outcomes.

Upgrading skills is not only about educating the future labour force, but also about providing training to those currently working. In respect of education and training for those working informally, a recent report by the French agency Agence Française de Développement (Walther, 2007) stresses the following three points:

— The need to offer training early on and acknowledge the fact that informal employment may be the only training, conducted on the job, some people get.

— Restructuring traditional apprenticeships to combine theory and practice. Various initiatives are currently taking place within the informal sector to transform traditional apprenticeships into dual apprenticeships. See Walther (2007) for details.

— Stressing the role of local governments in providing training in the informal sector as public vocational education and training focus mostly on skills needed in the formal sector, and neglect current labour market needs in Africa.

The priority of improving the quality and availability of training means that it is necessary to focus on reforming education and training systems so that they provide the skills and competences that will be needed to boost the growth of decent work in the formal economy (e.g. see the objectives of the revised South African National Qualification Framework in 2007[10]). Policy responses need to place emphasis on increasing the access of the poor to training, upgrading

ISBN: 978-92-64-05923-8 - © OECD 2009

apprenticeship training, and improving the relevance of training in public institutions. This could involve strengthening co-ordination and partnerships with the private sector and combining institution-based education and training with self-financed and self-regulated enterprise-based learning, i.e. formal apprenticeship.

Box 6.1. Technical and Vocational Training in Africa

The AEO (African Economic Outlook) 2008 Report (OECD, 2008c) provides a snapshot of Technical and Vocational Skills Development (TVSD) in 34 African countries at different levels of economic development and with different labour market needs. It demonstrates that opportunities offered by the private enterprise sector, including the informal sector, hold the greatest promise for the training of Africa's youth and the next generation of entrepreneurs likely to provide employment and prosperity. TVSD, it is argued, should be an integral part of any pro-poor economic growth strategy and more attention should be paid to the fact that 90 per cent of TVSD is done in the informal sector.

The report reveals that in the more developed African countries it is possible often to find a combination of high growth and productivity in some sectors and regions combined with low productivity and persistent poverty in others, mainly in the large informal economy. The role of training in promoting formalisation in many of these developing countries involves focusing on improving access to quality skills development outside high-growth urban areas; combining remedial education and employment services with technical training; implementing systems for the recognition of prior learning to open up jobs in the formal economy to those who have acquired skills informally; and targeting entrepreneurship training so that it encourages and enables the formalisation of small enterprises.

Microcredit represents an integral part of the means deployed to reinforce training and make it more effective. It plays a crucial role in helping informal-sector workers progress from the TVSD phase to enterprise creation, consolidation and development. The "First Job" law implemented in Angola since 2006 is a good example of how the Angolan Government aims to help trainees find work, which is a prerequisite for successful training schemes. Another example of good practice is the strategic partnership developed by the African Development Bank and the ILO to support growth-oriented women entrepreneurs, which has been applied in Cameroon, Ethiopia, Kenya, Tanzania and Uganda.

The livelihood of the large majority of workers in the continent depends on income-generating activities in the subsistence agriculture sector and the urban informal economy. Hence the importance of effective methods for improving access to high quality and relevant skills training in rural communities to improve agricultural productivity or to meet off-farm labour demand. Concrete actions should include: improving agricultural and rural extension services and combining technical and entrepreneurship training in local communities.

Important reforms in many African countries are under way to strengthen training systems to adapt them by introducing or strengthening partnerships between school-based training and apprenticeships in both the formal and informal sectors. For instance, Benin, Ghana and Mali are making important efforts to modernise traditional apprenticeship schemes and to integrate them into a national training system. These examples that take the form of dual apprenticeship systems, where craft enterprises co-operate with training centres to provide training and to issue certificates attesting to the skills possessed by informal sector workers, are promising and reflect a trend towards a more holistic approach to education, training and employment than in the past.

Sources: ILO (2008) and OECD (2008c).

Social protection and risk management policies

Besides improving productivity and the earnings of those working informally, a key policy concern is how to provide social protection in an effective and equitable manner to those who are not formally registered and are outside the reach of social security.

ISBN: 978-92-64-05923-8 - © OECD 2009

Typically, life risks such as illness, death, old age and disability are insured through job-related, often compulsory, insurance mechanisms. Informal workers who do not have access to such mechanisms therefore bear more risk than if they were formal. This is particularly true of those informal workers who, on top of their employment status, are in occupations that are themselves riskier or offer volatile returns.

The link between social protection and informality is a complex one and choices are linked to the question of what kind of welfare model a country is pursuing. Societies are likely to have different levels of tolerance for the cost of providing social assistance to informal workers or for possible increases in informality subsequent to the provision of social assistance services to informal workers. The provision of such services can foster the image of some participants in informal employment as free riders. This effect is to be balanced against the reduction in poverty that the extension of basic social insurance services can achieve.

Social assistance schemes that insure the poor against catastrophic risk can play a major role in reducing not only the level but also the severity of poverty. Moreover, they constitute important elements in increasing the productivity of informal workers.

Social assistance programmes

Social assistance programmes offer benefits to those not reached by formal social insurance mechanisms, including social security and contribution-based unemployment insurance. In practice, social assistance benefits are means-tested and encompass a wider set of benefits than those provided by social insurance. In particular, social assistance can take the form of cash transfers whether as part of income guarantee schemes or as a response to life events.

Recently, social cash transfers as a part of social assistance schemes have attracted a great deal of attention from policy makers, donors and researchers. They include conditional or non-conditional transfers, pensions, child support grants, disability benefits etc. Social cash transfers are closely linked to employment. Depending on the specific form they can influence labour supply and demand, human capital formation and other welfare variables. The overall evidence seems to support a positive impact on employment outcomes (Samson, 2007). They directly promote short term labour market participation and reduce unemployment (Devereux *et al.,* 2005; McCord, 2004, 2005). As an example, Chimai *et al.* (2008) find that through participation in the Zambian pilot cash transfer scheme, households were able to hire labour for land cultivation, creating jobs for local young people.

Cash transfers have often been presented as transitory measures to alleviate poverty in times of economic crises or trade regime changes, when more households are at risk of falling into poverty. The more critical and disputed issue, though, is the longer-term post-programme employment effects. Will workers be able to exit public works at some time to engage in their own livelihoods? The evidence so far seems to be too scattered and inconclusive to draw any firm conclusion. What one can say, however, is that cash transfers can durably guarantee a minimal income in certain situations (unemployment, old age), substituting for social insurance altogether. In Mexico, where no universal old-age insurance exists, old-age security is provided by various sources: at the federal level for the elderly in rural areas and by municipal governments in certain cities (including Mexico D.F.).

Among social cash transfers, conditional transfers have received much attention as a means of influencing behaviour, in particular in the benefit of future generations, without recourse to distortional and possibly paternalistic in-kind transfers and subsidies. Conditional cash transfer (CCT) programmes have spread throughout Latin America since the mid-1990s, but are also implemented in Africa (e.g. Zambia, Malawi). The best known in Latin America are *PROGRESA/ Oportunidades* (Mexico), *Chile Solidario* and *Bolsa Família* (Brazil). Despite differences in their design and scope, CCT programmes are characterised by their twin objectives of providing for the immediate needs of the poor (via the transfer), and of breaking the intergenerational transmission of poverty by investing in the human capital of the children of the beneficiary families (the conditions attached to the transfer). To achieve these, they combine a cash transfer

ISBN: 978-92-64-05923-8 - © OECD 2009

mechanism, a targeting system and a set of conditions, normally related to school attendance and compliance with healthcare programmes. The results of early impact evaluations bolstered the reputation of CCT programmes from the outset. These demonstrated definite improvements in education and health outcomes, some evidence of improvement in nutrition, mainly where the CCT was accompanied by the distribution of food supplements, and no negative impact on labour supply.

CCTs are particularly good at targeting, thanks to the combination of self-selection and appropriate identification of the population at which they are aimed. Such interventions are key to alleviating poverty and an important tool for future poverty reduction. They remain, however, generally too small to affect the well-being of informally employed workers when they represent the majority of employment.

Because of their relatively modest size (relative to the size of informal employment) and the focus on poverty alleviation, conditional cash transfers are not a sufficient tool to address the risk of poverty faced by many informal workers. Neither are they an impediment to the implementation of labour market policies and interventions. As shown by Samson (2007) for South Africa social transfers seem not to compete with labour market policies and interventions; rather to complement them.

Poverty reduction and promotion policies: distorting incentives?

In many developing countries high levels of poverty and inequality have prompted the creation of social assistance programmes. These cater to informal workers, either as part of their statutory framework or by self-selection, since formal workers have access to formal social security. If informal employment is voluntary and results from an analysis of the costs and benefits of being formal, providing services that are an alternative to contribution-based social insurance at low or zero cost will encourage informal work. In those countries with a high percentage of people belonging to the upper tier of informal employment, such social assistance programmes funded either through payroll taxes in the formal sector or general taxation may encourage informality, distort the allocation of other factors of production and threaten the viability of the contribution-based system (Levy, 2008). In turn, this can create segmented labour markets and the "missing middle" in an economy composed of many small and some large enterprises (Galiani and Weinschelbaum, 2006).

The debate in Mexico was prompted by the implementation of a large-scale health insurance scheme for those without access to social security. The *Seguro Popular (Sistema de Protección Social de Salud)* offers a basic health package with a subsidy that decreases as declared household income rises. In practice, about 90 per cent of the 5 million families that were beneficiaries of *Seguro Popular* at the end of 2006 received a full subsidy. Such issues are not only present in health insurance, but also in respect of pension finance. In Brazil, those earning the minimum wage can apply for an old-age benefit from age 65 (means-tested and equivalent to a minimum wage), therefore providing incentives for the aged to retire and work informally.

The relevance of these arguments depends on the degree to which informality is indeed voluntary in a given country and the effect that non-pecuniary benefits are likely to have on choice. Qualitative evidence suggests that non-pecuniary benefits, including such elements as freedom to be one's own boss, are relevant to the decision to become self-employed (see Perry *et al.*, 2007). However, the debate on the relative size of voluntary and rationed segments of informal employment is by and large unsettled.

The degree of mobility between different segments of the labour market is a highly contested topic. In a recent case study of Mexico, a country for which it has been found that there is substantial mobility in labour markets, Laiglesia *et al.* (2008) find that education and gender have a critical influence on mobility patterns. Individuals with fewer than six years of education are found to be significantly less likely to go from an informal to a formal job and also less likely to remain in formal employment[11]. Social contributions in Mexico are regressive (OECD, 2007), which indeed provides incentives to recruit low-paid workers informally.

155

From a theoretical standpoint, without market segmentation, providing certain benefits to informal workers might distort incentives to become formal. In practice, the size of such an effect remains an empirical question. Moreover, a certain perverse effect might be a reasonable price if the provision of better risk management can increase the productivity and earnings of poor informal workers.

The distorting effect of such programmes could also be minimised by adopting systems akin to those designed to "make work pay" in OECD countries (such as tax credits like the Earned Income Tax Credit in the United States or the Working Families Tax Credit in the United Kingdom). The maintenance of part of the subsidy for those in formal employment at lower earnings would ensure that their incentives to opt for formal jobs are not distorted. At low earning levels, labour supply is unlikely to be affected significantly by the corresponding wealth effect.

Similar schemes for pension finance can also be envisaged: by providing a progressive solidarity pension, eligibility criteria based on years of work could also be complemented by criteria based on capitalisation, thereby circumventing the problems posed by rigid criteria based on years worked – which are only relevant if worked in the formal sector.

Many of the most vulnerable are likely to have a low educational attainment and would have very low productivity in the formal sector. Attention to the potentially perverse incentives of social assistance programmes should not prevent addressing the needs of those who are indeed excluded. Providing basic social services to them, and especially to their families, remains imperative for poverty alleviation. It is particularly important in breaking the vicious cycle of persistent poverty. Fostering the employability of the low-skilled also remains relevant. Initiatives in this direction can include setting social security contributions for low-paid workers at levels that do not make them unemployable, and encouraging human capital accumulation not only before but also after entry into the labour market.

Voice and recognition: The role of non-state actors

Public policy can do much to promote workers in the lower tier of informal employment, opening up new opportunities and providing means for increased productivity. Non-state actors also have a role to play in promoting workers and their rights. Being in informal work adds a particular challenge in trying to establish workers' organisations that are credible and representative. However, these obstacles can be overcome, as shown by informal worker associations throughout the world. The best known is perhaps SEWA (India's Self-Employed Women Association) which is not only engaged in advocacy but also provides a wide range of services to its members[12].

Membership-based organisations throughout the developing world represent individuals in such typically informal activities as street vending, transport (especially taxis and micro-buses) and domestic work. Such organisations can critically provide a public voice for individuals who find themselves outside the formal economic and legal framework and, accordingly, without access to the formal procedures to defend and establish their rights.

Workers' organisations can be critical in establishing the voice of their members in the economic discourse. The importance of Peru's National Federation of Domestic Workers in the passing of legislation providing domestic workers with social security and healthcare coverage and establishing the duration of the working day is a prime example. They can also help generate social dialogue in those countries where informally employed workers – especially salaried workers – are legally covered by minimum wage provisions, as in the case of India (Saget, 2006).

ISBN: 978-92-64-05923-8 - © OECD 2009

BEYOND INFORMAL EMPLOYMENT AND POVERTY REDUCTION: TOWARDS A SOCIAL CONTRACT AND IMPROVED POLICY COHERENCE

Informality can be seen as a symptom of a broken or non-existent social contract[13]. A social contract is generally an implicit theoretical construct, although occasionally it is partly embodied in constitutions or specific multi-stakeholder political agreements. Formality frames many of the economic interactions between citizens and the state: from tax payments to the adherence to trade and labour regulations and the use of public goods – in particular the protection of private property and the enforcement of contracts. The recognition that informality is symptomatic of a broken link between economic actors – producers and workers – and the state calls for strategies in which formalisation is less a legal imperative than a tool of economic transformation to be used in pursuit of better outcomes for all, including those currently in the informal sector. Informal workers are not informal *per se* but chiefly workers and entrepreneurs. Giving them more rights, access to services and a voice, while reminding them of their duties as citizens, will not only contribute to the economic and social development of a country but also contribute to bringing a society closer together.

Formality and its various requirements are also often preconditions not only to service but to entitlements. The enforcement of basic economic rights, including the defence of private property, the right to unionisation and freedom to establish economic enterprises, are subject to registration and compliance with formal requirements. When such requirements are overly stringent, they give rise to segmentation that is not only the creation of two markets, but that of two legal worlds (de Soto, 2000; UN Commission on Legal Empowerment of the Poor, 2008). De Soto (1989, 2000), among others, has argued for simplified methods of recognition of the property of the poor on the basis of its incorporation, as capital, into the economy. Tokman (2007) goes further and argues for the extension of this approach to the recognition of other economic rights in employment, business registration and taxation. This approach has wide-ranging implications. In terms of employment relations, it calls for the formal recognition of oral labour contracts. With regard to business establishment, it implies legal means to separate business assets and providing them with protection comparable to that received by corporate property. Simplified methods that allow the recognition of economic rights would generate the conditions to mobilise assets and, ultimately, to be subject to the benefits of formal labour regulation. Finally, not only is formality a precondition for entitlement, certain of the requirements of formality can themselves contribute to the modernisation of economic units. For example, the accounting requirements of business taxation can help micro-entrepreneurs develop the tools to assess the value of business opportunities and the documents to convince financial backers (Tokman, 2007).

Just as formality is not a monolithic set of obligations and entitlements, informal work is far from homogeneous. Indeed, both informal workers and enterprises typically do not infringe all relevant regulations. For example, studies from Bolivia and Mexico found that informal firms were quite likely to have an operating licence from the municipality, but less likely to be registered for tax purposes (OECD, 2008b). It is therefore necessary to unbundle requirements in order to understand the composition of informal employment in any given country and to set priorities for public action.

Besides the need to look beyond sector policies, another important conclusion from this study is the need to achieve more coherence between different policies. In most countries there is only limited co-ordination between ministries dealing with employment and those responsible for "poverty reduction" or fiscal matters. This study does not call for creating yet another agency looking for more coherence across policy areas. But it argues that it would be beneficial to conduct more information campaigns within the government pointing to the side effects a certain policy in one field might have.

157

ISBN: 978-92-64-05923-8 - © OECD 2009

In poor developing countries the PRSPs should reflect more the link between employment and poverty reduction. Evaluations of the second generation of PRSPs highlight the need for an integrated framework that combines a focus on social sectors and well-targeted social interventions with an in-depth analysis of how productive sectors can better contribute to pro-poor growth (ODI, 2004). A more realistic strategy is needed to reach out to the millions of informal workers to provide them with the necessary tools (extension services, technology, inputs etc.) as well as develop an enabling local environment for business creation and an increase of productivity.

Informal will remain normal for a majority of workers worldwide for the foreseeable future. It is high time that policies be adapted to what some might perceive as an inconvenient truth. While the long-term objective of making informal jobs formal should be maintained, it should not prevent the improvement of the plight of those who are striving for better jobs within informal employment.

ISBN: 978-92-64-05923-8 - © OECD 2009

NOTES

1. See Chapter 3.

2. "False" self-employment refers to the situation where some "self-employed sub-contract every day to the same employer, but choose or are forced to operate as self-employed to bypass the legal requirements of a normal employer-employee relationship or reduce their tax liability" (OECD, 2008a). "Envelope payments" are a practice in which only part of workers' earnings are being declared to the tax authorities and social security administration, the rest being paid to them in cash (the "envelope payments") or in kind (Ghinararu, 2007; Albu, 2007).

3. For a review of arguments on the societal costs of informal employment see OECD (2004) and the referenced literature.

4. See Chapter 3.

5. The literature does not agree on what constitutes moderate inflation.

6. India is a very interesting case in which growth has been concentrated in services while in agriculture the growth is in comparison relatively modest. This is one of the reasons why despite growth rates over 6 percentage points the number of informally employed in India remains over 80 per cent.

7. Indeed, financial market depth is critical for the incorporation of "dead" capital (in the sense of de Soto, 1989) into the economy and for the formalisation of property in particular to have a major effect on the economy. This is by no means guaranteed in many developing countries.

8. The authors find for the Latin American-Caribbean region that increasing employment protection legislation (EPL) means labour markets have become more segmented with fewer chances for the unskilled, young and female workers to find a formal job.

9. See Saget (2006) and the discussion in Chapter 5.

10. See www.ilo.org/public/english/employment/skills/hrdr/init/sa_16.htm.

11. See Chapter 5 for details.

12. See Chapter 4 for a detailed discussion.

13. A social contract is the agreement by which individuals adhere to a common system of laws and government, possibly restricting their own freedom, in exchange for the greater good or for the benefits that are derived from such an arrangement, such as the division of labour, the respect of property, etc. The theoretical construct of the social contract that underlies the discussion in this section does not necessarily portray such a social contract as just or fair (contrary, for, example to Rawls's [1972] landmark discussion of justice in the context of the social contract).

ISBN: 978-92-64-05923-8 - © OECD 2009

REFERENCES

ALBU, L.-L. (2007), "A Model to Estimate Informal Economy at Regional Level: Theoretical and Empirical Investigation", *MPRA Paper* No. 3 760, Munich.

ALMEIDA, R. and P. CARNEIRO (2006), "Enforcement of Regulation, Informal Labour, Firm Size and Firm Performance", *Discussion Paper* No. 5976, Centre for Economic Policy Research, London.

AURIOL, E. and M. WARLTERS (2005), "Taxation Base in Developing Countries", *Journal of Public Economics*, Vol. 89, pp. 625-646.

BATRA, G., D. KAUFMANN and A. STONE (2003), "Investment Climate Around the World: Voices of the Firms from the World Business Environment Survey", *World Bank Report* No. 26103, World Bank, Washington, D.C.

BELL, L. (1997), "The Impact of Minimum Wages in Mexico and Colombia", *Journal of Labor Economics*, Vol. 15, No. 3, pp. S102-S135.

BERG, J. and D. KUCERA (2008), *In Defence of Labour Market Institutions: Cultivating Justice in the Developing World*, ILO, Geneva.

BETCHERMANN, G. (2002), "An Overview of Labour Markets World Wide: Key Trends and Major Policy Issues", *Social Protection Discussion Papers* No. 205, World Bank, Washington, D.C.

BRAUN, J. VON (2007), " Rural-urban Linkages for Growth, Employment and Poverty Reduction", Keynote address for the Ethiopian Economic Association's Fifth International Conference on the Ethiopian Economy, 7-9 June, Addis Ababa.

BRUHN, M. (2008), "License to Sell: The Effect of Business Registration Reform on Entrepreneurial Activity in Mexico", *World Bank Policy Research Working Paper* No. 4538, World Bank, Washington, D.C.

CARNEIRO, F. (2004), "Are Minimum Wages to Blame for Informality in the Labour Market?" *Empirica*, Vol. 31, pp. 295-306.

CHIMAI, B., N.FREELAND, B.MULENGA, S.NKUNIKA, E.SCHÜRING and G.TEMBO (2008), "Social Cash Transfers and Household Welfare in Zambia", Paper presented at the conference on Social Protection for the Poorest in Africa: Learning from Experience, 8-10 September, Kampala, Uganda.

COMMISSION ON GROWTH AND DEVELOPMENT (2008), *The Growth Report. Strategies for Sustained Growth and Inclusive Development*, World Bank, Washington D.C.

COOK, S., J HEINTZ and N.KABEER (2008), "Economic Growth, Social Protection and 'Real' Labour Markets: Linking Theory and Evidence", *in* KABEER, N. and S. COOK (eds.) *Economic Growth, Social Protection and 'Real' Labour Markets,* pp. 1-11, Institute of Development Studies, University of Sussex, Brighton.

CORD, L. (2007), "Promoting Pro-Poor Growth: Lessons from Country Experiences", *in IPC, Poverty in Focus, Analyzing and Achieving Pro-poor Growth,* UNDP Poverty Centre, Brasilia, pp. 10-11.

DEVEREUX, S., J.MARSHALL, J.MACASKILL and L.PELHAM (2005), *Making Cash Count: Lessons from Cash Transfer Schemes in East and Southern Africa for Supporting the Most Vulnerable Children and Households,* Save the Children UK, HelpAge International and Institute of Development Studies, London. Available at: www.ids.ac.uk/UserFiles/File/poverty_team/MakingCashCountfinal.pdf.

DJANKOV, S., R. LA PORTA, F.LOPEZ-DE-SILANES and A.SCHLEIFER (2002),"The Regulation of Entry", *Quarterly Journal of Economics* 117, No. 1: pp.1-37.

FIESS, N., M. FUGAZZA and W. MALONEY (2006), "Informal Labor Markets and Macroeconomic Fluctuations", *Working Paper* No. 2006_17, University of Glasgow, Glasgow.

ISBN: 978-92-64-05923-8 - © OECD 2009

FREEMAN, R. (2007), "Labor Market Institutions around the World", *NBER Working Paper* No. 13242, NBER, Cambridge, MA.

FREY, B. and B. TORGLER (2007), "Tax Moral and Conditional Co-operation", *Journal of Comparative Economics*, Vol. 35, pp. 136-159.

FRIEDMAN, E., S. JOHNSON, D. KAUFMANN and P. ZOIDO-LOBATON (2000), "Dodging the Grabbing Hand: The Determinants of Unofficial Activity in 69 Countries", *Journal of Public Economics*, Vol. 76, pp. 459-493.

GALIANI, S. and F. WEINSCHELBAUM (2006), "Modeling Informality Formally: Households and Firms", *CEDLAS Working Paper* 0047, Universida Nacional de La Plata, Argentina.

GHINARARU, C. (2007), "Thematic article on Undeclared Work in Romania", update review for the European Employment Observatory.

GOTTSCHALK, R. (2008), "A Macroeconomic Framework for Growth and Employment Creation", *in* KABEER, N. and S. COOK (eds.) *Economic Growth, Social Protection and 'Real' Labour Markets,* pp. 1-11, Institute of Development Studies, University of Sussex, Brighton.

GUTIERREZ, C., C. ORECCHIA, P. PACI and P. SERNEELS (2007), "Does Employment Generation Really Matter for Poverty Reduction?", *World Bank Policy Research Working Paper* No. 4432, World Bank, Washington, D.C.

HAMIDI, F. and K. TERRELL (2001), "The Impact of Minimum Wages on Wage Inequality and Employment in the Formal and Informal Sector in Costa Rica", *William Davidson Working Paper* No. 479, University of Michigan Business School.

HANOUSEK, J. and F. PALDA (2002), "Why People Evade Taxes in the Czech and Slovak Republics: A Tale of Twins", *CERGE-EI Discussion Paper* No. 85, CERGEI, Prague.

HECKMAN, J. and C. PAGÉS (eds.) (2004), "Introduction" *Law and Employment: Lessons from Latin America and the Caribbean*, University of Chicago Press, Chicago, Ill.

HULL, K. (2008), "Understanding the Relationship between Economic Growth, Employment and Poverty Reduction", Paper prepared for the OECD DAC Task Force on Employment and Labour Markets.

ILO (2006), *Labour Inspection*, ILO, Geneva. Available at: www.ilo.org/public/english/standards/relm/ilc/ilc95/pdf/rep-iii-1b.pdf.

ILO (2008), "Report V. Skills for Improved Productivity, Employment Growth and Development". International Labour Conference 97th Session 2008, ILO, Geneva.

INFANTE, R., A. MARINAKIS and J. VELASCO (2003), "Minimum Wage in Chile: An Example of the Potential and Limitations of this Policy Instrument", *ILO Employment Paper* No. 2003/52, ILO, Geneva.

JARAMILLO, M. (2005), "Minimum Wage Effects under Endogenous Compliance: Evidence from Peru", Paper presented at the IZA-EBRD International Conference on Labor Market Dynamics, the Role of Institutions and Internal Labor Markets in Transition and Emerging Market Economies, University of Bologna, 5-8 May.

JONES, P. (1998), "The Impact of Minimum Wage Legislation in Developing Countries where Coverage is Incomplete", *Centre for the Study of African Economies Working Paper* No. 98-2, Oxford University, Oxford.

KABEER, N. and S. COOK (eds.) (2008), *Economic Growth, Social Protection and 'Real' Labour Markets,* IDS Bulletin Vol. 39 No. 2, Institute of Development Studies, University of Sussex, Brighton.

KAPLAN, D., E. PIEDRA and E. SEIRA (2007), "Entry Regulation and Business Start-ups: Evidence from Mexico", *World Bank Policy Research Working Paper* No. 4322, World Bank, Washington, D.C.

ISBN: 978-92-64-05923-8 - © OECD 2009

LAIGLESIA J. DE, R. BAZILLIER, R. S. PARKER, U. QUIJANO, A. SARACHO, A. and V. SCORZA (2008), "Work and Wellbeing in Mexico: Integrating the Employment and Social Development Agendas", Draft Report prepared for the Mexican Ministry of Social Development, OECD Development Centre, Paris.

LEMOS, S. (2004), "The Effects of the Minimum Wage in the Formal and Informal Sectors in Brazil", University of Leicester Department of Economics *Working Paper* No. 04/8, Leicester.

LEVY, S. (2008), *Good Intentions, Bad Outcomes*, Brookings Institutions Press, Washington, D.C.

LOAYZA, N., A. OVIEDO and L. SERVÉN (2005), "The Impact of Regulation on Growth and Informality: Cross-Country Evidence", *World Bank Policy Research Working Paper* No. 3623, May, World Bank, Washington, D.C.

MCCORD, A. (2004), "Policy Expectations and Programme Reality: The Poverty Reduction and Labour Market Impact of Two Public Works Programmes in South Africa", *ESAU Working Paper* No. 8, Overseas Development Institute, London.

MCCORD, A. (2005), "Win-win or lose? An Examination of the Use of Public Works as a Social Protection Instrument in Situations of Chronic Poverty", Paper presented at the conference on Social Protection for Chronic Poverty, University of Manchester, 23-24 February. Available at: www.gsdrc.org/go/display/document/legacyid/1718.

MCKINLEY, T. (2008), "Economic Policies for Growth and Poverty Reduction: PRSPs, Neo-liberal Conditionalities and 'Post-consensus' Alternative", *in* KABEER, N. and S. COOK (eds.) *Economic Growth, Social Protection and 'Real' Labour Markets,* IDS Bulletin Vol. 39 No. 2, pp.93-104 Institute of Development Studies, University of Sussex, Brighton.

ODI (2004), "Second Generation Poverty Reduction Strategies", PRSP Monitoring and Synthesis Project, Overseas Development Institute, London.

OECD (2004), "Informal Employment and Promoting the Transition to a Salaried Economy", Chapter 5 in *Employment Outlook*, OECD, Paris.

OECD (2006), *Promoting Pro-Poor Growth: Agriculture*, OECD, Paris.

OECD (2007), *OECD Economic Surveys: Mexico*, OECD, Paris.

OECD (2008*a*), *OECD Employment Outlook 2008*, OECD, Paris.

OECD (2008*b*), *Latin American Economic Outlook 2009*, OECD, Paris.

OECD (2008*c*), "Technical and Vocational Skills Development in Africa" *in African Economic Outlook* Report 2008, OECD, Paris.

PARLEVLIET, J. and T. XENOGIANI (2008), "Report on Informal Employment in Romania", *Working Paper* No. 271, OECD Development Centre, Paris.

PERRY, G., W. MALONEY, O. ARIAS, A. FAJNZYLBER, A. MASON and J. SAAVEDRA-CHANDUVI (2007), *Informality: Exit and Exclusion*, World Bank, Washington, D.C.

RAWLS, J. (1972), *A Theory of Justice*, Harvard University Press.

SAFAVIAN, M. and J. WIMPEY (2007), "When Do Enterprises Prefer Informal Credit", *World Bank Policy Research Working Paper* No. 4435, World Bank, Washington, D.C.

SAGET, C. (2006), "Wage Fixing in the Informal Economy: Evidence from Brazil, India, Indonesia and South Africa", *Conditions of Work and Employment Series,* No. 16, ILO, Geneva.

SAMSON, M. (2007), "Social Cash Transfers and Employment – a Note on Empirical Linkages in Developing Countries", Note for the OECD Povnet Task Team on Employment and Labour Markets.

SCHRANK, A. and M. PIORE (2007), "Norms, Regulations and Labour Standards in Central America", CEPAL *Serie Estudios y Perspectivas* No. 77, United Nations, Mexico.

SLEMROD, J. (2007), "Cheating Ourselves: The Economics of Tax Evasion", *Journal of Economic Perspectives*, Vol. 21, No. 1, pp. 25-48.

ISBN: 978-92-64-05923-8 - © OECD 2009

Soto, H. de (1989), *The Other Path: The Invisible Revolution in the Third World*, Instituto Libertad y Democracia, Harper and Row, New York, NY.

Soto, H. de (2000), *The Mystery of Capital. Why Capitalism Triumphs in the West and Fails Everywhere Else,* Basic Books, New York, NY.

Straub, S. (2005), "Informal Sector: The Credit Market Channel", *Journal of Development Economics*, Vol. 78, pp. 299-321.

Tokman, V. (2007), "Modernizing the Informal Sector", *DESA Working Paper* No. 42, United Nations, New York.

Toye, J. (2008), "Macroeconomic Policy, Labour Markets and Growth in Developed and Developing Countries" *in* Kabeer, N. and S. Cook (eds.) *Economic Growth, Social Protection and 'Real' Labour Markets,* IDS Bulletin Vol. 39 No. 2, pp. 112-120, Institute of Development Studies, University of Sussex, Brighton.

Treichel, B. (2004), "The Ten Steps for Strengthening Labour Inspection", *Labour Education*, Vol. 3-4, No. 140-141, pp. 74-78.

UN Commission on Legal Empowerment of the Poor (2008), *Making the Law Work for Everyone*, Report of the UN Commission on Legal Empowerment of the Poor, United Nations, New York, NY.

Walther, R. (2007), "La formation professionnelle en secteur informel", *AFD Notes et documents,* No. 33, June.

World Bank (2001), *Globalization, Growth and Poverty: Building an Inclusive World Economy*, World Bank and Oxford University Press, Washington, D.C.

ISBN: 978-92-64-05923-8 - © OECD 2009

DATE DUE

MAR 0 2 2010	
JAN 0 2 2012	